Other Books by GARY EMERY

Rapid Relief from Emotional Distress (with James Campbell, M.D.)
Own Your Own Life
New Directions in Cognitive Therapy, editor

GETTING UNDEPRESSED

How a Woman Can Change Her Life Through Cognitive Therapy

GARY EMERY, Ph.D.

Foreword by
Aaron T. Beck, M.D.

The Revised Edition of *A New Beginning*

A TOUCHSTONE BOOK
Published by Simon & Schuster Inc.
NEW YORK • LONDON • TORONTO • SYDNEY • TOKYO

Grateful acknowledgment is made to the following:

Random House, Inc., for permission to use excerpts from *The War Between the Tates,* by Alison Lurie, copyright © 1974.

A. S. Barnes & Company, Inc. By permission of the publisher. Copyright © 1955 Harper & Brothers. Publisher A. S. Barnes. From *The Ballad Book,* editor, MacEdward Leach. All rights reserved.

Revised Touchstone Edition, 1988

Published by Simon & Schuster Inc.
Simon & Schuster Building
Rockefeller Center
1230 Avenue of the Americas
New York, NY 10020

Originally published as *A New Beginning*
TOUCHSTONE and colophon are registered trademarks of Simon & Schuster Inc.

Designed by Irving Perkins and Associates
Manufactured in the United States of America

10 9 8 7 6 5 4 3 2 1 Pbk.

Library of Congress Cataloging in Publication Data
Emery, Gary.
[New beginning]
Getting undepressed: how a woman can change her life through cognitive therapy / Gary Emery: foreword by Aaron T. Beck.
p. cm.——(A Touchstone Book)
Originally published: A new beginning. 1981. With rev. and updated introd.
Bibliography: p.
Includes index.
ISBN 0-671-65891-3 Pbk.
1. Depression, Mental. 2. Women—Mental health. 3. Cognitive therapy. I. Title.
[RC537.E43 1988]
616.85'2706—dc19   87-26621
                             CIP

To Pat and Zachary

The names of patients in case histories have been changed to protect their privacy.

Contents

Foreword

DEPRESSION is a puzzling and even paradoxical disorder. An acknowledged beauty, suffering from depression, may beg for plastic surgery in the belief that she is ugly; an accomplished musician may conclude that her talent is worthless. Severely depressed patients may seek punishment, humiliation, and death despite outward signs of achievement and social success. Yet, unless suicide intervenes, the chances for the depressed patient's recovery are excellent, and complete remission of an episode of depression occurs in seventy to ninety-five percent of cases (although recurrences are common).

My ideas on depression have changed radically over the years. For example, not too long ago a well-known author came to me for a consultation regarding her depression. When I told her I admired and enjoyed her books, she broke into tears. I asked her what was going through her mind; she said, "I was thinking, 'Oh, no, I fooled him, too. He doesn't know how worthless my work is.' "

In my early days of practicing psychoanalytic psychiatry, I would not have accepted such thoughts at face value. (I also probably would not have inquired about them.) Instead, I would have moved immediately to exploring underlying emotional conflicts such as a repressed hatred.

However, over the years I have come to the conclusion that such negative interpretations of positive statements and events and exaggeration of negative occurrences are responsible for keeping this author and others like her depressed.

My formulation of the distorted thinking, or cognition, in depression evolved from a variety of sources—clinical material, such as

9

the dreams, free associations, and reports of feelings of patients in psychotherapy, controlled experiments, and psychotherapeutic studies. Since thinking is an aspect of cognitive processes, I attached the labels "cognitive model" to the theory and "cognitive therapy" to the treatment.

My present theory represents the end product of a zigzag series of investigations, formulations, and reformulations. I started by trying to validate Freud's theory that depression was caused by the patient's turning anger inward. The findings didn't support this position. I concluded that the cognitive model made more sense out of what patients told me and what I had found in the many research studies.

I discovered that in their dreams and early memories and in projective tests, depressed people see themselves as "losers"—deprived, frustrated, humiliated, rejected, or punished in some way. The psychological "cause" of depression did not appear to be buried deep in the unconscious but was related to this type of mistaken thinking.

I've called this constellation of negative perceptions of *the self, the world,* and *the future* the Cognitive Triad. The emotional, motivational, and behavioral changes in depression seem to flow directly from the depressed person's belief that he or she is worthless, the world is barren, and the future is bleak—no matter what efforts he or she makes to improve the situation.

Cognitive therapy is an outgrowth of this theory. This new approach to treatment uses a variety of techniques that directly or indirectly correct the depressed person's faulty thinking. Through controlled studies at the Center for Cognitive Therapy of the University of Pennsylvania and elsewhere, we have found cognitive therapy is an effective treatment for depression.

WOMEN AND DEPRESSION

Depression among women is a serious, widespread health problem. A number of theories attempt to explain the high frequency of depression in women. One view holds that the social roles given to women—their subservient employment as secretaries, nurses, and assistants, and those duties that relate to housewifery and mother-hood in the current American social scheme—are inherently de-pressing. According to this view, depression is a "normal" response to a bad deal.

There is another more optimistic way of understanding the prob-lem of depression in women. According to the formulation, it is not necessary to prove that women in contemporary America are ob-jectively oppressed. It is sufficient to show that they believe they are dependent, helpless, and deprived.

And, indeed, studies have shown women have a culturally in-duced tendency to regard themselves as weak and ineffective. They tend to conceptualize difficult situations in terms of their own help-lessness and powerlessness rather than from a more adaptive perspective. Whether or not their original perception of "copelessness" is founded on objective fact, they interpret the re-sulting depression as evidence confirming that perception. So per-haps women may be *more bound by their stereotyped negative expectations than by insurmountable obstacles to their happiness and success.*

Consider the following:

> So hard is the future of poor womankind—
> They are always objected, always confined;
> They are controlled by their parents until they are made wives,
> And slaves for their husbands the rest of their lives.*

It is true that throughout history women have been offered only a narrow range of alternatives in choosing their lifestyles. Relatively few women had the opportunity to direct their own lives, to realize their personal conception of happiness and fulfillment. Recently, however, the injunction that marriage and motherhood are the only proper goals for a young woman has been relaxed. The possibilities for change inherent in current attitudes go far beyond what has already become incarnate in social habit and legal actuality. Yet the incidence of depression in women has not declined.

Women, both as a group and as individuals, will make few gains unless they reach a critical decision—that is, despite socialization

* "The Wagoner's Lad," a traditional folk ballad, in MacEdward Leach, ed., *The Ballad Book* (New York: A. S. Barnes and Company, Inc., 1955), p. 738.

and precedent, they must take control of their lives, goals, families, careers, and psychological problems. The women depicted in the folk song undoubtedly suffered from manipulation and abuse; yet, it's likely that their modern counterparts would emerge in an era of relative liberation still ruled by the habits of mind that reduce even partial new freedom to a new level of enslavement.

Women, in fact, may be no more predisposed to suffer from depression than are men. What distinguishes male from female depression is that the events which typically "trigger" depressions tend to be sex-typed. While a man is more likely to become depressed at critical junctures in his career or business life, women tend to experience these crises during marital turmoil, after childbirth, when children leave home.

Middle-aged women, for example, may feel victimized by a fear of death and aging, by their children's apparent indifference, by financial insecurity, or by anxiety about new jobs and living arrangements. The fundamental challenge remains what it has been all along—to master and modify trying circumstances and thereby transform them into an acceptable and even rewarding way of life.

Knowing that these and other crises will have to be negotiated in the future, women will do well to concentrate on preventing future depressions by cultivating habits of *self-respect* and *self-reliance,* by leading a balanced life, and by participating independently in a variety of activities rather than depending on family ties for emotional and intellectual sustenance. In other words, women must integrate as their own the goals of independence, productivity, and enjoyment, rather than the limited goals of serving their employers, husbands, and children and deriving vicarious satisfaction from the accomplishments of others.

Woman after woman has come to the Center for Cognitive Therapy with the complaint that she can't exist without a man. But when we inquire, we find nearly all have survived some time without men. And in fact they often get along much better without a man.

In their need to please others, women are vulnerable and continually on the defensive, overvaluing appearance and attractiveness and panicking when they think them threatened. Finally, by restricting their attention to the "feminine" sphere in the age of supertechnology and the "global village," women sacrifice a sense of the objective reality that exists beyond domestic confines.

It is hard to dispute the contention that our culture tends to view women as ineffectual, dependent, and overemotional, and troubled or depressed women as pathetic or manipulative. No doubt the fact that the culture confirms her negative self-evaluations is an added obstacle to the woman who becomes depressed. Yet women can reeducate themselves to recognize these prejudices for what they are—attitudes that may rule masses of people but which need in no way affect an individual's estimate of her own worth.

We have found that self-defeating thinking and attitudes can be changed—no matter how deeply rooted. Patients who are usually discerning when evaluating matters of little personal concern may not question the validity of their perceptions of their own worth or effectiveness: They need to be reminded that "Thinking does not make it so." When the patient begins to subject her perceptions to "reality testing," the downward spiral of negative thinking and depression can be reversed.

Dr. Gary Emery has worked closely with me for the last five years at the Center for Cognitive Therapy at the University of Pennsylvania. He has been an extremely innovative member of our team in developing and refining cognitive therapy. He has collaborated with me in writing several technical books and manuals on cognitive therapy.

He was a therapist in some of our earliest treatment-outcome studies. In the last several years, he has been involved extensively in teaching other therapists cognitive therapy—both in the United States and abroad.

Most popular books on depression merely describe the problem. This book is unique in that it clearly spells out proven techniques that we have used to help people in overcoming depression. Thus, it can help women to weather the crises of depression and lay the groundwork for more effective responses in the future.

—Aaron T. Beck, M.D.

Introduction:
Overcoming Depression

I went to a graduate school at the University of Pennsylvania, where a large part of my training to become a psychologist was spent treating clients. Occasionally I would come across someone severely depressed. I remember in particular Sally Thompson.*

Sally started off our first session by asking how many tranquilizers she'd have to take to kill herself. She was a twenty-year-old college sophomore and had been depressed for six months—ever since her boyfriend broke off with her. She'd decided she couldn't live without him and had concluded suicide was the only way out.

I was baffled by how to treat someone like Sally: My normal counseling helped most people, but it didn't work with the severely depressed. And I was unnerved by the possibility of suicide.

My supervisors generally advised me to refer these cases to a psychiatrist. They pointed out that since psychiatrists, unlike psychologists, are M.D.s, they can prescribe medicine and if necessary hospitalize the person. I referred Sally to a psychiatrist.

But I began to think that rather than just throw up my hands and refer depressed clients to someone else, I should try to learn more about depression. I began by reading what was considered the authoritative textbook on the subject—*Depression, Causes and Treatments,* by Aaron T. Beck, M.D.

The book contained a great deal of scientific material, but what excited and encouraged me was a short description of a new *psychological* treatment for depression. Dr. Beck wrote that he was

* Not her real name.

15

developing this new treatment, cognitive therapy, in the medical school at the University of Pennsylvania—the same university I was attending.

I decided to go over to the medical school and see Dr. Beck. I wanted to find out more about depression and to ask about being trained in this new treatment. During our discussion he told me that after many years of research and clinical experience with depression, he had concluded that the best way to treat it was with cognitive therapy.

He was planning some outcome studies to test cognitive therapy's effectiveness and agreed to train me if in return I would be a therapist in the outcome studies. This started my study of depression and cognitive therapy. I've continued to study and work in this area for the past twelve years.

What have I learned about depression? First, depression is a serious emotional disorder and a significant health problem. Suicide, a byproduct of depression, is a leading cause of death. Researchers now estimate that one out of seven people with a severe depression will commit suicide. Up to forty thousand people do so every year; nearly all are depressed.

Depression is not an isolated problem. Worldwide, over 100 million people are depressed. In your lifetime you run more than a twenty percent risk of having a major or minor depression. And if you're a woman, the odds are higher, for depression strikes many more women than men.

What is depression? Many people have come to see me over the years and said, "I'm depressed." But when I question them further, I find many aren't clinically depressed. Some are confusing normal mood changes with depression; some are unhappy with current circumstances, such as their marriages or jobs; some aren't getting what they want out of life; and still others confuse another problem, such as anxiety, with depression. But they aren't depressed. (Interestingly, while many people mislabel their occasional blue or down-in-the-dumps feelings as depression, they often downplay real depression when it follows a loss, such as the death of a loved one.)

Part of the misunderstanding about what true depression is comes from the way people talk. They often exaggerate and escalate the seriousness of everyday concerns to make a point. Psychological terms are ready-made for such exaggerations. For example, when people are suspicious, they say, "I'm paranoid"; when excited, "I'm hysterical"; and when unhappy, "I'm depressed."

Used like this, psychiatric terms developed to describe clinical disorders begin to lose their original meanings. This has happened to the term *depression.*

In the past, psychiatrists and psychologists themselves supplied a second source of confusion about depression. Until recently, they classified depression by presumed causes, such as *involutional melancholia,* thought to be a special type of depression caused by aging, or *endogenous depression,* thought to come from within a person, as opposed to *reactive depression,* thought to come from stressful events.

The major problem with the old classification system was that it was unreliable: Professionals couldn't agree on which category fit which person. So a new official system of classifying depression was developed and recently adopted.

The new system is purely descriptive: It doesn't make statements or implications about causes. Depression is defined by the person's signs and symptoms—what the person does, thinks, and feels. The descriptive method, although it has its drawbacks, not only makes it much easier for professionals to agree, but also provides a much better way to define depression.

What are the symptoms? Depression is a group of enduring symptoms that can last anywhere from a few weeks to years. They can be broken down into four general symptom clusters: *how you act* (slowed down, apathetic), *how you feel* (sad, guilty, anxious), *how you think* (a negative view of yourself, the world, and the future), and *how your body reacts* (trouble with sleeping and your appetite).

This distressing state can develop rapidly or come on more slowly over a period of weeks. Some depressions are mild; you're able to go through your normal steps but you feel bad and lack energy. At other times, people may become so depressed and suicidal that they must be hospitalized.

The most common symptom of depression is the inability to shake your blue moods. Your bleak moods hang on until they begin to color all of your experiences. You may cry a great deal. Or even worse, you want want to cry but can't. Simple chores require great effort, as though trying to swim in wet cement. Everyday problems seem overwhelming. One writer aptly described depression as a "season in hell."

Once depressed, you become your own worse critic. You may blame yourself for everything—your dishwasher's breaking down, your children's low marks in school, the family dog's tearing up your neighbor's flowers. You may believe that you're being punished. And you may become so pessimistic about your future that you consider ending your life.

Are you depressed?   Suppose you're unhappy and have some of these symptoms. Does that mean you're depressed? Not necessarily. Remember, depression is a *group* of specific enduring symptoms. I use two methods to see if a person is depressed: a clinical interview and psychological tests. In the clinical interview I want to find out if the person meets the criteria for being depressed. I use what is called the Research Diagnostic Criteria (RDC). The RDC is well established and used at nearly every depression research center.

Based on the RDC, you would be considered depressed if you could answer yes to two broad questions: *One,* have you had a distinct period of feeling down and unhappy or a distinct period of overall loss of pleasure and interest? And *two,* have you suffered from five of the following eight symptoms for at least two weeks: (1) appetite or weight change, (2) sleep problems, (3) excessive tiredness, (4) physically slowed down or agitated, (5) loss of interest or pleasure in usual activities, (6) feeling guilty, (7) slow thinking or indecisiveness, (8) thoughts of killing yourself. You can use these two questions as a guide to discover whether you're depressed or not.

The other way to measure depression is through psychological tests. The tests ask you the same questions you'd get in a clinical interview, but in written form. Both clinical interviews and psychological tests try to assess which symptom clusters you have. As I mentioned, there are four general symptom clusters: how you act, how you feel, how you think, and how your body reacts. This book is written and designed to help you overcome these specific symptom clusters one at a time.

If you're depressed, what can you do about it?   Most people don't do anything: They muddle through the best they can. And because depression usually is self-limiting, their depression does lift—although this may take a while. But you can do more than just wait. A range of effective treatments for depression, both medical and psychological, has been developed that means you can minimize your suffering and get over your depression much more quickly.

MEDICAL TREATMENTS

Indirect medical treatments.   Since certain physical problems—among them infections, cancer, epilepsy, vitamin deficiencies, some forms of arthritis, and disorders of the endocrine system—are associated with the symptoms of depression, the depression symptoms are secondary to the physical problems. Generally, if you treat the physical problems medically, the depression will clear up.

Similarly, side effects of some drugs may be the real problem Antihypertensive drugs, cardiac drugs, birth control pills, and steroids can bring on the depression syndrome. If safe to do so, the removal or change of drugs will clear up the depression. For these reasons, if you suffer from depression you should have a physical examination and have any current medications you're taking checked out for depressive side effects.

Electric shock therapy (EST).   Although once used extensively to treat depression, EST is used much less now. No one knows quite why EST works, but it does help some people—although the improvement often is temporary. EST is used mainly as a last resort when other treatments haven't worked or when the person is an extremely high suicide risk.

Lithium. Biopolar depression, or manic depression, character- ized by fluctuating periods of mania, is the one form of depression that most likely has a biological basis. The disorder, which affects only a small portion of depressives, is believed to be inherited, although stress can bring on attacks.

The manic state is one of constant excitement. A manic person believes he or she is so great that anything can be accomplished. I saw one forty-five-year-old manic patient who believed he could do just about anything. He'd go into police stations and ask if they had any crimes he could help them solve. He told me he didn't need my help but if I had any difficult cases to call him and he'd give me a hand. He was hospitalized when he began to think he could stop cars simply by walking in front of them.

A drug, lithium, can control this disorder, but since there seems to be a psychological as well as a physical component to the problem, the best treatment is often a combination of lithium and psychotherapy.

Antidepressants. While there's been no breakthrough in drug treatment of depression over the last fifteen years, researchers are finding better ways to use the drugs currently available. And new drugs are being tested all the time. Among the antidepressant drugs, tricyclics are by far the most commonly prescribed. (They're called tricyclics because of their chemical formation.) The best known are Tofranil, Norpramin, and Elavil. You must take the drug for about two weeks before it starts working. Studies have found drugs are helpful sixty to seventy percent of the time.

The second major category of antidepressants is known as MAO Inhibitors. Among this group are Parnate, Marplan, and Nardil. They often work when the person doesn't respond to tricyclics; however, they are less safe than the tricyclics and need close medical monitoring.

Researchers aren't quite sure why drugs work. They seem to improve the physical symptoms of depression: sleep difficulties, lack of energy, and appetite problems. People with marked physical symptoms do the best on antidepressant drugs. Because the symptoms of depression are interrelated, improvement in one sympton cluster leads to improvement in the other clusters.

Antidepressant drugs do have drawbacks. All drugs have side effects, such as drowsiness, dizziness, and dry mouth, which many people find uncomfortable. Older people in particular are sensitive to the side effects. Others with certain physical problems such as hypertension can't take the drugs.

A harsher criticism is that drugs give only a temporary cure for the problem, like having a drink to calm your nerves. When you mask your symptoms of depression with drugs, you aren't motivated to see what's wrong with your life that needs changing.

Over a dozen research projects studying the effectiveness of cognitive therapy have found that the vast majority of people can overcome their depression without drugs. But because depression is a serious problem, I do recommend drugs if the psychological methods aren't working.

Even if you do find relief with antidepressants, you can still benefit immensely by learning how to use psychological methods to lift your moods.

PSYCHOLOGICAL TREATMENTS

Psychological (as opposed to medical) therapy is the other major form of treatment for depression. Despite the differences among the range of therapies available, they can be broken down into three types: traditional or insight, behavioral, and cognitive.

Insight therapy. The goal of traditional therapy is to provide you with insight into and understanding of your problems. The type of understanding depends on the therapy. In analytic therapy the focus is on understanding your early childhood experiences; these experiences are believed to cause your depression. Other traditional therapies focus on getting you to understand and accept what are thought to be your true feelings. This is based on the belief that when you're depressed you're really angry at someone else. Because you can't express this anger, you turn it inward and become depressed.

Whether or not traditional therapy works as well as antidepression drugs isn't known. The evidence is conflicting and unclear. But there's increasing research evidence that together they work better than either one alone.

Behavior therapy. Traditional therapy has been criticized for spending too much time on talk and too little on action. While traditional therapy often downplays current concerns and problems, behavior therapy is almost exclusively focused on them. Behaviorists believe that your depression is caused because you have too few positive experiences (reinforcers) and too many unpleasant experiences. The solution is to increase pleasant experiences and through problem solving to decrease unpleasant ones.

Several studies have found behavior therapy more effective than traditional therapy with depression. However, behavior therapy has been criticized for not helping the person gain psychological understanding of his or her problems, and for not helping uncover and correct thinking habits and underlying beliefs that may lead to depression in the first place.

Cognitive therapy. In a sense, cognitive therapy is a hybrid of the other two approaches. Like behavior therapy, it is interested in action and solving present concerns. And like traditional therapies, it tries to unearth dysfunctional beliefs. However, cognitive therapy places much more emphasis on actively correcting faulty beliefs than traditional therapy does.

Specifically, cognitive therapy, developed at the University of Pennsylvania by Aaron T. Beck, M.D., and his colleagues, is based on the cognitive model of emotional disorders. The basic principle of the cognitive model is this: *How you evaluate or think about your experiences determines how you react emotionally.* If you think you've lost something, you'll feel sad; if you think you're in danger, you'll feel anxious; if you think others have treated you wrongly, you'll feel angry. Recent research has found that people with emotional disorders systematically distort their experiences. The direction and type of cognitive distortion determines the nature of the emotional disorder. If you distort your experiences in such a way that you see conspiracies everywhere, you become paranoid; if you misinterpret your neutral experiences as signs of danger, you become anxious; and if you distort your experiences in a manner that leads you to conclude you're a loser, you become depressed.

Though cognitive therapy was developed specifically to treat depression, it clearly has application to other emotional problems. It teaches the person how to identify, correct, and "reality-test" cognitive distortions. For example, the depressed person learns to master problems and situations she previously believed were impossible by learning to reevaluate and change her mistaken thinking. To get the most out of cognitive therapy, you need to grasp at a deep level two basic principles. The first is that you create your psychological reality by your thinking. The second is that your state of mind is directly related to your mood. When you are in a low state of mind and not thinking clearly you need to raise your mood so that you can more accurately see what is going on.

Cognitive therapy is brief, directive, and highly structured. You first learn how to obtain relief from symptoms; later, after your state of mind has risen, you learn how to identify and change the dysfunctional beliefs that led you to distort your experiences in the first place.

Before describing cognitive therapy and outlining how you can use its techniques and principles to overcome depression, I'd like to talk about women and depression.

DEPRESSION IN WOMEN

Some writers have estimated that six to ten times more women than men suffer from depression. These high estimates are misleading—because they're based on who seeks treatment. And because fewer men go for help, many aren't counted.

When looking at the number of depressed women versus the number of depressed men, you have to take into account self-disclosure. Men are more reluctant to admit to being depressed, partly because many believe it's unmanly and partly because it's not as socially acceptable for men to talk about being depressed. In a study at UCLA, researchers found that women are encouraged by friends and relatives to talk about their depression while men are actually discouraged from doing so.

When depressed men do go for help to the family physician or a therapist, they're less likely to be diagnosed as depressed. Many men, particularly older men, mask their depression by describing it as a physical problem, such as headache. As a result, their depression is often overlooked. Further, more depressed men than women drink to control their depression and so are more often diagnosed as alcoholic rather than depressed.

Even when taking all this into account, women *are* depressed more often than men. Well-designed community surveys in the United States and other countries have found that women clearly have the lead in depression. At least twice as many women as men are depressed.

Maggie Scarf, a science writer, has investigated this thoroughly and concludes, "The evidence is clear and overwhelming, females from adolescence onwards are far more vulnerable to depression than are males. It turns up in virtually every study carried out anywhere and everywhere."*

Why so many depressed women? Researchers have spent a great deal of time trying to answer this question. (Many depression researchers prefer to study women because subjects are easier to find.) But no general answer has been found.

The answer is most likely in the social/psychological area rather than in the biological. Studies have found that female hormones, which can affect moods, can't account for so much depression among women. The one subgroup of depression (manic-depressive) that has the most evidence for a biological cause is made up mostly of men.

There's not one but many reasons for the high rate of depression among women. These reasons or causes come together in special ways for each person. Each person's situation is unique, but the cultural, social, and psychological themes are the same.

Our culture accounts for some of the reasons why more women

* *Psychology Today,* April 1979, p. 45.

than men become depressed. By culture, I mean way of life, the way people customarily act—how you raise your children, your reactions toward the opposite sex, and what you expect of other people. Cultural influences starting at birth are continually at work. For example, baby girls are seen as being smaller and weaker than boys of the same size.

Cultural influences are crystalized into social institutions: work, marrige, family, leisure, politics, religion. Social institutions in turn affect you in real ways—how you think, act, and feel and what opportunities and resources are open or closed to you.

Many aspects of our culture encourage dependency in women. Women are given the message from childhood: *To be accepted and appreciated you must be relatively passive, submissive, and anxious to please.* in other words, *dependent.*

A number of writers have talked about the role excessive dependency plays in causing depression, especially for women. They argue that females are *not* encouraged to act independently: rather, they're raised to please others. As a result, they become emotionally dependent on others' opinions. They feel good when others like them and bad when they don't. When they lose or don't have the good opinions of others, they are more vulnerable to depression. There's a good deal of merit to this argument.

While traditional cultural values contribute to depression among women, part of this upsurge is associated with rapid social change. Many women find themselves in marginal positions. They aren't sure where they stand. There are strong pressures to achieve and develop a career and equally strong counterpressures to raise a family and be more traditional. Many believe they're caught up in a no-win situation; no matter which way they turn, they lose.

Despite social changes, most women still place more emphasis on traditional family roles of wife and mother than on building a career. Perhaps for some women this makes them more vulnerable to depression. Community surveys have consistently found housewives to make up a large portion of depressed women.

Work outside of the home appears to protect some women from depression. In a major study carried out in London, investigators found that women who didn't work outside of the home were twice as likely to be depressed as women who did. A study in the United

States found similar results. Young mothers who didn't have outside jobs were much more lonely and unhappy than young mothers who did.

There's one other piece of evidence that a job plays an important role in depression: Women outdistance men in depression at all ages until men reach sixty-five. Then the numbers start to equal each other—just when many men are retiring and leaving their jobs.

If employment affects women this way, why? What reasons would account for this? Obviously, if women are underemployed and make less money than men, even for doing the same job, women often have fewer resources to meet everyday demands.

The problems of lower-paying jobs are often compounded by the problem of child care. Many women have to raise children on their own after a divorce or separation. Fewer resources and increased demands can contribute to depression.

The high incidence of depression among housewives may be due to the lack of structure and recognition in the job. The tasks are continuous, without beginning or end. The other family members automatically expect the toilet bowl to be clean, fresh socks in the drawers, the breakfast mess tidied. These completed chores are rarely recognized. When a woman has an outside job, her life is more structured and she is rewarded with a paycheck.

Self-esteem.   Many of the jobs women have, such as housewife, bring low social status. There are signs this may be changing, but it hasn't so far. Society is still status- and achievement-oriented.

A person's job provides one of the most common ways used to build self-esteem. The person's relationships provide another. Because women often have less investment in their careers, they're more vulnerable to depression if their relationships go bad. Unlike many men, they don't have careers to fall back on.

What does this mean? Must you have a high-prestige job to avoid depression? Or go to work if you're a housewife? Not at all. Many more women, working or not, aren't depressed than are. And this doesn't mean female sex roles are bad and male sex roles are good. Except for depression, men lead in just about every other emotional and behavioral disorder. Popular opinion polls over the years have found that women report being happier than men.

It does mean that you must be careful about what cultural messages you choose to adopt as part of your personal philosophy—messages like "If you don't have an important job, you're nothing." It's only when these beliefs become incorporated into your psychology that they can be dangerous.

Way of looking at the world. Growing up as men or women, people learn to look at the world in different ways, to develop different psychologies. Many women, for example, learn to take on excessive responsibility for others. When her son develops a cold, a mother thinks, "It's my fault. I shouldn't have let him go out without a coat." When her employer is having business trouble, a secretary thinks, "It must have been something I did."

The social influences I've mentioned before can play a big part in strengthening these beliefs and attitudes. For example, women can be used as handy scapegoats. When a teacher is unable to handle a student, she can complain, "It's the mother's fault." When a husband gets lost, he can say, "My wife gave me the wrong directions." And when the employer fails to get a letter out on time, he can alibi, "My secretary must have lost it." Many women allow themselves to be used as scapegoats and compound the problem by automatically assuming they are responsible for everything that goes wrong in the world.

Ruth Greenberg, at the University of Pennsylvania, has written on the role of depression among women. She stresses the importance of women's believing they have mastery over their lives.

Researchers *have* found that women underestimate their degree of influence over events. Men do the opposite: Men believe they have more control over a situation than they actually do. This is one of the reasons women become depressed more often than men: *Women overestimate their responsibility and at the same time underestimate their ability to master the situation.*

I saw an extremely depressed woman who was a good illustration of this. She was convinced she was worthless. Her proof? Her husband was cheating on her and her teenage son had been kicked out of school for fighting. In both cases she believed it was totally her fault and she was helpless to change either situation. It was only after she was able to see that she did have some choices over how the situation turned out that she was able to get better.

Why a book for depressed women? Over the years I have treated patients with both depression and intake disorders (alcohol and drug dependency and obesity). These people fought their black moods off (at least for a while) by drinking, taking pills, smoking marijuana, or overeating. Most were women.

From this experience, I helped develop procedures and strategies for people caught in this double bind. The emphasis was on self-management: ways the person could manage her depression as well as what she put into her body. I put these ideas into a manual for other therapists—and then moved on to another problem, depressed older people.

Around this time, Betty Ford disclosed that she was addicted to alcohol and Valium. Her disclosure was followed by a government report that said that alcohol and drug dependency among women has reached epidemic proportions. A silent problem was becoming less silent. Newspapers and radio stations began to contact the Cognitive Therapy Center. Had we found a similar problem with alcohol and drugs among the depressed women we treat? We had.

Most of the depressed patients I had seen were women. Cognitive therapy was developed and tested largely with women. Some groups of our patients, such as the elderly, are almost entirely women. And, as I mentioned earlier, women are at *twice the risk* of becoming depressed as men. Further, women are more inclined to admit they are depressed and more willing to do something about it.

I wanted to address in detail the common concerns and issues women face. Though men and women have the same feelings—both get depressed—persons of the same sex share common experiences and situations that lead to different reasons for each becoming depressed. Men, for example, become depressed more often over career problems and loss of sexual powers. Women, on the other hand, are more likely to become depressed over relationship problems—problems with boyfriends, husbands, parents, and children.

While this book is geared to women, men can get just as much out of it. The principles and techniques of cognitive therapy apply equally to men and women.

I've organized this book as if you had come to see me for help with your depression. First, I explain what depression is and how cognitive therapy can help. Then I focus on how you can get immediate relief from your symptoms (inactivity, negative feelings, thinking problems, and physical problems) and raise your state of mind. Next, I discuss ways to overcome common complications of your depression (weight gain, alcohol and drug dependency, and relationship problems).

After this, I describe ways you can avoid future depressions by working on the psychological causes of depression (underlying negative beliefs and ineffective ways of handling stress). Finally, I talk about how you can lead a more self-reliant and self-directed life, which I believe is the key not only to avoiding future depressions but to leading a better and happier life.

When I told a friend I was writing this book, she said in effect, "How could a book help someone get over depression? It seems to me that she'd have to go to a therapist."

I disagreed with her. I believe people can learn from written as well as spoken words. I know I learn more from reading than from listening. So do many others. I've noticed this in therapy. At times I've struck out trying to get an idea across to a patient, but the person readily understands it when she reads it. Granted, many don't enjoy reading and many don't learn from reading, but others do.

In therapy, the goal is for the patient to learn to master her emotions and actions. Gaining information makes up a large share of this learning. Because reading is one of the best ways to gain information, I encourage patients to read material that's to the point. Throughout therapy, I give patients books and articles to read. Sometimes I suggest the patient read the therapist's treatment manual. Cognitive therapy is essentially education. And people can learn in a variety of ways, including reading.

Over ninety percent of depressed people ignore or self-treat their depression. This book can benefit those who don't go for treatment. By following the suggestions, the severely depressed patient can get herself moving again and gain encouragement to get more help if it's needed.

However, if you're depressed, you're probably mildly so (you feel bad and aren't functioning well—but you are still functioning). This may be a recurring problem: the mild depression hangs on for days or even weeks, and these periodic depressions occur three or four times a year.

Although cognitive therapy was developed to help severely depressed people, it's very effective in knocking out mild depressions. The suggestions here—if followed—are sufficient to beat a mild depression. The procedures can also be used to eliminate your normal down moods that aren't true depressions, but are painful nonetheless.

To defeat depression you have to do the work—no matter if you see a therapist or read this book. One or two hours a week talking to a therapist isn't powerful enough *by itself* to defeat a longstanding depression. You can learn what you have to do by reading this book or by talking to a therapist, but *you* have to translate the method into action.

Teachers have been saying for years, "Do your homework." I tell patients the same, "To get rid of your depression, don't just work in the office—work at home. Do your homework."

One of the few patients who didn't get better with cognitive therapy said, "This proves your stuff doesn't work." In her case, I never found out if it worked or not because she never really tried it. I've found that patients who follow through on their homework get better.

By using the self-management procedures outlined here, you're buying insurance against future depressions. Once you learn how to use these methods, you can catch your depression before it becomes full-blown. True, a therapist can give encouragement and direction, but when it finally comes down to results—it's up to you.

I

How Cognitive Therapy Works

COGNITIVE therapy stresses the importance of looking at the facts
—good or bad. In keeping with this policy, we at the Center for
Cognitive Therapy have asked ourselves from the beginning: *Does
cognitive therapy work?*

First, we started by keeping careful track of our patients: We
found most recovered from their depressions rapidly. And when
we contacted them up to two years later they were still doing fine.
This was great, but it still wasn't proof—case studies aren't scientific
proof.

The case studies did show cognitive therapy had promise. Because of this, the government gave the Center enough money to
study cognitive therapy systematically. We decided to compare
cognitive therapy to treatment with antidepressant drugs, shown
over the years to be an effective treatment for depression.

Our reasoning: If cognitive therapy did as well as drugs (an effective treatment), this would show cognitive therapy worked. Further,
many people refuse to take antidepressant drugs (or any other type
of drug), others can't take drugs because of side effects, and antidepressant drugs don't help everyone that's depressed. So perhaps
we could show an effective alternative to drug treatment or depression.

We studied forty-one depressed patients. One group was treated
with drugs, the other with cognitive therapy. The average patient
had been depressed off and on for eight years; twenty-five percent

had been hospitalized for depression in the past and seventy-five percent were suicidal. We used standard measures of depression before and after treatments.

What happened after twelve weeks of treatment? The drug treatment did as expected: Nearly everyone who stayed in treatment (some dropped out because of side effects) improved, and five of the twenty-one people in this group were completely symptom-free after treatment.

The cognitive treatment, however, didn't do as expected—*it did better*. Patients treated with cognitive therapy showed more improvement across the board, and fifteen out of nineteen had no symptoms at all after treatment. We followed the patients for a year, and those treated with cognitive therapy still did better than those treated with drugs. Twice as many who used drugs relapsed compared to those treated with cognitive therapy.

Researchers in different locations, including the University of Toronto, Michigan State University, the University of Western Ontario, the University of Oklahoma, and Queens University in Canada, report similar successes.

Cognitive therapy has also been found to be more effective than behavioral and traditional therapy. In one study, cognitive therapy was compared to brief traditional therapy. The subjects in this study were thirty Black depressed women. Both treatments worked better than no treatment, and cognitive therapy worked best.

In a recent study at the Center, we tried to see if adding antidepressant drugs to cognitive therapy would improve its effectiveness. Half of the patients were given cognitive therapy plus drugs, the other half had cognitive therapy alone. We found that those who had cognitive therapy alone did just as well as those who had cognitive therapy plus drugs; drugs didn't add to cognitive therapy's effectiveness.

I now can tentatively answer the question—does cognitive therapy work? Yes. Over a dozen studies have shown it works, and that it works better than other forms of treatment. (All studies have limitations—and there are no *absolute* ways of proving anything.)

Aside from suffering, depression costs Americans millions of dollars in lost time and in health care. If a national health-insurance plan comes about, the treatment of depression will be a great expense. The government wants treatments for emotional problems that work.

With this in mind, the National Institute of Mental Health has funded a multimillion-dollar project to study the treatment of depression. Cognitive therapy is one of the treatments being studied. This project (being conducted on a national level) is a vote of confidence in cognitive therapy. In a time of dwindling research funds, this is the largest psychotherapy research project ever funded.

Britain has even less money for research; yet they have the same problem: Depressed patients put a heavy strain on the health-care system. For this reason, their Research Council has funded a study to see if cognitive therapy will work with their depressed people. The study is being conducted at the Department of Psychiatry at Oxford University, under the direction of Dr. John Teasdale, a senior researcher at Oxford. Studies of cognitive therapy are also being conducted at the University of Edinburgh in Scotland and in West Germany.

THE CAUSES OF DEPRESSION

Part of what I do in cognitive therapy could be considered educational—I pass on to patients what I've learned about depression as a therapist and researcher. But patients often have their own ideas on why they're depressed. Some believe their depression is caused by events ("I lost my job") and others believe it's caused by personal traits ("I'm ugly"). They'll concede what I've found about depression may apply to others—but insist their own situations are different. Kelly Ward was like that.

Kelly was a first-year law student when she came to see me. She was convinced that her depression was caused by a simple fact: namely, that she was too stupid to have realized she was too stupid for law school. She was one of the most skeptical patients I have ever seen; she spent the first session cross-examining me about depression. She had some good questions about this puzzling phenomenon and it took me a good while to answer them all.

Logic of depression. Why have people from the beginning of time suffered from depression? On the face of it, it doesn't make sense. Take sadness for example—feeling sad and blue is the chief sign of depression, yet feeling this way goes against a basic human drive to achieve happiness.

The depressed person seems to have lost this drive. Kelly, for example, avoided the things that used to bring her pleasure—parties, visiting friends, going to plays and movies.

The purpose of life, if nothing else, is to survive—to go on. Yet depression goes against this life force. The depressed person stops fighting. She may even go completely against the will to survive and kill herself.

Consider the puzzle of the depressed person's symptoms. She feels overwhelmed, yet stops trying to solve problems. She works at half-speed when she should be doing more. She has trouble remembering everyday concerns but can't forget past bad experiences. She has a general problem in concentration, but can concentrate intensely on her flaws. She has a strange type of fatigue. She does less but feels tired. Rest makes the fatigue worse—and despite the fatigue, she can't sleep.

Depressed people stand their qualities on their heads. A former beauty contestant believes she's ugly, a college professor believes she's stupid, a loving mother believes her children would be better off without her.

Dr. Aaron Beck has spent the last twenty-five years trying to make sense out of the puzzles and paradoxes of depression. He started out to prove Freud was right (people are depressed because they're angry at someone else) and ended up discovering Freud was wrong—depressed people in general are not angry at others.

His research was not armchair speculation but painstaking and systematic. In the end, he discovered depression and its symptoms to make perfect sense—once you look at the depressed person's thinking.

Distorted Thinking. What leads to a typical depression? First, you run into some type of stress (a loss, anxiety on the job, ending of a relationship) or a build-up of small stresses. Most people don't like setbacks but can handle them; others react by switching into negative thinking. It's as if a mask slips over them—an internal force that magnifies the negative and filters out the positive. Sylvia Plath described this as living under a bell jar with its curved glass warping and distorting what you see.

This internal force *warps* your perceptions and causes you to react in an excessive and inappropriate way. *Perception warping* is made up of a series of negative beliefs that revolve around sensitive areas: success/failure, rejection/acceptance, health/sickness, gain/loss.

This negative force begins to color all of your experiences. Experiences that would normally undermine negative ideas are twisted to support them. You begin to prejudge your experiences and because this prejudice is in your private thoughts, there's no one to argue for the other side.

A *negative view of self* is at the heart of depression. If you're depressed, you believe everything about yourself is worthless—past, present, and future. Your depression symptoms can be traced back to this basic underlying notion—"I'm a loser."

If this were all there is to it, overcoming depression would be a snap. Just list the ways you aren't a loser, and presto, you're no longer depressed. However, this doesn't work. And here's the rub: Depression muddles up not only how you feel and act ("I feel too bad to go to Mom's birthday party"), but how you think as well ("A good daughter would go"). When you become depressed, you *distort your experiences* in such a way that your thinking reaffirms your negative opinion of yourself ("I'm no good").

When you're depressed, you see the world in a way that supports your own negative conclusions. Events are misheard, misperceived, and misconstrued to fit the prevailing negative line. The distorted thinking that keeps you locked into depression acts as a kind of Procrustean mold—an arbitrary standard to which you force exact conformity. (Procrustes was the mythical Greek villain who either stretched his guests or chopped off their feet to fit his bed.)

Assumptions. Why do some people respond in such a self-defeating way to stress when others don't? The answer can be found in people's assumptions and beliefs. Everyone has learned a set of assumptions about herself and some can lead to depression. Self-defeating beliefs usually stay in the back of your mind ("I'm unlovable" . . . "I should be the best" . . . "Everyone should always like me"). But if the right buttons are pushed, they jump forward. When you encounter setbacks that touch on these negative beliefs ("John didn't ask me out again"), the beliefs come alive ("I'm unlovable"). If you're prone to depression, you probably have many more of these self-defeating beliefs.

Assumptions, for the most part, are silent. You're unaware of them unless you're specifically asked—and even then you may not realize you hold them. Beliefs about yourself often grow out of childhood experiences. Many are based on family rules. A parent may tell a child, "Mary, be nice or others won't like you." The child may repeat this to herself—out loud at first ("Mary, be nice") and later silently to herself. After a while she develops the unspoken rule or assumption, "My worth depends on what others think of me."

Some patients develop negative beliefs after a painful experience. One woman's parents divorced when she was eight. Like many children, she thought it was her fault. This led to the belief, "When bad things happen, it's my fault." Years later, after ending her own relationship, this negative belief reappeared in full force and led to a severe depression.

Feedback. Is there more to it than this? Yes, and that's the concept of feedback. As shown in Table 1, stress (a loss of a relationship, a setback on your job) activates negative beliefs that lead to distorted thinking and the symptoms of depression. The symptoms then feed the negative beliefs and keep them alive.

In Kelly Ward's case, she had been an academic star in high school and college. But when she ran into tougher competition in law school, she didn't do as well. This was stressful to her and activated old beliefs ("If I'm not the best, I'm nothing"). Her father had wanted a son who achieved great heights. Since there were no boys in her family, she took on this burden and pushed herself to excel. Her experiences in law school activated the old belief that she had to be the best or she was nothing, leading to thinking distortions and depression.

TABLE 1

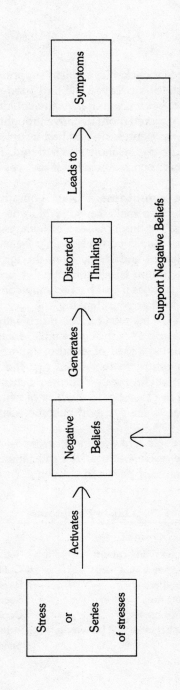

Here is the feedback: Her sadness supported the idea that everything was bad. (She believed she had good reason to be sad.) Her feelings of sadness were so heavy she couldn't think of much else. The sadness triggered more negative thoughts. She became slowed down during her depression and had trouble getting tasks done, so her school work and relationships suffered. The feedback from her symptoms supported her belief that she was basically inadequate.

Reasons for symptoms. Once your thinking is understood, depression starts to make sense. What you think determines how you feel. Negative thoughts lead to feelings of sadness and dejection. For example, if you mistakenly believe others dislike you, you'll feel rejected and lonely even though most others may like you. Similarly, if you falsely think you've done something terrible, you'll feel as guilty as if you had *actually* committed a terrible act.

When you look at your thinking, the symptoms make sense (see Table 2). You see the world as too much with you and you become passive. Tasks you once thought simple, such as getting the kids off to school or doing a load of laundry, appear insurmountable. You may want to return to work, but just the idea of going for an interview overwhelms you. You may believe you have to take a drink or a pill just to cope. In the face of what you see as the sheer weight of your difficulties, you become apathetic and feel beaten down.

Avoiding people and wanting to escape—the extreme being suicide—are the results of negative expectations. You see your future as a continuation of pain and suffering. You're without hope and

TABLE 2
Relationship of Thinking to Symptoms

Thinking	Symptoms
I lost something very important.	Sadness
I shouldn't have acted that way.	Guilt
Everything is too hard.	Passiveness
People won't like me.	Social withdrawal
I need the help of others.	Dependency
No matter what I choose, it'll be wrong.	Indecisiveness
I'm a loser.	Sense of worthlessness.

convinced nothing will satisfy you, so you avoid the people and activities you once enjoyed.

You believe you're incompetent, so you seek help from others and become dependent. You believe any decisions you make will be wrong and become indecisive. You're bombarded with negative thoughts, and as a result you have trouble concentrating and remembering everyday details. And finally, you even blame yourself for having the symptoms of depression ("I'm worthless. I can't remember anything, make simple decisions, or get myself to do anything"), and this self-blame makes you even more depressed.

I outlined this theory to Kelly. She thought Dr. Beck's observations might help explain her own depression. However, she wanted scientific facts to back the theory up. (This scientific attitude, once applied to her own problems, allowed her to recover from her depression quickly.) I was glad to show her the studies because the primary message I try to get across to patients is the necessity of checking out the facts. Don't assume something is true merely because you believe it or because someone says it is; rather, investigate.

As I've said before, investigations, in addition to our own studies, have been conducted at leading universities and research centers. Researchers have interviewed large numbers of depressed individuals and given them a variety of psychological tests. In some studies, sophisticated experimental manipulations were used. Researchers have even studied the dreams of depressed patients. The results are remarkably consistent in supporting Dr. Beck's original observations about depression—depression is a thinking disorder.

Table 3 outlines some of these studies. Rather than go into all of them, I'd like to discuss studies that investigated the effect of thinking on moods. In a sense, this forms the basis for cognitive therapy. I believe that if you can control your thoughts, you can change your mood.

You may have had an experience similar to the following: You're waiting for someone to come home; it gets later and later. The person usually calls but hasn't this time. You imagine all kinds of disasters—traffic accidents, muggers, and so on. You're thinking that the person may be in danger, and this leads to feelings of

TABLE 3
Studies Comparing Depressed and Nondepressed Persons

Studies	Depressed Person	Nondepressed Person
Dream studies	Sees self in dreams suffering as result of inadequacies.	Normal range of dreams; sees self as competent in dreams.
Story-completion tests (person imagines self in story and completes it)	The person in the story comes to a bad ending. Chooses unrealistic and improbable answers.	The person in the story is successful; chooses realistic answers.
Memory tests	Can recall unpleasant memories but not good ones.	Can recall more pleasant memories.
Expectancy tests	Sees future as hopeless.	Sees future in realistic terms.
Experimental studies (person performs task in laboratory) measuring recall	Downgrades and underestimates how well did. Underestimates how many times rewarded for doing it right.	Accurate in recall of how well did and number of rewards.
Experimental studies measuring performance	Tries less when fails or thinks has failed.	Tries more when fails or thinks has failed.
Attitude studies (example: "If I make a mistake, I'm a failure")	Has many negative attitudes and the more depressed, the more believes them.	Few negative attitudes.
Studies of thinking processes	Rigid thinking; sees events in black-or-white terms.	Flexible thinking; sees the grays in between.

anxiety. Then you hear the person's car pull up outside and you think, "Thank God, nothing has happened."

How do you feel now? Probably relieved and happy. You changed your thoughts (no more danger), and your mood changed. But what often happens when the person walks in the door? You start to think and probably say, "Why didn't you call? Do you know how worried I was?" Your thinking changes the mood once again—this time to anger.

In early studies, researchers observed and reported on situations like this. Later the studies became more complicated. Dr. Ron Coleman, for example, had people read positive statements about themselves ("I'm a likable person") and negative statements ("I'm not reliable"). He found when people read positive statements they became happy and when they read negative statements they became sad. A series of similar studies turned up the same results.

In a more sophisticated study, all of the subjects were purposely failed on a task. Half were led to believe they failed because they were incompetent; the others were led to believe it wasn't their fault. Those who thought the failure was their fault became sad; the others didn't. The tasks didn't lead to the mood changes, but their *thinking* about how they performed did.

Kelly Ward said, "I don't have any thoughts before I get sad. The sadness just comes. How does this fit in with your theory?" In her case, she was unaware of her thinking. Once she started tuning in to what was going through her mind, she came to see what her thoughts were. But sometimes you might not have specific negative thoughts right before your unhappy feelings. Your thinking may take a more general form in terms of the *meaning* you give the situation. For example, one patient was sad about not getting an editorial job on a magazine. She said she had no specific negative thoughts about the loss. But when I asked what losing the job meant, she said, "It means I'm inadequate and I'm never able to do anything. I won't advance my career and I'll never be happy." Her crucial, but unexpressed, meaning was about the negative consequences of not getting this job—and this fed her depression.

People place private meanings on their daily activities. These private meanings are usually not expressed fully in their thoughts.

Generally, the more the private meaning of an event differs from the public meaning the greater the chance for emotional problems. Some patients believe this theory is too simple—others think it's too complicated. One housewife said, "I know I look at things in a negative way, but I can't change my whole personality."

I told her that depression is a psychological state, not a part of your character. I don't believe there's such a thing as a depressive personality. Even the most chronically depressed person isn't depressed all the time. To overcome depression you have to change specific mistakes in thinking and acting, not your whole personality. (That wouldn't be possible, anyway.)

Kelly believed, however, that there were justifiable reasons for her depression. Most depressed people believe this to some extent. After our first meeting, Kelly asked, "What if everything really is bad—like in my case. Wouldn't anyone become depressed?"

I told Kelly, "I'm not sure the situation is as bad as you may think. Later, we can check this out. First, we want to find out which problems are practical and need practical solutions and which are self-created and need psychological solutions."

So the first part of Kelly's statement ("Everything is bad") may or may not be true. But I think the second part ("Anyone would become depressed") is wrong. Most people may become frustrated and momentarily unhappy over setbacks and misfortune, but they don't become clinically depressed.

Kelly knew of several people who had a lot of problems but hadn't become depressed; she was even able to come up with incidents from her own life when setbacks didn't automatically lead to depression.

HOW COGNITIVE THERAPY WORKS

The idea that emotional problems are caused by faulty thinking is not new. Early Greek philosophers argued that it isn't situations that upset people but their interpretations of the situations. Many writers have been saying essentially the same ever since.

Cognitive theory is new in that it's more detailed. The exact thinking errors that lead to specific emotional problems are spelled out. This leads to direct ways you can correct your emotional problems. The other approaches were too global—and didn't allow for specific ways to correct the errors.

Interestingly, you don't have to buy the theory completely to get over your depression. But what you must do is use the method that grew out of this theory.

How does cognitive therapy work? When Mrs. Barconi came for treatment, I asked her a number of questions. I wanted to find out what her main symptoms were and how they were affecting her life. She saw herself as a total failure. To her, this was obvious. Every day she had hundreds of negative thoughts, each one confirming that she was a loser. When her husband didn't call from work, she automatically assumed he no longer loved her. She considered this further proof that she was unlovable. When she didn't get her daughter out of bed in time for school, she thought, "This just proves what a lousy mother I am." And when a neighbor complimented her on a meal, she jumped to the conclusion, "She's humoring me because the food was bad. I can't even cook anymore. People think I'm so weak they don't even tell me the truth." She didn't just have these thoughts once, but over and over again.

I've seen many people like Mrs. Barconi. And as I said earlier, I've found a common thread running through all of the cases—the person's mistaken way of looking at the world is keeping her depressed. Not events, and not emotions gone mysteriously haywire, but *her thinking* is keeping her depressed.

If this is true, it will be good news. Because while it's tough, if possible at all, to *change* directly your emotions from feeling bad to feeling good, or change situations or events, you *can* learn to *control* your thinking and thus your depression.

At her first session, Mrs. Barconi and I went over her symptoms in detail. She complained most about her lack of energy and said she had trouble completing jobs around the house. She was apathetic and lacked motivation. So we worked on this symptom cluster first. The symptoms of depression are interrelated: Improvement in one area leads to improvement in other areas. And this is what happened to Mrs. Barconi.

She put into practice my suggestions (mainly ways to challenge the thoughts that kept her apathetic) and followed the guidelines we had worked out together. She became more active and began to have more energy. She then started to show improvement with symptoms that hadn't been focused upon.

For example, she had trouble getting to sleep. This symptom of her depression wasn't directly worked upon. However, once she started to become busier during the day and spent less time watching television, she fould that she was physically tired at night—and this allowed her to fall asleep. There were still other symptoms she had to work on.

You don't stop working once you get over your symptoms. This would leave you vulnerable to future depressions. You must change the mistaken thinking that brought on the depression in the first place. But the symptoms of depression can be so painful and distracting that you can't think of much else. For this reason, you have to get control of your symptoms before attacking underlying causes. In the long run, it's more important to *get* better than to *feel* better, but in the short run, you must feel better before getting better.

I can't overstate the enormous role your wrong thinking plays in bringing on depression. Thinking errors are the pitfalls and quicksand that lead down into depression. In therapy, patients practice sidestepping these errors and pulling themselves up if they slip. I encourage you to take charge over your thinking. This is the best way to *get out* and *stay out* of the grip of depression.

If you're depressed, you believe these fictitious negative ideas—and will go on believing them *unless* you actively and strongly challenge them. You need to learn how to confront these thoughts head on. You can teach yourself to do this. Mrs. Barconi was able to start effectively answering her automatic negative thoughts within a couple of weeks.

For instance, when her daughter was late for school, her negative thought was, "This proves what a lousy mother I am." One of the best ways to answer negative thoughts is to write your response out. She wrote: "First, just because Melissa was late for school doesn't prove anything—except that she was late for school. I actually woke her earlier and she didn't get out of bed. I just didn't go back. She has some responsibility for not getting out of bed in time. And even if I did make a mistake (by not going back) that doesn't make me a lousy mother. That's an overgeneralization. Really, I'm making a big deal out of nothing."

Realistic thinking. Mrs. Barconi's answers not only made her feel better, but they were closer to the truth—they reflected reality. This brings up an important point: *Cognitive therapy is not a rehash of the power of positive thinking.*

Many people make this mistake. Granted, there are surface similarities. Both stress the importance of thoughts and ideas, and both warn against the power of negative thinking. (I once had a patient who said he liked being depressed because he got a clearer picture of the negative side of things.) But the similarities between the power of positive thinking and cognitive therapy stop there.

What's wrong with the power of positive thinking? Nothing, except positive thoughts aren't always true! You can trick yourself for a while with false positive thoughts. But in the end you'll feel worse. Positive thoughts lead to positive consequences only when you believe the thoughts are true, *and only when they turn out to be true.*

Some people suggest repeating over and over, "Every day in every way, things are getting better and better." Why should you believe everything is going to get better and better? There's no proof things will. And it's highly unlikely *everything* is going to get better.

Don't be an optimist—be a *realist.* Optimists are continually getting themselves into trouble by assuming the best. They believe that they can make the trip on half a tank of gas and that their bald tires will see them through. They break down and get themselves into jams over and over again by overlooking real problems. Or as the social philosopher Max Lerner put it, "To believe either that everything is bound to work out or that nothing will ever work out is equally an exercise in mindlessness."

I'm for the power of realistic thinking—not positive thinking. A glass of water isn't optimistically half full or pessimistically half empty. Rather, it's four ounces of water in an eight-ounce glass. When you have accurate information (the good and the bad), you can make the right decisions. And leading a happy, productive life means making good choices.

In positive thinking you're replacing one global judgment ("I'm no good") for another ("I'm wonderful"). My suggestion: Shift away from *all* vague moralistic labels. Look for specific situations and problems you can change. When problems are broken down to specifics, solutions start to appear.

Beliefs such as "It's my fault if anyone I love is suffering," "I'm basically inadequate," and "I can't be happy unless I'm loved," are common themes that lead to depression, but you may have your own unique set of rules or assumptions that leads you down into depression.

Children form an assortment of beliefs about the world. Some make sense—others don't. Mrs. Barconi was the oldest child in a large Italian family. Her parents believed the older children should take care of the younger ones. When one of her brothers or sisters broke a dish or cried, her parents often blamed her. Over the years she developed the belief, "It's my fault when things go wrong." She set herself up for depression by believing this.

Awareness is the first step toward change. Once Mrs. Barconi brought her beliefs out into the open, she was able to turn them around. She continued to chip away at these beliefs even after treatment ended. At a six-month follow-up, she said, "When anyone had a problem, I used to feel guilty as though it were my fault; but I decided to stop being the big sister to all of the world's problems. Now I force myself to stop taking on everyone else's problems as my own."

Many people suffer from one depression after another—like a series of common colds. What's the best way to immunize yourself? Change the beliefs that lead to depression.

DEPRESSION AND BIOLOGY

Some people have said, "I've read that depression is a biological problem and I wonder how it could be treated with cognitive therapy." While there is strong evidence that the manic-depression disorder has a biological cause, there isn't the same type of evidence for a biological cause of straight depression.

Depression often runs in families, but this could be learned as well as inherited. If over the years you've watched your mother react to stress by getting depressed, how will this affect you? Probably this increases chances that you will react in the same way.

When you become depressed, you may have real biochemical changes. But this is *no* evidence that these changes take place before your depression. Further, psychological factors (what you see, feel, think, and do) can lead to physiological changes.

For example, suppose you're driving home from work and the car in front of you suddenly veers off the road and hits a pedestrian. The accident you just saw is likely to cause marked physiological changes. Your eyes will dilate, your muscles tighten, and there will be a rise in your gastric acidity. Adrenalin will begin to flow through your body, leading to further physiological changes. Hence, what you see, feel, think, and do can cause physiological changes as well as the other way around.

While drugs do help some depression, this doesn't prove depression is caused by a lack of them. You may have a cough for many reasons. Cough syrup may improve your cough, but it doesn't mean you began coughing because you didn't take cough syrup.

There's usually more than one way to solve a problem—no matter what the cause. In the example I just gave, you experienced arousal and internal changes after you'd witnessed a car accident. Chronic arousal can lead to hypertension, heart disease, ulcers, and other physical problems, so you'd want to bring these changes back to normal.

How could you do this? You could use chemicals by having a couple of drinks or taking a tranquilizer when you get home. You could exercise, jog, or play tennis. You could calm yourself down by talking to a friend or talking to yourself in a quiet, rational way. All of these would have the same effect of bringing your internal changes back to normal.

I'm uncomfortable pitting psychology against physiology because this type of argument keeps the myth going that the mind and body are separate. This is an outdated idea that doesn't add to understanding. In reality, people react as a whole: Every part affects every other part. The mind and body are really one.

Perhaps drug treatment and cognitive therapy aren't that far apart. In cognitive therapy, I teach people how to change their thinking. This could be seen as a physiological intervention because thoughts are made up of chemical/electrical impulses—there's nothing else in the brain. Others have suggested antidepressant drugs work because they change thinking, which in turn changes the symptoms of depression. In any case, the mind and body work together as one. Even the outcome of a dramatic physical intervention such as surgery often depends upon what surgeons call the patient's "will to survive."

The question is not, "What gets people over depression—psychology or drugs?" The question is, "What is the best way to help a particular individual?"

GUIDELINES FOR OVERCOMING DEPRESSION

When you become bogged down in depression, the solution is clear: Correct your thinking. This, of course, is easier said than done. You may not believe you're making any thinking errors. You may think, like Kelly Ward, "Others might become depressed because they distort things, but I'm depressed because everything is rotten." Every depressed person believes this to some extent since ideas are taken for facts: If you didn't believe you were a loser, you wouldn't be depressed. Only when you recover will you fully realize the extent of your errors.

I recommend you take Mrs. Barconi's lead in overcoming your depression. *She was willing to entertain the possibility—however slight—that her conclusions about herself were wrong.* She believed she was basically a loser, but she was able to suspend this belief while she fought her depression.

She began to search for alternative explanations. In the past, she took the first negative idea that popped into her head as the final word. *She decided to test out many of these negative ideas.* When she thought, "I won't enjoy myself at the movies," instead of staying home she went to the movies to see if this was really true or not. *She gave the procedure a chance to succeed.* This was crucial: She didn't abandon a strategy without first giving it a fair try.

In summary, cognitive therapy has helped hundreds of patients like Mrs. Barconi and Kelly Ward defeat their depressions. Unlike traditional psychoanalysis (that takes years to complete), this approach is active, fast, and effective. Patients, many of them severely depressed, are over their depressions in a matter of weeks. And unlike drug treatment for depression, it teaches methods and strategies you can use to avoid future depressions.

To get the most out of this book, first read the whole thing. Then go back and review the sections that most apply to you. Remember, to get the best benefit you have to translate the suggestions into actions.

If, after trying these methods, you still can't shake your depression, go for counseling. But first, I suggest you give the approach here a strong and fair try.

II

Changing Distorted and Self-Defeating Thinking

Sue Berlie was baffled. She'd moved to Philadelphia with her husband and two children from Arizona when he was transferred. She'd heard jokes about how bad Philadelphia was and thought she might have a little trouble adjusting, but the deep depression she developed caught her by surprise. She didn't know how to get over it.

I suggested she approach this mystery as a scientist. Scientists change mysteries into problems because problems, unlike mysteries, can be solved. I urged her to see her depression as a series of manageable problems to be solved—not as one global problem.

The best way to beat your depression is to consider each symptom as a separate problem to be solved. Then change the thinking that's keeping the symptom going. It takes effort, but with practice, changing your negative thinking can become second nature.

The steps to changing your thinking, while not easy, are simple. First, become *aware* of your self-defeating thoughts; second, *answer* these with more realistic ones; and third, *act* on the new thoughts.

If you use the three A's *(awareness, answering,* and *action)* you can overcome the symptoms and causes of your depression. Take Sue's case, for example. Her negative feelings were a major symptom of her depression.

She was sad much of the time. To overcome this, she first became *aware* of the thoughts that came with the sadness ("I don't have any friends in Philadelphia and I never will"). Next, she began to *answer* them ("I don't know for sure that I'll never make any friends. If I go out and try to meet people, I'm bound to make friends. I always have in the past"). She then *acted* on the new thoughts (she signed up for a tennis clinic and called an old school friend who lived in Philadelphia).

By using the three A's over and over again, she eventually got over her depression and learned, if not to love Philadelphia, at least to tolerate it.

Awareness

Symptoms of depression. How do you go about learning to use the three A's? First, you have to recognize your symptoms. This is the first level of awareness (even before you start working on your thinking). Depressed people often don't recognize the symptoms of depression. They miss or misinterpret them. They believe acting and feeling depressed are natural parts of their personality—not symptoms of an emotional disorder.

Many depressed people believe their feelings are dead. They don't see this as a sign of depression, rather they see it as a sign that they are uncaring. Others deny and cover up their negative feelings. Sue, for example, covered up her feelings of sadness with false cheerfulness. When people asked how she was feeling she would answer, "Oh, just fine, thank you," even though she was painfully sad.

So, first you must become aware of your symptoms: those times when you're acting and feeling depressed. This is crucial because it sets the stage for change. Below are some ways you can become more aware of your symptoms:

1. *Pay attention to your mood changes.* When you start to feel *sad, gloomy, ashamed, bored, lonely,* or *rejected,* tune in to what's going on, to how you're feeling. These are also important clues to your thinking.

2. *Own your own feelings.* If you're having trouble recognizing your feelings, start talking about them. Tell people how you're honestly feeling at any given moment. Sue started by having an honest talk with her husband.

3. *Be alert to your body.* This is a clue to your emotions. Butterflies in your stomach can be anxiety; heaviness in your limbs can be a clue to sadness. Notice your posture, your facial expression, how you're walking and moving.

4. *Label your avoidance.* Keep a lookout for people, places, and activities that you once enjoyed but are now avoiding. Forget about the reasons *why* you're avoiding them, just see *when* you do.

5. *Watch for times when your confidence disappears.* Are there times and places when you ask others for help? Ask yourself, were you able to handle this on your own before? Remember, this loss of confidence can be a symptom of depression.

6. *Look for activities that require great effort.* Do you have to force yourself to make or return phone calls? Or have trouble completing tasks around the house?

7. *Become aware of those times you have trouble concentrating or making decisions.* Do you vacillate over simple decisions? Second-guess yourself? These can be symptoms of depression.

Automatic negative thoughts. The second level of awareness is catching the thoughts that come before your symptoms. Dr. Beck calls these *automatic negative thoughts.* During depression, your automatic negative thoughts become turned up louder and louder until they drown out more sensible thoughts.

Imagine a telephone conversation with yourself. When you're not depressed, you have normal conversations with yourself that are under control ("You're doing a good job" . . . "The house looks nice"). You may occasionally hear something else on the line —perhaps a low buzz—but you don't pay too much attention to it. When you become depressed, that low buzz (which is really a string of automatic negative thoughts) becomes so loud that it drowns your usual voice out. The normal conversation was under your control, but these automatic thoughts aren't. Automatic thoughts lead to many of the symptoms of depression as well as symptoms of other disorders.

People think continually. Thoughts are used to monitor feelings and behavior. They're used to initiate action and anticipate events. Your thoughts tell you what to do and often how to feel.

You're having some thoughts right now as you read this. For example, you might be thinking, "This makes a lot of sense; I can see what he is saying," or it could be the opposite. Perhaps your mind is on something completely different—what you're having for dinner or what you're going to do at work tomorrow. The content varies, but you *are* thinking something.

You may have seen the movie *Annie Hall*. One scene is a good illustration of automatic negative thinking. In this scene, Annie Hall and Woody Allen nervously meet for the first time. They make awkward small talk, which you hear on the soundtrack. Meanwhile, under each is a subtitle of what they're really thinking—ideas such as, "Why did I say that? I can't believe I'm such a jerk." Their automatic thoughts keep the couple anxious. And this type of automatic thinking keeps *you* depressed.

What is the chief characteristic of negative thoughts? *They're generally wrong.* They don't reflect reality, they reflect depression. (Table 4 outlines typical errors found in this type of thinking.) Most feelings of sadness or dejection are preceded by negative thoughts. Automatic thoughts aren't wanted, they just appear. They're exaggerated negative conclusions about yourself, your world, and your future ("I'm no good" . . . "Life has no meaning" . . . "Everything bad happens to me" . . . "I'm a failure and I'll always be one").

Automatic thoughts make you depressed; and the more depressed you become, the more negative thoughts you'll have—and the more likely you are to believe them.

Sue Berlie is a good example of someone who learned to become aware of her thinking. But she had to work on it. I remember when she came to one of her early sessions. She was quite depressed and said, "I felt okay when I woke up—then I just started to feel down from then on."

I asked her, "What were your thoughts?"

She said, "I didn't have any. Waves of sadness just came over me."

To find out what you're thinking, you may have to question yourself in more detail, just as I questioned Sue. I asked her to imagine herself going through her steps that morning.

She said, "Okay. I got out of bed and fixed myself some breakfast."

"What was going through your mind?" I asked.

"I was thinking I didn't want to drive downtown—that I hate Philadelphia traffic—that it'd be too hard."

TABLE 4
Thinking Errors

Type of Error	Examples
Personalizing	Thinking all situations and events revolve around you. "Everyone was looking at me and wondering why I was there."
Magnifying	Blowing negative events out of proportion. "This is the worst thing that could happen to me."
Minimizing	Glossing over the saving and positive factors. Overlooking the fact that "nothing really bad happened."
Either/or thinking	"Either I'm a loser or a winner." Not taking into account the full continuum.
Taking events out of context	After a successful interview, focusing on one or two tough questions. "I blew the interview."
Jumping to conclusions	"I have a swollen gland. This must be cancer."
Overgeneralizing	"I always fail—I fail at everything I ever try."
Self-blame	"I'm no good." Blaming total self rather than specific behaviors that can be changed.
Magical thinking	"Everything is bad because of my bad past deeds."
Mind reading	"Everyone there thought I was fat and ugly."
Comparing	Comparing self with someone else and ignoring all of the basic differences. "Cher has a better figure than mine."
Catastrophizing	Putting the worst possible construction on events. "I know something terrible happened."

"Okay. Then what happened?"

"Well, I got ready, but then I couldn't find my keys."

"What were you thinking?"

"I was thinking, 'I can't remember anything. I lose everything.' And, 'Why does everything happen to me?' "

"Did you find your keys?"

"Yes, I found them. But when I went outside, it was about to rain and I thought, 'Jesus! It always rains in Philadelphia. Why does everything bad happen to me?' "

"Then you drove here?"

"Well, the worst thing was when I got my car, there was bird crap on the windshield."

"And what did you think as you were driving here?"

"I was thinking, 'What's wrong with me that I have to go to a doctor for help with my stupid problems? It just proves what a loser I am.' I was also thinking about the traffic and so on."

I then asked her, "With all these negative thoughts, is it any wonder you feel sad now?"

She answered, "I'm beginning to see what you're saying."

One way to become more aware of your thoughts is simply to count them. This will help you realize that they just appear—they're automatic and not a reflection of reality. If negative thoughts stay underground, they cause more harm than if they're brought out into the open. The idea is to become more aware of them.

You can count negative thoughts in several ways. The best is to use a wrist golf counter which you can get in sporting goods stores. Golf counters look like wrist watches and you click the button each time you're aware of negative thoughts. You can also use a plastic grocery-store price counter or a small stitch counter that's sold in knitting shops. Some people change money from one pocket to another: a penny is one thought, a dime ten thoughts, and so on. Or you can simply make dashes on a three-by-five card.

These gimmicks will remind you to become aware of your thinking. You'll discover that you have the same thoughts over and over again. Counting your thoughts also will help you become aware of your feelings.

Remember, *don't blame yourself* for having a lot of automatic thoughts; they're a sign of depression, not a sign of character weakness. Don't be alarmed if you seem to start having more of them —this is probably a sign that you're getting better at catching them. But in the long run, counting them usually cuts down on the number of negative thoughts you have. Remember, you don't do anything with the numbers, you just tally them.

The most simple and elegant way to become aware of your thinking is to *focus on your negative feelings and see what's behind them*. When you start to feel bad, stop what you're doing. Ask yourself, "What's going through my mind at this moment?" Because automatic thoughts are fast and are at the outer edges of your awareness, you can easily miss them. But with practice you'll be able to catch them.

Here are some additional methods you can use to become aware of your automatic negative thinking:

- *Give yourself a goal of collecting fifty negative thoughts.* One patient said, "I couldn't collect any before, how can I possibly bring in fifty?"

  I asked her, "What did you think when I just said bring in fifty negative thoughts?"

  She said, "I thought, 'I can't do it. It's too much. I'll fail at it. He'll think badly of me. I can't do anything.' "

  I told her, "Well, you already have five—that leaves only forty-five to go."

- *Use an instant-replay technique.* If you have some negative feelings and can't quite catch the thoughts, replay the feelings over and over until you catch the thoughts.

  If you can remember what happened, imagine the event *as if* it were happening right now. You might find replaying the situation in slow motion helpful.

- *Look for the meaning of the situation.* Ask yourself, "What is the significance of the situation . . . what are the consequences?" By doing this you can usually become aware of your thought. The meaning of events revolves around what you think it adds or subtracts from your life. Tell yourself, "This means I'm _____." Then fill in the blank.

- *Set aside a specific time to collect negative thoughts.* You may find sitting down at a regular time, such as from 7 to 7:30 p.m., helpful. During this half-hour period, write out some of the negative thoughts you had during the day. You might want to limit the thoughts to specific problems or situations. One person, for example, wrote down all of her negative thoughts that had to do with her children.

• *Write out your thoughts.* Have you ever written a letter and in the process discovered what you really thought about a topic? Putting your thoughts down on paper is one of the best ways to become aware of them. When you're writing them out, force yourself to go beyond the obvious thoughts that first come to mind. By doing this you can find out what your whole range of thoughts are.

Be careful of the excuses that keep you from collecting your thoughts ("This isn't the time—this is different" . . . "I'll do it later"). You may have a strong urge not to look at your negative thoughts. Most people don't like to think through the unpleasant events; but this is one of the best ways to get over your depression. Your thinking gets you depressed, but it can also get you undepressed.

Use the excuses you come up with to avoid collecting negative thoughts as cues to swing into action. This way the excuse can become an early warning signal.

Underlying dysfunctional beliefs. In addition to awareness of your symptoms and thoughts, there's a third level of awareness— awareness of the beliefs underlying your negative thoughts. In chapter X, when I talk about avoiding future depression, I'll discuss how you can bring your silent beliefs out into the open. Once out in the open they can be changed.

ANSWERING

Once you begin catching negative thoughts, you can begin answering them. The secret to answering negative thoughts is to realize there are different interpretations of any event and some are closer to reality than others. When answering your thoughts, try to consider a wide range of possible interpretations, not just the negative ones.

It's human to confuse thoughts with facts. Almost everyone does this. But the depressed person does it more often and makes bigger mistakes. Once you stop this confusion, you're on your way out of depression. If you're depressed, it's particularly important to separate thoughts from facts, since you will have more distorted thoughts. And when you believe and act on distorted thoughts, you become more depressed.

Sometimes I ask depressed patients what they were thinking right before they came into the session. I want to find out how they're looking at the world. Once I was late and the patient thought, "He's late because he doesn't want to see me." Another time a patient thought I started the session early because she needed more help. When I started the session on time, a patient thought, "He's running the sessions like an assembly line. He doesn't care about me." No matter what the experience, it can be turned around to look bad. You can see how negative thoughts lead to sadness and discouragement. For this reason, try to answer as many as you can.

Questions. When I talk to patients about their thoughts, I often ask them questions. I did this with the patient who thought I started the session late because I didn't like her. I asked her if there might be any other reason for starting late. She came up with the true answer—an earlier session had run over.

What I most like to hear from a patient is, "That's a good question. I haven't looked at it that way before."

The best way to open up closed logic is to ask yourself good questions. This is essentially what I do in therapy. I ask questions that make the person think more clearly. For example, in one case a patient was anxious about giving a talk. I asked her what she expected would happen.

She said, "People will think I'm a fool."

I asked, "What do you base this on?"

"I don't know. I just think that'd happen."

"What's your evidence?"

"Well, it's something I haven't done before."

"Do you think doing something different would be reason enough for people to think you're a fool?"

"Well, they might not think I'm a fool. They might just think I'm acting a little odd."

I asked her, "For the sake of discussion, even if they thought you were a fool, what negative results would this have?"

She said, "I don't know. I just think they might . . . but as we're talking about it, I see it's probably not too likely."

In this short interchange I asked her five questions. Eventually she learned to question her own distorted thoughts.

Learning to ask yourself good questions is an art. Socrates brought learning through questions to its highest form. You can follow his lead. Use the Socratic method yourself: Question your negative thinking so you can pry open your closed logic. Questions can spark your interest in trying, increase your motivation, and allow you to think in fresh, new ways.

In a sense, people are scientists. They make predictions ("If I go to work, I'll be paid" . . . "Cars will stop at red lights" . . . "It rains in the springtime") and then act on their predictions (buy a TV on time payments . . . start across the intersection on the green light . . . buy a spring raincoat).

People use the results of their experiences to support or change predictions. When you're depressed, you're like a scientist gone wrong. You form beliefs first and then distort experiences to support the beliefs—rather than letting the *actual* experience prove or disprove the belief.

When scientists have trouble with their experiments, their best move often is to sit down and ask themselves good, hard questions. This is also a sensible move if you're depressed.

This can be much like playing Twenty Questions. Rudolph Flesch is an authority on thinking and writing ability. He believes the strategy of asking twenty questions offers a way to solve everyday problems and possibly even to solve the most important problems of our age.

The following are twenty questions you can use to generate answers to your negative thoughts:

1. *What's the evidence?* Ask yourself, "Would this thought hold up in a court of law, or is it circumstantial?" Just because the newspaper is late one day doesn't mean you can't count on anything. Give yourself a fair trial before you convict yourself.

2. *Am I making a mistake in assuming what causes what?* Determining causes is rarely simple. Example: Many women think they're fat because they have no willpower. Scientists have been studying obesity for years and they don't know what causes it. They know the determinants are partly biological, social, cultural, psychological, familial and economic. Saying lack of willpower causes obesity is an oversimplification. Specifics are difficult to pinpoint.

3. *Am I confusing a thought with a fact?* This can lead to trouble —especially if you call yourself names and then believe them as gospel. There is an old story that makes this point: "How many legs would a dog have if you called the tail a leg? Five? Wrong. The answer is four. Calling a tail a leg doesn't make it so." Don't be *dogmatic* about your thoughts—look for the facts.

4. *Am I close enough to the situation to really know what's happening?* One woman said, "The bosses upstairs don't like our department's work and want to get rid of us." Who knows what they're thinking upstairs? You're not up there with them. You have to rely on what you know as fact. The woman's worry turned out to be a false rumor in this case.

5. *Am I thinking in all-or-none terms?* Do you see the world in either/or terms ("I'm ugly and everyone else is beautiful")? Just about everything is in degrees and on a continuum. Even a person's physical sex (male or female) is not always a clearcut issue; some people's hormonal makeup is such that it's a toss-up whether they're male or female.

6. *Am I using ultimatum words in my thinking?* ("I *always* should be nice or *no one* will like me.") You place unfair ultimatums on yourself with these words. In Table 5 I outline problems with words like this. This isn't "just semantics," but relates directly to how you feel and act.

7. *Am I taking examples out of context?* One student believed she'd been given a bad letter of recommendation. She thought the teacher said in the letter that she was narrow and rigid. When she reread the letter, she saw the teacher had written, "She has high principles." It was really a positive letter and she'd taken this part out of context.

8. *Am I being honest with myself?* Am I trying to fool myself—denying the truth, making excuses, and misplacing the blame? One depressed woman, speeding on the freeway, thought, "I hope they catch me and put me in jail." When she thought about it for a moment, she realized she didn't really mean this.

TABLE 5
Language Errors and Answers

Negative Thoughts	*Answers*
He *shouldn't* have left me for another.	I don't like it, but he *should* have left because he did. For all the reasons I know of and all the reasons I don't know of, he should have left. I don't have to like it, just accept it.
I *need* him.	I want him back, but I don't *need* him. I need food, water, and shelter to survive. I don't need a man to survive. Thinking in "needs" makes me vulnerable.
This *always* happens to me, and it will *never* change.	Just because it happened in one case doesn't mean it has happened or will happen in *every* case.
This is *terrible, awful, horrible.*	These are labels I add to the facts. The labels don't change anything and they make me feel worse.
I *must* have someone to love me.	It's nice to love and be loved, but making it a condition to being happy is a way of putting myself down.
I'm *too* ugly and *too* fat to find anyone else.	*Too* is a relative concept, not some absolute standard. Thinking like this is self-defeating and stops me from trying.
I *can't stand* being alone.	I can stand difficulties—as I have in the past. I just don't like them.
I made a *fool* out of myself.	There's no such thing as a fool. *Foolishness* is only an abstraction, not something that exists. This mislabeling doesn't do me any good and makes me feel bad.
He *made* me depressed.	No one can make me feel depressed. I make myself depressed by the way I'm thinking.

9. *What's the source of my information?* Consider your sources. People have their own reasons for what they tell you. "Am I depending on unreliable sources and spreaders of gloom to tell me how it is? Why let them define reality for me?"

10. *Am I confusing a low probability (a rare occurrence) with a high probability?* One person, a mailman, thought, "They'll probably fire me for missing three days of work." But after he reflected on it, he asked himself, "When was the last time they fired *anyone* at the post office?"

11. *Am I assuming every situation is the same?* Are you taking into consideration time, location, and subtle differences? "Just because I dropped out of school twenty years ago doesn't mean I'll fail this time."

12. *Am I focusing on irrelevant factors?* Patients attempting to build a case for their depression have asked me. "What about Uganda, starving children, and Hitler?" It's highly unfortunate that there's misery and evil in the world. But it's irrelevant to being depressed. Do what you can to alleviate the suffering of others, but getting depressed over it won't help.

13. *Am I overlooking my strengths?* When people become depressed, they overlook the problems they have solved in the past. I am continually amazed at people's ability to handle adversity once they turn their thinking around. Ask yourself how you handled situations like these in the past.

14. *What do I want?* What are my goals? Do I want to be happy and get the most out of life? Is this thinking ("Everything's bad") getting me what I want? Is it doing me any good?

15. *How would I look at this if I weren't depressed?* Would I think a cold sore is the worst thing that could happen? How would others (nonpartisan viewers) interpret this situation? Imagine how you'll react to it once you're over your depression.

16. *What can I do to solve the problem?* Are my thoughts leading to problem solving (generating solutions) or to problem blockage? If your kids are fighting and the plumbing is stopped up, thinking about the "unfairness of it all" doesn't lead to any solutions.

17. *Am I asking myself questions that have no answers?* ("How can I redo the past?" . . . "How can I be someone different?"

. . . "How can a relationship that's ended not be over?")
Questions like these often can only be answered with questions. "Why should this happen to me?" Answer: "Why shouldn't it?" "What if something terrible happens?" Answer: "So what if it does?" Asking yourself unanswerable questions is another way of demanding the world be different than it is.

18. *What are the distortions in my thinking?* Once you pinpoint the errors, you can correct them. Are you jumping to conclusions? Painting everything black? Are you confusing your behavior with your worth?

19. *What are the advantages and disadvantages of thinking this way?* I asked Sue Berlie if there were advantages in thinking, "I hate this house, I hate this neighborhood, and I hate this city and everything in it." She said, "Probably few." The disadvantage is that this type of thinking can stop you from getting your share of pleasure.

20. *What difference will this make in a week, a year, or ten years?* Will anyone remember (let alone care) in ten years that I made a stupid remark at a party or had dandruff on my sweater? People often believe that their mistakes will be frozen forever in others' minds.

After you write down your negative thoughts, question them. You'll believe them at first, but with good questions you can correct the errors in your thinking.

Interpretations. Back in the 1700s, Immanual Kant believed all mental disorders resulted from people's substituting private meanings for public meanings. His reasoning: public meaning, unlike private meaning, has the benefit of being checked out against the facts. But unproved private meanings keep the person disturbed.

Kant was right. To overcome depression, you have to change some of the basic meanings you give to events. Many depressed people latch onto one meaning and don't look for alternative ones. All of your experiences are subject to a variety of meanings. You can decide what you want to make of any experience.

When you're having negative thoughts, it's important that you consider other interpretations. One woman's addiction to alcohol and tranquilizers started after her son was killed on his bicycle. She thought the accident meant she was a bad mother. She believed she had caused the accident by not teaching him to ride safely. She finally was able to accept the possibility that her son was killed because he hadn't developed good riding judgment; this was due to lack of experience—not to her negligence. She changed the meaning of the accident; she no longer thought it meant she was an evil mother. Once she came to accept the more reasonable interpretation, she was able to control her drug and alcohol problem.

Another woman's depression was related to a sticky divorce she was going through. She was twenty-one and had a new baby. Although her husband had a good income, he, like many husbands before him, told the judge at the first hearing that he was almost broke. As the divorce proceeded she discovered through friends that her husband was spending large sums of money on his new single lifestyle. She placed a negative, frightening meaning on this ("He's going to spend all of his money and there won't be anything left for the baby and me"). She would then become anxious and sad.

She came to realize that by spending freely her husband was contradicting what he had told the judge; the more he spent, the more evidence she would have that he had lied about his income. His extravagant living would increase her chance for a fair settlement, not decrease it. This alternative explanation helped her control her sadness. After she adopted this new point of view, she didn't become sad and frightened every time she thought about her husband off somewhere spending more money. She instead attached a positive meaning to it.

The written technique. Writing down alternatives to negative thoughts lets you reflect on them and forces you to become more objective. You're able to stand back and take a fresh look. You'll need to write out at least fifty situations with alternative answers before you can do it in your head—if then.

Keep in mind that there are different ways of looking at any event—but you have to look. Take for example a recently divorced woman I saw. After being turned down for a job interview, her automatic thoughts were, "I'm no good. I'll never find a job. I'm just not as good as other people."

She was able to challenge these thoughts by writing them down and telling herself (on paper): "The fact that I didn't get one job doesn't mean I'm no good. That's a gross overgeneralization. All it means is that I didn't get one job. It's ridiculous to compare myself with others on the basis of a job. Really, it's ridiculous for me to compare myself with others for any reason."

By repeatedly challenging her automatic negative thoughts, she was able to maintain enough encouragement to look for a job until she found one.

Writing your answers out helps you challenge even your most strongly held beliefs. Negative ideas are so powerful that if you try to answer them in your head, they'll immediately erase the answers. But once you get the answers down on paper, the negative ideas have a hard time overpowering them.

Most people can't add too many numbers at one time, so they write them down and add them on paper. Disputing distorted ideas is more complicated than adding a row of numbers. So you must write them down.

Here's how Sue could have written out the answers to the thoughts she had the morning she got so depressed:

Thoughts	Answers
I can't remember anything.	It's not true that I can't remember anything. That's an overgeneralization. While it's true my memory is a little bit off, this is just a symptom of depression.
It's raining. Why me?	It's raining because it's the rainy season. That has nothing to do with me. I'm taking everything too personally.
The bird crapped on my window. Everyone craps on me.	This isn't anything personal. I just parked my car under some trees. Focusing on everything bad is just going to make me depressed.

Other ways you can use this two-column technique are: Write down the thought in one column and stress the thinking error in the other ("Because I have to go for help, this proves I'm inadequate." ERROR: Jumping to conclusions). Or write as if you were an objective observer instead of a participant ("Look at all of this traffic; it's not fair that everything happens to me." OBJECTIVE OBSERVER'S INTERPRETATION: She's a person driving in relatively heavy morning traffic).

You probably can think of other ways you can use this written technique. Keep in mind that answering negative thoughts is a skill, and like any skill it develops over time with practice.

Postponing answering. What if you can't think of answers when you become upset? This can happen. You can be so upset that you have trouble coming up with answers. If this is the case, try not to have thoughts that make it worse ("This doesn't work—nothing works" . . . "I can't stand feeling this way").

You can handle this problem in several ways. Plan a short delay before writing your answers out. One woman waited an hour before writing out her answers. While she was calming down, she diverted herself by sewing and talking to herself. She eventually learned with practice to calm herself down much quicker and this gave her the most confidence.

Another way to handle this is to set aside a specific time every evening to write out your negative thoughts. When you have negative thoughts during the day, tell yourself, "I'm not going to think about this now. I'll work on it tonight." Then make a note of the thoughts—so you can remember which ones to work on.

One patient expanded on this idea. She heard of a strategy called a Wednesday Box. During the week she wrote down thoughts and ideas that bothered her and put them in the Wednesday Box. On Wednesday, she opened up the box and tore up those that were no longer problems. For the ones that were still problems, she would work on them and then put them back in the box. She discovered that what seemed like an insurmountable problem on one Wednesay would often look like a mere inconvenience the next Wednesday.

Accepting your answers. When patients first start answering their negative thoughts, they often say, "I believe my answers intellectually but not emotionally." I think they're making a semantic mistake—they're misusing the words. Emotions are feelings and sensations, so a person can't believe anything emotionally. They're really talking about *degree of belief.*

For example, let's say you make a mistake. You may believe in general that making a mistake is human, yet you may also believe it's unacceptable to *you.* You have two minds about it. Of the idea you believe *least* ("I'm *not* inadequate"), you say, "I believe it in my head." Of the idea you believe *most* ("I *am* inadequate") you say, "I believe it in my heart."

Once you start actively challenging your negative and distorted ideas, you start changing the balance between distorted and realistic thinking.

ACTION

Just answering your thoughts won't get you over your depression. *You must act on your new thoughts and beliefs.* By acting differently, you can change old thinking habits and strengthen the new ones.

Suppose you tell yourself, "I'm a loser. I can't do anything right." You probably will feel sad. The first step to overcoming the sadness is to answer your thoughts ("That's not true. It's an overgeneralization. I do quite a bit right"). You can then *act* on your answer by *writing* out what you have accomplished, or you can act on it by *doing* some task right now.

Another example: When you're afraid and answer yourself ("There's no reason to be afraid"), you can start to really believe this by *acting* as if you're not afraid (although you may still be afraid). You act on your answer by approaching what you're afraid of (touch the dog . . . give the speech . . . ask for a promotion).

You have to *do* something to challenge your automatic thoughts. For example, if you think, "I've completely forgotten how to type," get the typewriter out and find out whether you can type. It may turn out that you need to brush up on your typing. But by actually sitting down and typing, you know for sure. Some of your most successful challenges take this form of reality testing. Some other examples of how action can change thoughts are in Table 6.

TABLE 6
Role of Action in Changing Beliefs

Negative Thoughts	Answers	Action
I can't do anything about my depression.	If I try, I can beat it.	Write out answers to negative thoughts. (Strengthens belief you can control your emotions)
I don't enjoy anything.	Maybe if I do something I used to do, I'll have fun.	Go to a movie. (Strengthens belief that thoughts aren't facts.)
It's too hard for me to finish my term paper.	I'll try an experiment and work on it for ten minutes.	Work on it ten minutes. (Strengthens belief that it's best to test out negative predictions.)
I bet this lump is cancer.	I'd better see a doctor to check it out.	See doctor. (Strengthens belief it's best to have good information.)
I can't think of the answers to this test. I'm going to fail.	Stop thinking about failure. Think about the questions.	Focus thinking on test questions. (Strengthens belief you can control thinking.)
I'm ashamed of how I talk.	Shame is self-created. If I don't think it's shameful, I won't feel like it is.	Give a public speech. (Strengthens belief you can control painful feelings.)
If I disagree, she'll think badly of me.	I have survived the disappointment of others quite well before.	Express your disagreement. (Strengthens belief you are an adequate person.)
I made a terrible mistake. What if people find out.	It's a mistake to think I can never make a mistake. So what if they find out. It won't be the end of the world.	Tell someone about the mistake. (Strengthens belief you don't have to be perfect.)

Get the facts. One of the best answers you can have for a negative thought is, "I don't know that for sure—I don't have all the information." The *action* that follows this answer is to get more information—ask others, go to the library, make a phone call, do some leg work.

Sue Berlie put the principle of gathering information into practice. A friend hadn't responded to her letter so Sue thought she must be angry. She forced herself to call her friend—and learned she'd been wrong. The friend had been out of the country. Another time, she didn't believe she could take a night class at a local university because of her average grades. Again, she went after the facts. She talked to a counselor and found that she *could* take a class.

Lack of information (or too much misinformation) can heighten your depression. You exaggerate the odds in favor of failure, overlook resources, and let help pass you by.

Many of the patients I've seen were helped by getting the right information. Linda Doyle was a good example.

After five months of nursing school she was going to drop out because she thought she wasn't cut out for it. After talking with her supervisor she decided to stay and eventually ended up an exceptionally good nurse. Without the right information she would have left the profession. She was embarrassed to approach her supervisor, but she finally did. *She erred on the side of inclusion—doing too much rather than too little.*

Like Linda, you may feel uncomfortable asking others for information, but if you're going to make a mistake it's better to err on the side of inclusion rather than exclusion. For example, if you're not sure whether or not you're invited to a party, it's better to risk embarrassment and ask than to miss your chance to go to the party. You may find the information isn't good news. But it's almost always better to have the right information than no information.

I have asked patients to go to the library to look up information. A secretary at the university was divorced and had two little girls. She was depressed because she thought no one would ever want to marry a divorced woman with children. I told her I didn't agree with her, but she didn't believe me.

She knew of a couple of instances where a divorced woman with children had remarried, but she considered these flukes. I suggested she call up the sociology department and ask someone who taught family and marriage courses. She wouldn't do this, but she did go to the library to look it up. She found that a divorced woman has a greater chance of marrying then does a single woman of the same age. And divorced women with children have the greatest chance.

This started her thinking. Maybe some of her other ideas were wrong, too. I saw her a year later; she was now *really* convinced someone would marry a divorced women with kids. She had just remarried.

The experimental approach. A powerful way to act on your answers is to test them out—see if they're true or not. Sue, for example, didn't believe she could make any friends. But she was willing to test this out by going where she could meet new people. She tested her ability to go to a new place and also her exaggerated ideas of being rejected by others. This was an experiment to "get the evidence."

Try to see your thoughts as possible—but not given. Possibilities can be tested out, givens can't. You'll find some negative thoughts may be partly true, but mostly untrue. For example, "I cannot spell." *Truth:* "I make mistakes in spelling, but *most* of my spelling is correct."

This is how I used the experimental approach with Sue. When I first suggested she write down her negative thoughts, she didn't think it would work for her. I told her it was good that she was questioning the technique. There's no reason she should automatically believe everything I told her. I'm not 100 percent sure any one technique will work. But I have hunches—or hypotheses—that certain techniques will work.

She asked, "What do you mean, test the hypothesis?"

"I have a hypothesis that this will help you. You have a hypothesis it won't. I don't know for sure who's right, do you?"

"No, I don't."

"I suggest you run an experiment for a week—get some facts, and see which point of view or hypothesis is right. What do you think?"

She said she would give it a try. At the end of the week, she began to see the results. The technique helped her and she changed her mind.

Making unrealistic predictions is at the heart of depression. Usually if you can see one dire prediction after another not coming true, your thinking will change.

In summary, keep the three A's in mind. Become *aware* of your symptoms and the negative thoughts that come before them. Write these thoughts down so you can bring them out in the open.

Answer your automatic negative thoughts. Look for the errors and search for more balanced alternatives. Fill in the holes in your logic by asking good questions.

Then *act* on the answers. "Reality-test" the distorted thoughts by getting more information and testing them out.

III

Overcoming the Behavioral Symptoms of Depression

BETH Rogers was the first woman in her company (an electronics firm) to become a sales representative. At thirty-eight she was energetic, personable, and effective. She was happily married and had a son. Then, several big sales fell through and one of her best friends at work died. She gradually became more and more depressed. She became passive, withdrawn, and ineffectual. She was barely hanging on to her job when she came to see me.

She had trouble getting herself organized. She stopped going out to see new customers and didn't return phone calls. She didn't want to see anybody, and spent days at home watching television. She said she felt as if she had weights tied to her: Every move was an effort. Because she was so apathetic and slowed down, one of her first goals was to get control over this "symptom cluster."

The behavioral symptoms of depression, which revolve around how you act, are quite common. Does it take extra effort to do your work? Do you have to push yourself to get started on tasks? Do you tire more easily? Do you feel as if you're physically slowed down? Have you lost interest in your activities, either hobbies or work? Do you spend less time in your activities or has your productivity decreased?

I ask patients questions like these to see if they suffer from this symptom cluster. The key is *change* in the level of activity. If you're normally inactive, then low levels of activity wouldn't necessarily mean much. But if you're usually active and there's been a change, this is a different story.

Why become more active?   Nearly every depressed person has tried to become more active. Friends and relatives may have urged and even harrassed you to get out and do more. This was true in Beth's case: Her friends urged her to act like her old self. This failed, as it usually does, because people don't understand depression. First, you need motivation—good reasons *why you should be more active.* The reasons have to be strong enough to make you try. Second, you have to *challenge the thoughts and ideas* that are stopping you from doing so.

I discussed the advantages and disadvantages of becoming more active with Beth. Below are some of the advantages I pointed out:

- *Increasing your activity is a major way to change your thinking.* Depression is a vicious cycle: You do less—and then blame yourself for doing less; you believe you're inadequate, lazy, and worthless for slowing down and not finishing your tasks. One of the best reasons for becoming more active is to challenge these ideas. By becoming more active, you're providing yourself with evidence that this is not so; you're showing yourself that you *can* start and complete projects, that you *can* get out of the chair and effect change.
- Even the most depressed woman feels better once she becomes more active. Studies support the fact that *activity improves your mood.* Spend a few hours working in the yard and you'll probably feel better. To test this out, chart your moods and activities. You'll probably find the more you do, the better you'll feel. Activity gives you relief from painful feelings. If nothing else, it provides a good diversion from your sadness and anxiety by taking your mind off unpleasant thoughts.
- *Activity counteracts the fatigue found in depression.* When you're not depressed, rest revives you. Only one of the many paradoxes of depression is that when you're depressed, you have to *do more* to *get more* energy. This is especially true with physical work.

- Different controlled studies have found that *activity increases your motivation.* When a depressed person has a successful experience—even a simple task like making a phone call or writing a letter—she becomes motivated to do more. A depressed person's motivation works backward. You have to do what you don't feel like doing before you feel like doing it.
- *Activity improves your mental ability.* You not only change your situation by action, but you stimulate yourself to think. You think more and you think better. Solutions to what seem like unsolvable problems come to mind after you begin moving.
- *Once you become more active, people are likely to get off your back.* Usually, others will respond positively to your attempts to become more active. Stifling others' nagging can be a big benefit and shouldn't be taken too lightly.

I may not have completely sold you on trying to do more—but I hope I've sparked some interest in at least trying, which is the first crucial step. Think of becoming more active as an experiment. Try it and see what happens.

ACTIVITY RECORDS

An activity record (see sample chart, p. 75) is an hour-by-hour record of what you do and the satisfaction (rated from 0 to plus 5) you get from doing it. One purpose of the record is to help you become aware of what you accomplish and how you feel about it.

The first step in becoming more active is finding out what you're doing now. Realize you're always doing something. Instead of writing, "I did nothing," it's more accurate to write, "I sat on the sofa, drank coffee, and listened to the radio." A passive activity is still an activity. If you're misleading yourself by thinking you're doing nothing, correct your thinking.

Beth began by recording what she did as she did it (wash her hair, do the dishes). She found she was more active and successful than she thought, but her pessimism and discouragement had previously stopped her from recognizing her accomplishments.

For example, she'd been spending most of her weekends in bed,

Weekly Activity Schedule

	M	T	W	Th	F	S	S
9–10							
10–11							
11–12							
12–1							
1–2							
2–3							
3–4							
4–5							
5–6							
6–7							
7–8							
8–12							

but over one weekend she decided to drive down to south Jersey to visit her sister. When she came in for her next appointment, I asked how it went.

She said, "Terrible. I was sick, I think I had the flu. It was a terrible weekend."

I thought she must have spent the weekend in bed again. This isn't unusual when you've been depressed. It takes real effort to get moving, and first attempts might be unsuccessful. But when I asked if she'd stayed home in bed, she said, "No, I went down to see my sister."

I asked if she felt any satisfaction from going—even though she was sick.

She said, "I guess I did, but only about a plus two (out of five) because anyone can drive to the shore." She went on to say it had been a rotten drive.

"I had a flat tire on the turnpike and had to walk two miles to a gas station—and I was feeling bad."

I asked if she found any satisfaction in handling this problem.

"Well, yeah, I guess. I was glad I was able to handle it—a little proud. The guy at the gas station tried to sell me a set of tires. I didn't let him con me into buying them."

I asked if she felt any pleasure while she was visiting her sister. "Yes, my sister and I went for a walk. I did enjoy that. I like the ocean in the winter."

The conversation went on like this; she continued to list a variety of activities that had given her satisfaction or pleasure over the weekend. So I asked her, "How does what you're telling me fit in with what you said earlier about having a terrible weekend?"

She said, "Well, this weekend was an exception. Most of the time things really are rotten . . . but now that I'm looking back on it, I can see I did more and had a better time than I thought I did."

This is why writing down what you do is so important: *When you're depressed, you don't remember the positive as well as you remember the negative.* The overall purpose of recording your activity is to show yourself that you still enjoy things, and that you often accomplish more than you think you do.

You must keep track of your daily activity—you can make all of the right moves and still not benefit from them if you don't take time to record them. If you make records, you'll be aware of what you're doing.

I used to have patients record their activities for only a week or two to help them become more active. But getting more active usually won't cure your depression by itself. You have to change your mistaken thinking as well. To do this, you must confront your thoughts with facts; and a record of your activities is one of the best ways to get the facts.

One woman, for example, said she ignored her children all week. But a look at her activity schedule showed that she had in fact spent considerable time with them that week.

Another woman said she stayed at home because she didn't like to be with people. She looked over her activity schedule and discovered she was happiest during time she spent with people and unhappiest during the time she spent alone.

I now encourage patients to record their activities until they get their depression under control. It will take some effort, but it's one of the best ways to get on top of your depression.

First, record hour-by-hour what you do for a week. Next to the activity, rate how much satisfaction you felt on a scale from 0 (for none) to plus 5 (for a great deal). By monitoring yourself, you'll have a truer picture of what you accomplish. You can use this information to see what gives you pleasure and satisfaction, no matter how small. Then you can increase this pleasurable activity when you begin scheduling your activities on a daily basis. This is the next step.

SCHEDULING ACTIVITIES

By planning your day on an hour-by-hour basis, *you're retaking control of your life.* A rational workout schedule is a powerful antidote to depression.

When you're depressed, you're unfocused, indecisive, overwhelmed. What you need most is structure, since poor use of time is symptomatic of depression.

Indecisiveness is also a symptom of depression and one of the biggest thiefs of time. When you schedule your day, you're using the lazy person's way of making decisions: You're making one decision (to draw up and follow a plan) that frees you from having to make many smaller ones. And when you're depressed, any decision is usually better than no decision.

Motivation. *A schedule of your daily activities can also increase your motivation.* If your tasks are laid out in black and white, they don't seem as formidable as when they're in your head. When you lay out a daily plan for yourself, you can see what has to be done. This cuts down on ambiguity.

Keep in mind that when you're depressed, motivation works backward. Beth Rogers thought, "I don't want to wash my hair. What difference does it make if it's stringy and dirty or not?" But she scheduled an hour to take a bath and wash her hair. Afterward, she found she felt much better. And this motivated her to start doing more for herself—she ended by scheduling some time during the next day to shop for a new dress.

Awareness of self-defeating thoughts. Another benefit of an activity schedule is that it gives you two opportunities to catch self-defeating thoughts that might keep you at a standstill—first, when you preview your scheduled activities for the day, and next, when you're actually in the planned situation.

Here's how you can discover thoughts that might possibly block you. Before you attempt the planned activities, close your eyes and imagine going through each one, step by step. Look for the reasons why you can't do it.

Beth had been putting off paying her bills. So she scheduled time to do this. I asked her to imagine doing it and see if there was any reason why she couldn't.

She said, "I can see my desk. It's such a mess I can't find anything . . . this is too much . . . I don't even know how much money I have . . . What's the use?"

After she became aware of these thoughts, she realized they could stop her from even starting the job of paying her bills. This helped her prepare arguments for each negative thought ("Of course my desk is a mess, that's why I want to clear it up. I'll work at it for fifteen minutes and not be distracted by negative thoughts").

You usually have to answer your thoughts before you can start to be more active. In Table 7, I've listed common activity stoppers and answers for them.

Planning your schedule. You won't have to schedule your time so tightly once you're moving again. But it's an excellent way to get started.

- *Plan with flexibility.* Your schedule is meant to be a general guide, not a god; you can't always follow it exactly. If the unex-

TABLE 7
Ways to Keep Yourself Passive and Answers to Them

Thoughts	Answers
It's too hard to find out about taking classes.	It's as difficult as it is—no more, no less. I've done many more difficult things.
I won't know what schools to call or what questions to ask.	The idea is to do it—not do it perfectly. It's better to do a poor job, to try to find out, than not to try at all.
I don't want to do it. I hate making phone calls.	That's what I think now—but earlier I wanted to. So whether or not I want to do it now is irrelevant. I'd better do it now for my own good.
I don't think I'm up to doing it. I'll wait until I feel more like doing it.	I don't know for sure. I'm not a mind reader. I'll experiment and see what I can do. Inspiration comes from activity, not the other way around.
I've wasted so much time already. When I start to do it, it reminds me of wasted time.	I didn't waste time. I just did something different with that time. Now the question is, what do I want to do with this time—more of the same or something different?
I can't decide which school to call first.	Call the one that comes first in alphabetical order. Calling the least helpful is better than not calling one at all.

pected happens (a relative comes in from out of town or a friend can't make lunch), you may want to change the schedule.

Build in alternative plans in case this happens. If you have plans to go on a picnic, make contingency plans in case it rains. Leave in an unplanned hour to use for the unexpected.

- *Stick with the general plan.* If you can't do the activity for some reason (you planned to clean the bedroom in the morning and you were unable to), don't go back and try to make it up later. Just proceed with the schedule. If you have thirty minutes scheduled for reading magazines, go ahead and read. Replan the activity you missed for the next day.

  If you finish an activity earlier than planned, don't begin the next activity scheduled. Rather, do something pleasurable with the extra time.

- *Schedule activities in one-hour and half-hour intervals.* Don't plan activities that are either too specific or too general. Planning to go shopping for the day is too general. Listing every department in every store you plan to visit is too specific. Shoot for something in between ("Go to shopping center, meet mother there at noon and have lunch, go by post office . . .").

- *Plan for quantity, not quality.* Write down activities you're going to undertake and the amount of time you're going to spend on them (gardening, one hour; walking, thirty minutes). *Don't* write down how much you're going to accomplish (trim all the roses; walk to town and back).

  How much you accomplish is often related both to forces outside yourself (interruptions, mechanical failures) and to internal forces (fatigue and ability to concentrate). For example, if you want to refinish a piece of furniture, plan to work on it for a specific period of time (one hour). Don't plan to complete the job. (If you do complete it, fine, but don't set yourself up for failure.) Also, keep in mind: *Anything worth doing is worth doing poorly.* If stripping the chest of drawers is worth doing, you don't have to do it perfectly.

- *Be task oriented.* Remember your immediate goal is to follow the schedule, not to get rid of your depression. If you think, "I'll keep this schedule and then I'll be over my depression," you're likely to get discouraged. But if you continually work on becoming more active, you'll eventually feel better. Your goal is *to try* to follow your schedule. This is similar to a smart weight-loss diet: You don't work directly on your weight but on changing your eating habits. The weight loss will follow. If you work on changing how you think and act, improvement will follow.

• *After you've completed a planned day, write down how you did.* Look at what you did right and where you can improve. Again, don't expect to follow the schedule perfectly.

If you don't completely follow the schedule, use this fact to your advantage. Tell yourself that *trying* is what's important, but look for the reasons why you didn't follow through. Don't experience it as a failure; rather, change it into a learning experience. Experience consists of mistakes from which you learn. Failure consists of mistakes from which you don't.

If you put yourself down for not following the schedule ("I'm lazy and no good"), think of it as good material ("Calling myself names won't help. I'll just have to find out what stopped me so I can be prepared tomorrow"). Try to turn disadvantages to advantages. By learning from your mistakes, you can make an activity schedule a no-lose proposition.

Set aside a specific time each evening to plan the next day. A person who was hesitant to use the activity schedule at first, later said, "I've learned I can control my depression if I plan my work and work my plan."

Graded tasks. You may have been avoiding some big jobs or you may see everything as a big job. In either case, break the task into specific smaller tasks that you can handle. Do the tasks in order, going from easiest to most difficult. Keep reducing the job until the steps seem manageable.

For example, if you have to clean the yard and this looks insurmountable, don't plan to "clean the yard." Rather, plan to: (1) get the yard tools out, (2) pick up the trash, (3) mow the lawn, (4) rake the grass, and (5) put the tools away.

If your house is a mess, don't attempt to put it all in order at once. Concentrate on one room. List the jobs that have to be done —dusting, vacuuming, polishing, picking up, and so on. Do the easiest ones first and then gradually move on to more difficult ones.

Be sure you don't discount the difficulty of the task. Activities that may seem like a walk in the park when you're not depressed may look more like climbing a mountain when you are depressed. When you feel good, cleaning the house may seem like nothing, but when you're depressed, it can be a real chore.

Beth used graded self-assigned tasks to tackle her problems at work, which were severe. She had stopped going into her office, calling instead from her home and saying that she was out in the field. To begin with, she gave herself the assignment of going into the office and sorting her papers for just one day.

This turned out to be too difficult. She had to back up and give herself the assignment of going in for only forty-five minutes—just to make an appearance. By doing this, she was able to go to her office for the first time in several weeks.

She came in to see me after achieving this and discounted it, "Anyone can go into her office for a few minutes. It's no big deal. I *should* be out making contacts and sales—not going to work for only forty-five minutes."

I asked her if it had been difficult for her to go to her office before she became depressed. She said it wasn't difficult at all. She was doing what many depressed people do: judging herself by her past standards (and finding herself lacking). I advised her to revise her standards to better fit her current situation.

Beth, by breaking her problems down into smaller steps, started to put her affairs in order. But she still couldn't go out and face customers. So again I suggested she set up a graded task assignment. Who was the easiest client she could see? An old friend she felt comfortable with. Her assignment was to go to his office for a short visit.

Fighting off internal negative forces.   When she came to the next session she was as depressed as she had been in the beginning. It seems she started to drive to her client's office, but turned around before she got there.

She said she didn't know why—she just turned back. She went home and spent the rest of the day in bed crying. She thought she was a hopeless mess, beyond help.

I asked her, "When you were driving out there, did you feel like you were being invaded by a strange force?"

She said, "That's exactly how I felt . . . like I didn't have any control."

I said, "When this happens, in a way you *are* being invaded—you're being invaded by internal forces. Do you see any benefits in giving in to these forces?"

"No, but I don't know how to do anything else."

I told her most people give in to these forces when they're depressed. Other luckier ones don't, and they're all the stronger for it. But you can learn to fight off these forces.

First, see them as an invading army, whose first goal *always* is to capture the radio station—so communications can be controlled. To keep control of your own internal communications, give yourself *loud, direct,* and *simple* orders that tell your body specifically what to do. ("Legs, move!" "Arms, pick up the phone!" "Keep going!")

These orders have to be loud enough to drown out the enemy's orders; and *you have to act immediately.* If you wait too long, the enemy will take over. By actively talking to yourself like this, you won't have time to think of all the reasons why you can't do it.

Beth was dubious, but she was willing to give it a try to see if it would help. She called her client from my office—no time like the present—and made an appointment to see him that afternoon. (Making commitments helps you to follow through. Promises are self-rewarding when you keep them and self-punishing when you don't.)

Beth called me that evening. She was back on her feet. She said the visit went well. There was one point when she had almost turned back, but she told her muscles to "keep driving," and was able to fight off the urge.

Beth was able to handle what I call a *critical incident.* When you're attempting to control any of the symptoms of depression—negative feelings, inactivity, and so on—you'll find that some times are particularly important to your improvement. These moments, or critical incidents, represent opportunities when you can *choose* to control your symptoms. You can give in to the situation, or you can fight—you have a choice.

The best way to handle critical incidents is to *do the opposite of what you instinctively feel like doing.* Your first instinct is nearly always the worst strategy. Your first thought will be to defend yourself and put the worst light on the situation. But the paradox is that the more you try to defend yourself, the more vulnerable you become.

If you're prone to anxiety, you'll want to run and hide. You'll feel more weak in your own and others' eyes. If you're prone to anger, you'll want to attack others, which will put you in a vulnerable spot. If you feel beaten down, your first instinct will be not to try. If you must make a decision, your first instinct will be to avoid doing so. So when you're in trouble, think reverse. Take the opposite tack to get back on track.

What eventually happened to Beth happens to most depressed people once they start moving. Her courage came back. Once she rejoined the human race, other people began to respond positively to her. Old customers she dreaded seeing were glad to see her. She found she enjoyed the contacts. Shortly after this, she became an effective sales representative again. Her commissions went up and her fellow workers complimented her success.

Beth didn't lose any ground in her career because of this depression. A year later she was promoted to district manager. She was able to get back in step on her job and not be penalized for her depression because of her "social margin," the excess good will and points she had accumulated in the past. If you've been depressed, keep in mind that you probably have a social margin to draw on too. And like Beth, once you get back on your feet, you can quickly rebuild your margin.

BLOCKS

Once you start moving, always be on the lookout for blocks. Just when you think you have it made, they reappear. Watch out for these common traps.

I can't think of any activities to schedule. Is it that you *can't* or just that you're having trouble? Ask yourself, "If the life of a loved one depended on it, could I think of something to do?" In general, you can schedule three types of activities: (a) things you must do daily (eat, dress, etc.), (b) things that bring you pleasure (going to a movie, reading, shopping), and (c) things that bring a sense of satisfaction or mastery (answering letters, finishing projects).

Ask yourself specific questions ("What can I do between ten and eleven a.m. that might give me a sense of satisfaction?" . . . "What would I do if I weren't depressed?" . . . "What tasks or projects am I putting off?"). Your questions will generate a list of potential activities. Choose one or two from the list to try.

One patient couldn't think of any activities until she began to act like a consultant to herself. You might try this: If a person exactly like you asked for advice on how to get going, what would you suggest?

Practical problems stop me from carrying out activities. Life is a series of practical problems—cars break down, babysitters cancel, animals get sick and have to go to the vet, rents are raised—that are more difficult to solve when exaggerated by depression. Solving them often sets the stage for getting better.

One woman, Judy, had a practical problem that also happened to be a psychological problem because it stopped her from becoming more active. Her car wasn't running, so she didn't leave her house. She used a problem-solving approach that you can use with your practical problems. First, *identify the problem specifically.* Judy first had to find out what was wrong with the car. She called several friends to find a good mechanic. The mechanic told her she needed two hundred dollars' worth of repairs. She didn't have two hundred dollars. This turned out to be a specific problem.

Second, *think of a variety of solutions.* She could borrow the money from a friend, her sister, or the bank, or she could see if the mechanic would take payments. She could try to make do without a car by buying a second-hand bike or using the bus.

Third, *select the most promising solutions.* She thought the best would be to talk to the mechanic about making payments. You might as well try your first choice. The worst Judy could expect would be the mechanic's saying no.

Fourth, *try a solution and see what happens.* The mechanic said he would let her pay off half of it over a month, but she'd have to come up with the first hundred dollars.

Fifth, *if the first solution doesn't work, revise it or try another until you find the right one.* She was able to borrow the hundred dollars from her sister and with payments had her car fixed. By solving this practical problem, she also helped solve a psychological problem of inactivity.

You can use this five-step method with a range of problems. If, for instance, one of your children has a difficulty in school (his grades are slipping), find out what the actual problem is (he's having trouble with reading). Come up with several solutions (talk to his teacher . . . help him at home . . . get a tutor). Then, through trial and error, find out which one works the best.

Some of your practical problems may not be *your* problems. Many women who stay at home are expected to be on twenty-four-hour call and help out whenever they are needed, even if they have other plans. The solution might be to call your mother-in-law and say, "No, I don't have time to wait for the Sears man for you. I have something planned for today."

Some of your practical problems may require special knowledge. For example, if a business has cheated you, you may need to talk to a lawyer. Do not hesitate to get good information. If a lawyer costs too much, use problem-solving methods like Judy did to work around this obstacle.

I'm not a record keeper—I can't keep a schedule. Have there been times in the past when you've kept lists—when you were getting ready to go on a long trip or about to have a party? Keeping written records is a skill, and one you can learn. You may believe your depression is too complicated or deep-seated to be solved by simply keeping records. However, as simple as it may sound, this is the modern way to treat depression.

If you feel too confined by an hour-by-hour schedule, modify it to fit your style as Mrs. Thompson did. She was a real estate agent who listed all of her most pressing problems (reports due, clients to call) and made a rule to do at least one difficult task in the morning and one in the afternoon.

The key is to write down your activities in some form. Writing down what you plan to do can be a mastery experience in itself. A major symptom of depression is feeling you've lost control over your life. Your activity schedule counters this by increasing chances that you're doing both what you want to do and what's best for you.

I get distracted and sidetracked and don't follow through on my schedule. If this is a problem for you, see it as a challenge you can beat. Give these methods a try:

• *Get rid of distractions* that keep you from following your activity plan. Turn off the radio or television; don't have reading around that keeps you from planned activities. If a friend is continuously calling (and keeping you on the line), tell her you're sorry but you'll have to keep the call short because you're very busy.
  One student's bed was a distracting temptation. She would start to do her homework, but then she would see her bed and lie down. The bed was like a magnet. She solved this by taking the mattress off the bed in the morning and rolling it up and putting it out of sight.
• There is a general rule for depression, "Beds are for sleeping, sofas are for sitting." *Don't lie down during the day* if you're depressed. This really feeds the depression.
• *Use aids* to help you follow through on your schedule. One woman wrote out a contract with herself. She couldn't watch any TV until she had done some activity for thirty minutes. *Reward yourself with points for following your schedule.* See how many points you can accumulate in a day.
• *Plan activities for specific times* and make sure you follow through on time ("At ten p.m. I'm going to write a letter"). Set an alarm to go off at ten. If you say, "I'm going to read for fifteen minutes," set your kitchen timer for fifteen minutes and read until the bell goes off.
• *Develop cues* to switch into your activity. Stick signs up in your house as reminders, such as, "Get started." Use three-by-five cards as reminders—or any other gimmick that'll remind you to follow your activity plan. The more unusual, the better. One man

put a large elementary classroom activity schedule on his wall. After he finished an activity he wrote it on his chart.

• *Start your plan with a success experience.* Pick a task that's difficult but one you can complete. Gradually, try to do harder activities first. This will give you a boost to keep going.

I'm so overwhelmed with problems that I can't get started. Believing your problems are too much for you is part of depression. Don't be intimidated by this sense of being overwhelmed. When you're depressed, it comes with the territory. The *sense* of being overwhelmed is nearly always worse than the *reality* of the situation.

The general strategy is to pinpoint specific subareas of the problem. Then develop a constructive plan for dealing with each smaller part. Instead of thinking, "I'm overwhelmed," change this to "What are the specific problems and what are possible solutions?"

Bear in mind that you can only do one activity at a time. Don't try to pay attention to everything at once. Instead, list your problems and set priorities. Nearly every task is easier once it's under way.

I don't know what to do about my problems. At times creative problem-solving is needed. You may be blocked from thinking of solutions that would be obvious if you weren't depressed. Virginia, a new Ph.D. and college instructor, was blocked by the amount of work she had to do. She didn't know how she would be able to make up tests for her four courses, and grade the papers— in addition to preparing lectures.

She hadn't thought of asking the other teachers how they did it. When she did, she found that there were standard tests on file. She also discovered that the college had a computer service for scoring the tests. Simply asking colleagues for suggestions helped solve her dilemma.

You may be taking on more work than you need to. If your family is eating different diets and you're chasing around trying to please everyone, perhaps it's time to let them cook their own meals.

You may believe more is expected of you than really is. Check out your assumptions. One woman had taken on a series of volunteer jobs in addition to a full-time job. She believed it was impossible for her to get out of these commitments without alienating her friends. But once she told them the problem, she found they understood her position.

PACE

As you start becoming more active, you may try to do too much —especially if you've been depressed for a while. The drawback to becoming overly ambitious is that it can backfire, especially if you run into difficulty. You can become discouraged and think your spurt of energy was false hope. So stick to your plan and increase your activities *gradually*. You'll find your energy coming back daily.

IV
Controlling Sadness

NANCY Ong's depression began shortly after her second child, Billy, was born. She found being mother to one child a job, but being mother of two small children a burden. She had always been quiet and introverted, but with the depression she became even more so. She stopped going out of the house. When her sister would call to invite her to go shopping or to a movie, she would say no, she didn't feel like it. She didn't feel like doing much of anything.

At first her husband paid more attention to her, bringing small gifts and spending extra time talking to her. But when she didn't respond as she had in the past, he stopped making the effort and gradually withdrew from her. She said, "I feel like I'm locked out in the cold and I can never get warm again."

These periods of melancholy lasted for days. At times they were so bad she could barely force herself out of bed to take care of the kids.

Symptoms of depression aren't the same for everyone. Take, for example, the emotional (or feeling) cluster of depression. Nearly every depressed person experiences some dysphoria, or painful and uncomfortable feelings. But what form the dysphoria takes—irritation, discouragement, sadness, guilt, shame, worry, or fear—varies from one person to another. The most common emotional symptom of depression, however, is sadness.

You may only occasionally feel blue, or like Nancy, you may

experience a sort of paralysis, a heavy, tight feeling in your legs or in your back. Maybe you've been sad for so long that it feels natural —like the old blues song, "Been down so long it looks like up to me."

When you're depressed, your tolerance for any psychological or physical pain is low. Painful psychological feelings can become so uncomfortable that you have trouble thinking of anything else. The sadness continues to remind you that you're depressed. For this reason, it's a good idea to get relief as soon as possible.

SELF-CRITICISM

Self-criticism causes much of your sadness. When you put yourself down, you'll see yourself as a loser and you'll feel sad—much as a child does after being criticized. The first step in getting rid of sadness is to switch out of your self-critical way of thinking.

Self-sympathy. One way to handle self-criticism is to feel sympathy for yourself. Step back, take a look at yourself, and instead of thinking, "I hate that person," think, "She has gone through a lot and she feels really bad." You can't feel sorry for yourself and hate yourself at the same time.

I'm not saying pity yourself. I think the number of people with clinical depression who do this is rare; I've found many more people crippled by self-criticism than by self-pity. I *am* suggesting that you stop being so hard on yourself.

Self-sympathy is particularly helpful if, like Nancy Ong, you want to cry but can't. After Billy was born she felt sorry for herself and spent hours crying. But as the depression developed and she became more self-critical, she felt blocked up and wanted to cry but couldn't.

Talking about your feelings or expressing them through crying can make you feel better and more human. One patient was unable to cry over the death of his wife after a lengthy and painful hospitalization. I described my own painful feelings when my wife was hospitalized because of an accident; he then was able to feel sorry for himself and cry.

Nancy Ong imagined how she would feel toward another person in the same situation as hers. After this she was able to cry for the first time. Crying made her feel much better.

Anger. Getting angry, like feeling self-sympathy, can counteract feelings of sadness brought on by self-criticism, and for the same reason—you can't have both emotions at the same time. This is a constructive use of anger.

Jan's case was a good example of how anger can counteract sadness. She was a secretary for three lawyers who frequently criticized her work. Her usual response was to blame herself and become sad. She went out of her way to please them so they wouldn't criticize her.

One day she came in early to do extra work for one of the lawyers, and during her lunch hour she dropped some legal briefs off at the courthouse. In spite of her extra efforts, later that afternoon one of the lawyers started criticizing her typing. This time, instead of going to the bathroom and crying, she got angry and told him off. Afterward, she discovered she felt good about herself and, best of all, she wasn't sad. For Jan, getting angry was a turning point in helping her get control over her sadness.

I'd like to add a warning, however. Anger can be a useful emotion, but unless carefully controlled, it can harm relationships. So use it with caution. If you do use anger to counteract sadness, don't overdo it. Limit how long you stay angry. And don't blame yourself —most depressed people are self-critical about showing anger ("I must be a bitch").

Objectivity. At a time when Nancy Ong was most vulnerable to any criticism, she continued to criticize herself harshly. She, like most depressed people, didn't challenge these thoughts. When you're depressed, you may *believe* you should be held in contempt.

When I suggested to Nancy that her self-criticism might be exaggerated, she said, "You don't understand. I don't measure up . . . I'm only being truthful with myself." You may, like Nancy, believe this. If so, the trick is to become more objective about your criticism.

I asked Nancy to look for critical thoughts and write them down. She found them fairly easy to catch. When she felt her sadness increasing, she played back to herself what was going through her mind. She brought in this list: "(1) I'm a terrible mother. (2) I'm fat and ugly. (3) I'm making Bill [her husband] unhappy. (4) I'm boring. (5) I can't do anything right. (6) I'm a weakling for being depressed."

We discussed each of these self-criticisms. Was she a terrible mother from A to Z, and terrible all the time? Or did she occasionally do some good mothering? Would a terrible mother be sad over being a bad mother? Did she *really* mean she was a terrible mother, or did she perhaps mean she makes some mistakes for good reasons (such as she's tired or doesn't have the right information)?

I told her I'd never met a "terrible" mother. I have met women who have problems parenting, but never a "terrible" mother. For this reason, her claim to be a rotten mother was extra-ordinary, and an extra-ordinary claim requires extra-ordinary evidence. What was *her* evidence?

Her only evidence was that she had become discouraged about taking care of two small children. I asked her how many other women get discouraged over taking care of babies. She said, "Probably most of them from time to time." She concluded that she might have been too hard on herself.

If you think your self-criticism is deserved, consider the following:

- *Self-criticism by definition is an overgeneralization.* You're giving your *total self* a grade. There's no rational way that you can grade yourself. You're made up of millions of thoughts, feelings, and actions. You're not even aware of most of them. When you base your total worth, as Nancy did, on a few of these thoughts, you're drawing a gross conclusion from a few acts taken out of context.
- *Self-criticism rarely does you any good and can do you harm.* Nancy, for example, would overeat, criticize herself for it, feel bad because of the criticism, and then overeat again because she felt bad.
- *Criticism in general rarely does any good.* It's rarely constructive.

People usually learn more from success than from failure. Good teachers realize this and reinforce students' good points and ignore the bad.

• *Self-criticism can hamper your performance.* I asked Nancy how she would feel about someone following her around all day harping at her. What if every time she turned around this person were criticizing her? She said she'd feel bad and wouldn't try to do much because she'd be so self-conscious. This is what self-criticism can do.

• *Why be harder on yourself than you'd be on someone else?* I've asked many depressed people if they would be as critical of someone else in the same position. I can't remember many saying they'd be as critical of others as they are of themselves. Battering your self-image doesn't make much sense—this is the only life you have.

• *You're probably making another error:* believing you could or should have acted differently. This isn't true. Given the situation (you were anxious . . . you were tired . . . you didn't have all the facts), you *should* have acted the way you did, though you might not like it and it might not have been in your interest. The proof is that *you did act that way.*

• *Self-criticism won't eliminate mistakes.* People make mistakes for two reasons: They don't have the right information, or they don't feel right because they're tired, sick, or depressed. While it's a good idea to make as few costly mistakes as possible, it's impossible to eliminate them totally.

If you always feel well and have all the information, great! But you won't and don't, so you're bound to mess up. Everyone does.

Why waste your energy criticizing yourself for your mistakes? Better to use that energy to your advantage. If you drop an egg, make an omelet, don't blame yourself for being clumsy.

Self-criticism and the depression syndrome. Suppose you came to me for a consultation and asked, "How can I stay depressed?" I could give you an extremely effective strategy. If you would use it consistently and practice it at every opportunity, you could stay depressed for quite a while.

The strategy is simple: Criticize yourself for being depressed. Tell yourself you're sad because you're weak-willed; you're apathetic because you're lazy; you can't sleep because you're no damn good. Overall, believe you're depressed because you're a rotten human being.

No one has ever asked me how to stay depressed, so I've never given this advice, but I've no doubt that it would work. Many depressed people unwittingly follow it.

Most depressed people criticize themselves for being depressed. But look at the paradox. The more you blame yourself for being depressed, the more depressed you'll get.

You may believe you're inferior for getting depressed. But consider that at any one time over ten percent of the population suffers from depression. Few people haven't suffered from some depression at one time or another. Many historical figures—Lincoln was one—suffered severely.

I've often wondered why depressed people are so quick to blame themselves. I've concluded that people like their world to make sense—to see that A causes B. Because you're feeling bad and not functioning up to par, you want to know what causes it, to blame someone. In your depressed state of mind, who's a better candidate than yourself?

This has been called the "just world hypothesis"—the belief that justice will prevail. If something is wrong, someone caused it ("If my child has leukemia, I must have done something to cause it" . . . "If I'm depressed, I must deserve it").

The problem with the just world hypothesis is that *life isn't just*. There is a degree of order and symmetry in the world, but much of life is unbalanced, disordered, and unfair. Some people develop diabetes and others get depressed. It makes no sense to criticize yourself for suffering from either. People don't voluntarily choose to have diabetes or to be depressed.

The philosopher Epictetus said that when you stop blaming others, your education has started, and when you stop blaming yourself, your education is complete.

THE CLASSIC HUMAN CONDITION

I remember the first time I became aware of another common condition that often leads to sadness. I was sitting at my desk writing. Out my window I saw a young boy cleaning a neighbor's yard. This boy was about to experience the classic human condition, and his experience started me looking for other examples of it. I found them left and right—on large and small scales.

I started calling this the classic human condition because, frequently, being human means either *not* getting what we *do* want (and think we deserve) or *getting* what we *don't* want (and don't think we deserve). The classic human condition is made up of both of these elements at the same time.

I watched the boy cut the lawn, trim the bushes and trees, rake the leaves. After he bundled up the branches and sacked the leaves, he put them out in the street. Then he spent some minutes gazing at his work with pride. He came back several times to see if my neighbor had returned. He seemed eager to get complimented for his work and collect his pay. He finally sat on the porch and waited for her.

My neighbor pulled up. She looked pleased as she walked up, but when she got closer she seemed to get upset and quite angry at him. After a long discussion, I saw the boy walk away dejectedly.

Later, I talked to the woman and found out what happened. It seems that while he was cleaning the yard, he cut back to a stub a rare tree that took years to reach its height. She was so mad she didn't even pay him for the work he did.

This is a good example of the classic human condition. He expected to be rewarded for his effort; instead, he was punished. The classic human condition is more than just disappointment, which stems from not getting what you want. The boss not only doesn't *praise* you (disappointment), but he *criticizes* the work you are so proud of. You get the double whammy.

After becoming a victim of the classic human condition, people

often start to criticize themselves ("How could I be so stupid" . . .
"I can't even trust my own judgment" . . . "I wasted my time for
nothing"). This self-criticism leads to feelings of sadness and rejection.

Self-criticism is more intense if you're prone to depression. You
suffer more disappointment, self-criticism, and sadness. The depressed way of thinking is to attribute anything good that happens
to luck and anything bad that happens to yourself. The classic
human condition fits right into this thinking ("I tried my best and it
came to a bad end, so it must be my fault").

Prevalence. The classic human condition abounds. It happens
in everyday affairs. You work hard planning a weekend of camping, but everything on the trip seems to go wrong. It also happens
in major life events. Ann thought her marriage was okay, but she
wanted to improve it. She persuaded her husband, Hugh, to go for
marriage counseling. At first she thought this was great: Her marriage was really going to be strengthened. Then Hugh told her that
as a result of the counseling he decided to be honest with her; he
no longer loved her and wanted a divorce. She then became depressed.

Unexpected consequences. The classic human condition is
related to the observation that, "There're more tears cried over
answered prayers than unanswered prayers." In other words, what
you expect to bring you happiness may bring you headaches. The
dream house you finally buy, the new school you're accepted into,
the promotion you hoped for, don't bring the happiness you expected—instead they bring problems and unhappiness.

When Nancy Ong started her second pregnancy, she was happy
and looked forward to another baby to take care of, remembering
the joy of her first child. But when Billy was born she discovered
that taking care of two babies is three times as much work as taking
care of one. It seemed like she always had at least one crying and
needing her. She started to blame herself for wanting the second
child and talking her husband into it. She decided she would just
have to pay the price for making a bad decision—and pay forever.
This started her on the road to depression.

When she was on her way back from depression, she decided one day to clean the house well and make a fancy dinner for her husband, whom she had been ignoring while feeling down. She expected him to be pleased. When he got home he said he was, but he subtly criticized her throughout dinner. He made a number of references to her past depression, such as why hadn't she been cooking like this all along?

These are good examples of the classic human condition. In the latter, Nancy didn't get what she thought she deserved—praise and a good time from her husband. She *was* getting what she didn't want—criticism. However, this time she didn't let the situation throw her. First, she realized that this was the classic human condition. So instead of getting sad over it, she decided to see if she could learn from it. She saw it as good practice for future run-ins and disappointments.

She decided not to take 100 percent of the responsibility for dinner's going badly. She saw it as her husband's problem. Rather than passively suffer, she told her husband what she thought. She pointed out that she'd gone through a lot of time and trouble to cook this meal and he didn't seem to be enjoying it. Was there something wrong?

He told her that he was having a lot of hassles on his job. This led to a discussion of what he wanted to do with his career. Their conversation went on past dinnertime into evening; it was the first time in weeks he had talked with her about his job.

He felt good getting this problem off his chest. She felt good because she was helping *him* for a change with his personal problems. By responding actively to the dinner situation (rather than becoming passive and sad), she was able to turn it around and save the evening.

I've given the classic human condition a great deal of thought. Below are some ways you might handle it the next time you run into it:

1. *When you run into the classic human condition,* do as Nancy did. Rather than say to yourself, "Oh no," smile to yourself and *recognize it for what it is.* Ask yourself how you can best handle it.

2. *Take an active approach toward it.* Be assertive. Even if this particular run-in with the classic human condition means that you don't get what you want or expect, you'll feel better for confronting it. Part of your problem is the belief that you've lost control. By being assertive and active, you've regained some control. Success in any endeavor isn't usually based on *what happens*, but on *what you make of what happens.*

3. *Be careful not to take more than your fair share of responsibility.* My neighbor didn't give clear directions to the boy she hired, so part of the responsibility of what happened to the tree lies with her. Don't take all of the responsibility.

4. *Try to change the* disadvantage *of the situation into an* advantage. At the very least, you can learn from it. One woman bent over backward to please her boyfriend; he responded by treating her badly. Her relationship with him was one classic human condition after another. She finally learned her lesson and broke off the relationship.

5. *Keep your perspective.* Maybe what you *think* is a failure isn't really. One woman gave a party and she said it turned out terribly. Yet when she checked with other guests, she found she was wrong.

   You have time on your side. The classic human condition has a way of flip-flopping. How many times have you heard, "I was devastated at the time, but looking back on it, it was really the best thing that could have happened."

6. *Don't be overconfident.* My wife, Pat, a zookeeper, was transferred to take care of elephants with a reputation for hurting keepers. She called me at lunch one day and said, "I've really got those elephants under control now. They're starting to see who's boss." By the afternoon, she was in the hospital with a collapsed lung and five broken ribs—the classic human condition.

7. *Watch your expectancies.* Are you getting yourself too excited about how you're going to be rewarded? Are you being too optimistic, glossing over potential problems? Are you placing too much value on how others are going to respond? Look for ways in which you may be setting yourself up for the classic experience.

In general, *the more you can live in the present* (and not in anticipation of future rewards or in regret of past incidents) and *the more you can rely on yourself for happiness* (not on the opinions of others), the better you'll be able to handle the classic human condition.

DISTRACTING YOURSELF

Humor. Humor distracts you from feeling unhappy and gives you a better perspective on sadness. Humor has been called tragedy revisited, and a courage mechanism. Like many depressed people, you may have kept your sense of irony through it all. This is a resource to draw upon; one that can divert you from sadness. It's a good sign when you start to appreciate the humor in a bad situation—it's a sign that you're starting to cope.

I look for the humor in the situation when I start to get upset. Not too long ago a patient pleaded with me to see her on Saturday, my day off. She said she was going on vacation and couldn't survive it without talking to me first, so I reluctantly agreed to see her. I came into the office that Saturday. But after fifteen minutes she said, "This isn't helping me at all. I don't know why I bothered to come in. I'm wasting a Saturday." The irony of the situation kept me from getting too upset.

When you start to feel sad, look for the humor or irony in whatever is triggering your sadness. Some people draw cartoons to illustrate the humor in bad situations. One woman brought in a cartoon of herself in handcuffs. The day before, she'd been falsely accused of shoplifting by a department store and searched by security guards. After this happened, she looked for the irony in the situation—which was that she of all people, an overhonest person, was thought to be a crook. The amusement she found in this irony counteracted her sadness.

Depressed people take life and themselves too seriously. When you start to see the humor in life, you're usually getting better. For a while I half-seriously thought of doing "clown therapy." Dressed like a clown, I would jump up and down on my desk ringing a bell in front of the patient. What stopped me was that most depressed patients wouldn't think that it was funny.

Diversion. Humor is just one of the ways you can divert yourself (at least for a while) from feeling sad. Focusing on objects outside of yourself is also an effective diversion.

Try this experiment. Rate how sad you feel from 0 to 100. Then focus on some item in your room—a light-switch plate, a rug, a chair. Now describe it to yourself in great detail: size, smell, possible taste, color, texture, flaws, price, age. Think of the item in terms of the workers involved in creating it: an electrician put the light switch on, an engineer designed it, a factory worker made the plastic and the screws for it. Do you have the idea? Lose yourself in the object. After you've done this, rerate your sadness. You'll find your feeling of sadness has lessened to some extent.

If this seems to work for you, practice it. Whenever you start to feel sad, use the sadness as a cue to start distracting yourself. The distraction could be taking a walk, reading, talking on the phone, or just looking at your surroundings. You may only be able to distract yourself for a few minutes at first, but with practice you can increase the time.

Tune in to your senses. You can learn to divert your attention from sadness by increasing your sensory awareness. Become aware of your environment by focusing on taste, hearing, smell, body sensations, and heightened vision. This is a good technique if you're bothered by negative thoughts going around and around in your head.

A housewife I saw was able to use this technique effectively. She controlled her unpleasant feelings by increasing her awareness of her surroundings as she went through her daily tasks. The more senses she used, the fewer negative thoughts and the less sadness she had.

Visualize. Imagine pleasant scenes such as seeing yourself tan and healthy, lying on a Caribbean beach. You might try to picture a time in the future when you'll no longer be sad. The more detail you use in the image, the more effective it will be.

Distracting yourself is not the ideal solution to your problem of sadness. Eventually you must learn to change your thinking and attitudes. However, distractions can help you start feeling and functioning better so that you can work on more basic solutions. Just knowing you have a way of coping with sadness can increase your sense of control. This in turn can increase your sense of security and well-being.

THINKING AND SADNESS

The most elegant way to change feelings of sadness is to change your thinking. Some thoughts exaggerate the sadness ("I can't stand this" . . . "I'll always be unhappy"). Others directly cause these feelings ("I'm a loser" . . . "The future will continue to be bad").

I encourage you to become *aware* of these thoughts ("I can't stand the rock music my kids are playing"); *answer* them ("I find it unpleasant, but it won't kill me"); and *act* on the new ones ("I think while they're listening to the radio I'll go into my room and start that book I've been wanting to read").

PLEASURABLE ACTIVITIES

This may sound overly simple, but a good way to overcome sadness is to do something that's pleasurable. Dr. Peter Lewinsohn of the University of Oregon has found that depressed people stop seeking pleasant experiences and do more unpleasant activities. When the depressed person switches this pattern around again, she begins to see more pleasure and less drudgery and her mood improves.

Your thinking can keep you from making the switch. Nancy was telling herself she didn't deserve any pleasure and she didn't feel like putting out the energy to try to have fun. She began to answer these thoughts ("Who deserves pleasure more? I work hard taking care of the house and kids"). She acted on her new thoughts by taking the initiative and inviting her sister to go to a movie.

Killjoy thoughts. Try to weed out thoughts that take away from the pleasure of the moment—thoughts that minimize and discount the pleasure you're feeling. For example, one patient said she got little pleasure out of the movie *Rocky*, not because she didn't like the movie, but because it reminded her of Philadelphia.

One type of killjoy thought focuses on what's *not* there instead of what *is* there. One woman went shopping and was enjoying herself and her purchases until another shopper beat her to two pot lids she wanted. She spent the rest of the day thinking about the pot lids she'd missed and not about what she *did* buy.

Another type of killjoy thought discounts the enjoyment because it doesn't measure up to some imagined standard of pleasure. I call this the *"It's okay, but it's not Mick Jagger"* syndrome. This is based on a magazine article I read about a young woman who slept with many rock musicians, hoping someday to sleep with Mick Jagger. After each encounter she thought, "It was good, but it wasn't Mick Jagger." She eventually ended up in bed with Mick Jagger. The next morning she awoke disappointed and found herself saying, "It was okay, but it wasn't Mick Jagger."

Many depressed people have similar standards. Try to focus on the pleasure in activities. It makes little sense to pay five dollars to see a movie and then tear it apart like an overzealous movie critic.

If you're like most depressed people, chances are you overlook activities that bring you pleasure—something as simple as watching children play outside your window, listening to music on the radio. You probably underestimate the degree of pleasure you get out of mastery experiences as well.

By ignoring these moments of pleasure and mastery, you become more pessimistic and less willing to try something new or different. What you need to do is fan these sparks of enjoyment, not snuff them out. The more you become aware of your pleasure and mastery experiences, the greater the probability that your positive attitude will spread into other areas of your life. If you start recording what brings you pleasure, you'll probably be surprised by the results. Nancy did this for a week. She said, "I found I handled problems better than I thought I did. And you know, I completely forgot about the enjoyment I had watching TV and talking to my sister on the phone."

One of the symptoms of depression is forgetting and downplaying your positive experiences. When you do, you feel sadder and don't want to try anything. Also, people often don't know what brings them pleasure. They assume it must be fun if it's expensive or high status.

Sometimes their idea of pleasure is short-sighted. Elaine Robinson said, "The only thing I enjoy is taking sleeping pills so I can sleep and forget my troubles. Before my husband left me for another woman, I enjoyed lots of things like going to good restaurants, belonging to the yacht club, and buying expensive clothes. But without my husband's money I can't do any of these. There's nothing left for me."

After keeping track of her experiences for several weeks, she came to realize she enjoyed many activities—simple things such as talking to a friend on the phone or cleaning off her desk. Most importantly, she saw most of them didn't cost any money. She admitted to herself that she never *really* enjoyed putting on the dog with her husband. He was the one that said people needed a lot of money to be happy.

Depressed people avoid pleasurable activities for what seem like good reasons ("I don't deserve any enjoyment" . . . "I can't think of anything that is fun" . . . "Even if I could think of something, it wouldn't bring me any pleasure"). To overcome your sadness, confront these beliefs head on.

In our society, women frequently downplay the importance of their own pleasure. Your enjoyment comes somewhere after your husband's, your children's, your parents', and the family pets'. If everyone else is happy, you will then, and only then, consider giving yourself a treat. The depressed woman allows herself to become so intimidated by this artificial hierarchy that she finally concludes, "I don't deserve any pleasure."

Low self-rating is a bad policy. A large share of mental health consists of placing a high priority on your own enjoyment. Enjoying yourself is just plain common sense. If you discount yourself, others will do the same. By ignoring your own importance, you are training others to treat you as a second-class citizen. This treatment naturally leads to resentment on your part; and the resentment often worsens relationships.

You may be convinced that others come first, or that you're so "low-life" you don't deserve any fun. Even if you believe this, you can still *force* yourself to do pleasurable activities for the sake of others. Once you're working better, you become a better companion and parent, and generally an easier person to live with.

At this moment you may not be able to think of anything that sounds like fun. However, you can develop a list of potentially pleasurable activities by asking yourself the following questions:

What did you enjoy learning before you got depressed? (New recipes, crafts, languages.) What day trips did you enjoy? (Going to the shore, to the mountains, to the country.) What could you enjoy if you had no inhibitions about it? (Painting, acting in a play, playing the piano.)

What did you enjoy doing alone? (Long walks, playing the piano, sewing.) What did you enjoy doing with others? (Talking on the telephone, going to dinner with a friend.) What did you enjoy doing that costs no money? (Playing with my dog, going to the library, reading.)

What did you enjoy doing that costs under five dollars? (Going to a movie, riding in a cab, going to the museum.) What did you enjoy doing when money was no object? (Buying a new dress, going to New York, going out for a nice dinner.) What activities did you enjoy at different times? (In the morning, on Sunday, in the fall.)

After you generate a list of activities, rate each according to potential pleasure; then select the ones that are most likely to bring pleasure.

You may be thinking, like Jackie Cobb, "Oh, sure, there are *some* things I used to enjoy, like playing golf, but I don't enjoy them now. So why try? What's the point?"

This type of thinking will stop you cold. You have to suspend this disbelief to overcome your depression. No one can guarantee that a specific activity such as playing golf will be fun, but there's at least a chance, however remote, that you will enjoy yourself. However, if you don't try it, there's *no* chance.

You may have to do some problem solving to free yourself up enough to take part in pleasurable activities. One elderly woman had to buy new glasses before she could start sewing again. You may be exaggerating the difficulties and minimizing the corrective steps. When you do this, you end up not taking any action at all.

Jackie said, "Even if I could enjoy playing golf, there's nowhere

I could play." I asked her how she could solve her problem. She spelled out her difficulties; solutions started to appear. She eventually was able to make the necessary inquiries, started playing golf again, and found it to be as pleasurable as it had been in the past.

Granted, it's unrealistic to expect a long-standing depression simply to disappear by playing golf. But the road out of depression is a series of small steps. Simply attempting to make positive, concrete moves to help yourself can be a successful experience.

Some activities start out pleasurably but over the long haul become unpleasant. One teenage girl said skipping school made her happy but getting caught made her unhappy, so I recommended against it. Eating high-calorie foods can bring a short, fleeting burst of pleasure, but gaining weight is an unpleasant experience.

Be careful not to overindulge in any one pleasure, which often results in the loss of pleasure in other areas. Sleeping can be a pleasant, sensual experience. But if you do too much of it, you'll find other experiences aren't enjoyable. The same can be true of an excessive amount of sexual activity.

UNPLEASANT ACTIVITIES

Another way to combat feelings of sadness is to cut back on your unpleasant activities. Nancy stayed in the house, which she found unpleasant; she quarreled with her husband; she put off paying the bills; she watched endless game shows she didn't like. She discovered, however, that most of these unpleasant activities were under her control.

The following are some methods you can use to decrease unpleasant activities.

- *Avoid the situation.* Engaging in the opposite action often solves the problem. Nancy found getting out of the house relieved the unpleasantness of it. Oversleeping was unpleasant, so she started getting up earlier. She stopped watching the game shows. Many unpleasant activities can simply be avoided.
- *Change the situation.* Do some "engineering." One woman re-

turned home each night from a full day's work to several unpleasant activities. She found herself bickering with her husband each evening. And she hated having a constantly messy house. She tried to get her husband to help with the housework, but this led to more bickering.

This is how she solved these problems. She made a pact with her husband that neither would say anything negative (about their day or each other) until they had been home for one hour. They discovered that after they'd changed clothes, eaten dinner, relaxed, and felt comfortable, they didn't feel like arguing. As for the messy house, she went to an elderly couple in the neighborhood and asked if they would like a job straightening her house one hour a day. Because the elderly couple was on a fixed income, they welcomed the opportunity. This relieved the woman from one more unpleasant activity.

• *Plan.* Good planning can prevent many unpleasant activities. One woman I know disliked having her children wake her on Saturday morning, the one day each week she can sleep late. To get around this unpleasant activity, she has a babysitter come in that day. But because she knows people's plans can change, she always has a *backup* babysitter in the wings in case one can't come. Many unpleasant activities (running out of gas, falling behind in payments) can be avoided by good planning.

• *Say no.* Learn to say no to things you don't want to do. This is probably the best way to ward off an unpleasant event. If you don't feel like going door to door selling raffle tickets for your church, say *no thanks.* If you don't want to spend every vacation visiting your in-laws, say *no.* It's true that some people won't think you're "nice." But if you know in your heart you're going to resent the activity later, say *no* initially.

• *Master the problem.* Move toward an unpleasant activity instead of avoiding it. Embrace the activity and see if you can master it. If paying taxes is unpleasant, get a couple of books on it and put some concentrated thinking time into the task.

As a student I worked at a grocery store. Stocking the macaroni and spaghetti section was an unpleasant activity I tried to avoid. The boxes were difficult to mark and stack; there were so many different kinds of pasta that it was confusing trying to figure out where they went. All of the other clerks avoided doing it too—except for one, who loved putting up the pasta section. I asked him why and he said he liked knowing the different types of pasta and where they went. It was a challenge to him. I decided to try his method. I found by my becoming more involved in it, putting up the pasta became a pleasant activity. I started looking forward to it.

- *Limit the activity.* If you just don't like some activity, build a fence around it. Give yourself a specific amount of time to work on it and no more. Nancy used to fiddle with paying the bills all week long. She didn't know which ones she'd paid or which were due. She even lost bills.

  She decided to work on them only between ten and eleven a.m. on Wednesdays. She set herself up at a desk and promptly at ten a.m. each Wednesday, she would sit down at her desk and knock the bills out.

  Parkinson's Law is true: Work expands to fill the time available. So reverse this. If you have an unpleasant task, give yourself limited time in which to do it.

- *Be careful of your thoughts.* Many women become sad when they hear about children, animals, or others being mistreated. They feel more than just concern and empathy, rather a real, deep, painful sadness. I've found that they are usually projecting themselves into the situation. They see themselves somewhere in the suffering scene. A woman may visualize herself as the mother of a kidnapped child or the owner of a poisoned dog. She feels just as sad as if these things were actually happening to her. If you're bothered by *thoughts* of certain activities, separate the reality of the situation from what you imagine.

- *Use the three A's.* Become *aware* of thoughts and images that are making events more unpleasant, *answer* them, then *act* on the new ones.

V

Overcoming Anxiety, Guilt, Shame, and Anger

IF you're depressed, chances are nine out of ten that sadness is one of your symptoms. But this is only one of the many emotions of depression.

Depressed women are often burdened with *guilt;* they continually feel as if they've let someone down. They may have an *anxiety* about growing old that borders on panic. Many feel *shame* about their depression; they think others hold them in contempt for getting depressed and "acting like a big baby."

You can't tell if a feeling is a symptom of depression without looking at it in the context of how you normally feel. If you usually feel guilty, then guilt won't necessarily be a symptom of depression. But guilt does symptomize depression if it has become exaggerated —if you feel more guilt longer and more often.

The approach to all the symptoms of depression is the same: *See the symptom as a concrete target problem to be solved.* If you take one symptom at a time, depression can be beaten.

ANXIETY

A big problem I've found in doing research into depression is that many times the diagnosis is mixed: a person is both anxious *and* depressed. This could be diagnosed as either primary anxiety with depression symptoms or as primary depression with anxiety symptoms.

Although mixed diagnoses present a problem for research (because researchers want to report whether they're treating anxiety or depression), they're not a problem for treatment, which often includes ways to treat both sets of symptoms. Antidepressant drugs, for example, often include antianxiety agents. Similarly, I use cognitive therapy to treat the anxiety symptoms that are often found in depression.

Sadness revolves around past events ("The people at the party didn't like me"), while anxiety revolves around future events ("I'm afraid people at the party won't like me"). Many depressed people teeter between sadness and anxiety. When one goes up the other goes down.

You may experience anxiety in a number of physical ways. Anxiety has its own body language: You start breathing fast, your heart rate increases, you feel nauseated and dizzy, your hands sweat, your mouth feels dry, there's a tightening in your throat, and you feel pain in other muscles. When feelings of anxiety are prolonged or chronic, these frightening symptoms may seem to be a real disease or disability.

The most important point about anxiety to realize and remember is that the symptoms aren't dangerous—not the racing pulse, not the pounding heart, not the dizziness, not the nausea nor the desire to scream or hit the table.

None of these physical or emotional reactions means you're dangerously ill or "going crazy." They *are* uncomfortable, but you can both increase your tolerance for them and speed their departure by not getting anxious about your anxiety. Don't be afraid of your symptoms.

Aside from having your symptoms checked out by your doctor, what can you do?

Distract yourself. *Don't focus on the symptoms.* Ellen Zachary avoided other people because she was afraid they wouldn't like her. Her social anxiety could be traced back to her childhood. She'd felt odd about being Black and growing up in a white neighborhood. On top of that, her elderly grandmother had raised her on frightening stories of the old South.

She now had a range of fears that kept her from leaving her house and expanding her life. She was depressed when she stayed home and anxious when she went out. She didn't like going into the city because she was afraid of being mugged. She was afraid to meet new people because she thought they might reject her. She experienced her fears as visual images—actual mental pictures in which she was being murdered on the subway or humiliated by social encounters and unable to cope with it all.

Once Ellen became anxious ("I'll be a mass of nerves when I meet my new neighbors"), she would worry about the physical feelings her anxiety produced. This made matters worse. She'd feel dizzy and lightheaded and think, "What's wrong with me? This isn't real." *She stopped identifying with herself* ("This can't be happening to *me*"), which led to unreal, dreamlike feelings. Feeling as if she weren't a part of her body made her even more frightened. She saw this feeling as a danger sign, a warning that something terrible was about to happen. This created more anxiety, and more symptoms to worry about. She developed anxiety about her anxiety.

One of the best ways to stop your escalation of anxiety is to distract yourself from the symptoms as best you can. Ellen found this tactic extremely helpful. When she kept busy, the symptoms receded into the background until they disappeared.

Thinking errors. Most of the emotional symptoms found in depression are due to thinking errors. Anxiety is no exception. For instance, one of Ellen's mistakes was believing that she should never be anxious. She let her small fears ("I'll be nervous") build into full-blown attacks of panic. A certain amount of anxiety in an unknown situation is unavoidable, normal, and often helpful. For example, many actors find a degree of anxiety gives their performances an edge.

As Ellen came to realize this, she forced herself to go out more and more. Although still somewhat timid, she learned to control her anxiety. Her depression cleared up after her anxiety was under control.

Rita Larson was anxious about becoming old and unattractive. She was afraid her husband was going to leave her because of this. Many women share this anxiety over aging, which is worsened by cultural pressures. For example, I recently saw an ad for a skin-care business in the *Wall Street Journal*. The headlines screamed "IN-VEST IN FEAR" and the copy read: "The fact is, we're all afraid of growing older. Radio, TV . . . all blare out the message of the day —'Remain young and youthful looking.' " These kinds of cultural influences keep anxiety about aging alive.

Rita's fear caused her to notice and exaggerate all the new wrinkles on her face and neck, all her gray hair, and to compare herself unfavorably with every younger woman she met. She became too upset to make the most of her good features. She underestimated her husband's love and loyalty and didn't consider the fact that he too was aging.

Another example is Linda Spencer, who was anxious about how well she would do in graduate school. Before a test she would think, "What if I fail this? My career will be ruined before it starts. I'm so sick just thinking about it that I can't study. But I *must* study or. . . ."

Her symptoms were worse before oral presentations, which she imagined as catastrophes before they happened ("I can't give it tomorrow. I'm not prepared enough. I know I'll be so nervous I'll forget what I've planned to say. I can just see what it'll be like—all those eyes on me, all of them knowing how nervous and stupid I am"). She expected nothing short of total disaster in giving speeches and taking tests.

On the other hand, Beth Herman's anxiety caused her to avoid her customers. She feared the worst. She thought, "I can't face seeing them. If they see my panic they'll know I'm inadequate. I'm afraid I won't be able to answer their questions or complaints . . . I'll be humiliated."

In her anxiety, she forgot all of her past successes as a sales representative and anticipated only problems and unending suffering in the future. She also forgot that blowing a visit or two wouldn't make or break her career.

Visual images. The first time I talked formally about my work in treating anxiety was to a group of 500 psychologists, psychiatrists, and social workers. Several days before the talk I started getting anxious because of a vivid image I had. I saw myself standing before this group, scared to death, shaking and stammering while trying to tell them how I cure anxiety.

So I followed my own advice. To keep from getting too anxious over the upcoming talk, I watched for and became aware of visual images. Next, I answered them ("There's no evidence that I'll be that anxious. I've given talks to large audiences before—and even if I do become anxious, I can handle it").

I then acted on these answers. I closed my eyes and fantasized how I could control my anxiety. I would see myself starting to get anxious while giving the speech. Then I would change the fantasy so that instead of being overpowered by my anxiety, I would take a deep breath, focus on the content of my presentation, and talk more slowly.

Fortunately, fantasies are consistently worse than reality and I gave the talk with a minimum of anxiety. Try to be on the lookout for visual images (fantasies and daydreams) that may be causing your anxiety.

I've found that over ninety percent of anxious people have vivid images, often in color, of a catastrophe occurring. Watch for them. Once you're aware of them, you can fight them with coping images and other visual methods I'll talk about in connection with shame.

Self-monitoring. Another problem is that you may have distorted ideas about your anxiety ("I can't survive it" . . . "I can't avoid it"). If so, you need more information to get a clearer picture. Judith, a teacher, thought her anxiety was continuous and not related to events ("There's nothing that causes it. It just comes. I don't know how to stop it").

She tested this belief. When she started to feel anxious, she recorded it on a graph—0 was perfectly calm and 100 was a full-blown panic attack. She wrote down the time of the attack and the amount of her anxiety. She did this at half-hour intervals. She also recorded what brought on the anxiety attack.

She learned that her anxiety was related to *external situations* and was *time limited*. This was important information. One of the ideas that frightened her was believing the attack would never end.

If you'd rather, keep a diary instead of a graph. In any case, try to find out what brings on your anxiety. Record the time, place, and events, and most importantly, what you're thinking when you're anxious. Be an investigator and search for clues.

Judith was afraid to be with authority figures such as her principal and professors. She believed she couldn't control her anxiety, but she agreed to an experiment. She started keeping a list of attempts she made to be around authority figures. She recorded the degree of anxiety she felt in the beginning, how much time she spent with these people, and the degree of anxiety she felt at the end. She became more objective about her anxiety. She learned that she was able to increase her tolerance of the anxiety by staying with the situation. She also saw that her anxiety lessened by the end of the meeting. She now had evidence that she had more control over her anxiety than she thought.

The three A's. Just as your thoughts keep you sad, they also keep you anxious. You can use many of the techniques I have talked about already, such as counting your automatic thoughts, looking at alternative explanations, and testing your thoughts, to overcome anxiety.

An example of how this works was when Ellen was trying to improve her social life. She made a luncheon date to see Amy, an old friend, but the night before the lunch she started to get anxious.

She thought, "Amy won't want to see me . . . I'll be nervous and won't know what to say . . . She'll think I'm stupid to be so nervous and I'll feel so miserable it'll show . . . I might even cry." As these thoughts flooded her mind, she became more anxious. The only way she could think of to reduce this panic was to call Amy and say she couldn't make lunch.

She felt better for an hour or so, but then started hating herself for giving in to the anxiety and losing the chance to see her old friend. She became depressed for the rest of the evening and decided she was a loser.

This wasn't getting her anywhere, so the next day she began working on the problem again. First, she became aware of her inner voice ("I'm a loser") and answered it ("I'm capable of meeting people. I've been doing it my whole life"). She then acted on this thought by calling Amy back and setting up another lunch date.

This time she overcame her negative thoughts and anxiety about the meeting with Amy. She had a good time and realized her negative predictions had been far-fetched. She was also glad that she could start controlling her thoughts.

Review your own logic. You'll find it's one of the best ways to undermine anxious thoughts. Check out how you're interpreting your daily experiences. Do you see any errors or distortions? Spell out what you're afraid of, then decide if the evidence supports this fear. If it doesn't, you'll probably see that your logic is faulty.

Linda Spencer, for example, was extremely anxious over an upcoming examination. She'd taken and passed many exams, first to get into her program and then to stay in, but she still believed she would fail this one. She had plenty of evidence that this test wouldn't be any harder than the others, but still she got herself so worked up that she stopped studying. Studying reminded her that she might fail and that brought on more anxiety.

She became aware of her thoughts and examined the logic behind them. Based on her past experience with tests, she saw that she was jumping to conclusions. Simply knowing this allowed her to reduce her anxiety enough to go back to studying, which, in turn, distracted her from her anxiety even more. When she eventually passed the exam, she realized how close she had come to academic trouble by almost giving in to faulty logic.

Again, review your logic. You can scare yourself with poor logic. That's why answering your anxiety symptoms is both helpful and necessary to overcoming your depression.

Diet. Don't take an excessive amount of stimulants such as coffee, tea, or cola. For some people, even a single cup of coffee can produce physiological arousal which, often mislabeled as anxiety, can begin a chain reaction.

Try to cut back on alcohol if you're anxious. Many people drink to control their anxiety. The drinking, however, makes you more susceptible to anxiety and anxiety-like symptoms, and you become caught up in a vicious cycle.

Don't go too long without eating. Many of the symptoms of low blood-sugar level (hypoglycemia) are similar to those of anxiety and so can be mislabeled as anxiety. If you suspect you're developing low blood sugar, have some protein, a glass of milk, or a piece of fruit.

GUILT

Many depressed people are weighed down by their sense of wrong-doing. Mary Ralston, a mother of two, felt guilty about a whole range of negative events for which she frequently took on more than her fair share of responsibility. For example, she considered it her fault when appliances around the house broke down or her children were sick. She got over this habit by learning to look at the facts and stop criticizing and blaming herself automatically.

For example, her husband's younger sister, Christy, had lived with them for a while before going off and joining a religious cult. She felt guilty about Christy. She thought, "I *should've* been able to stop her from doing this . . . I *should've* known she was going to do it." After she thought about it for a while, she saw her mistaken thinking—she really had little control over her sister-in-law. Christy had never taken any of her advice before; why would she now? There was no reason why Mary *should have* known Christy would join the cult. Believing you should (or could) know the unknowable runs counter to the laws of nature.

Examine your thinking on the matter. Ask yourself: "Why am I totally responsible if something bad happens?" If you still have difficulty working out your share of responsibility, try this. Draw a circle and divide up the responsibility among all those involved.

For example, Allison Nelson believed she was worthless because her husband had a girlfriend and her teenage son had trouble in school. In both cases she believed it was *all her fault*. We discussed just how much she was responsible for these two people's actions.

She drew a pie representing her marriage. Conceivably, with respect to her husband's infidelity, she could deserve a slice of the pie. Marriage is a partnership, so if she had refused to have sex or told him to find sex elsewhere, of if she hadn't communicated her feelings to him, she could deserve a bigger slice. But this wasn't the case—she had worked hard at the marriage. Her husband was going through a period of self-doubt and was out to prove something to himself. She was finally able to accept this and cut a large slice of responsibility pie for her husband.

By taking the rap for her son's behavior, she was making the same mistake that she had made with her husband's affair. So she decided that instead of taking the responsibility for the whole pie, here too she would see who else had a slice. Her conclusion: Obviously her son was responsible for the biggest piece. He was the one who got into trouble and was responsible for his own behavior; there was no way she could have forced him to do something he didn't want to do.

Her husband, too, had some responsibility for their son's upbringing. She thought perhaps the school personnel were partially responsible, as were her son's friends who egged him on to fight. Also, on the "it takes two to tango" principle, she concluded that the boys her son fought were partly to blame for taking part in the fights.

She didn't duck her own responsibilities. She realized that she did have some responsibility as a parent in her son's problem, but she took a more realistic share.

She acted on her new thoughts by having a noncombative talk with her son. She wanted to see what role, if any, she might have played in his school problem. She discovered that her son thought she was fed up with him and wanted him out of the house. This was a distortion on his part that may have accounted for part of his problem. She reassured him that this wasn't true and explained that she had been depressed. She told him that one of the symptoms of depression is difficulty in showing positive feelings toward others, but that she still loved him and wanted him around. As a result of this discussion, their relationship improved greatly.

Remember to act on your new way of thinking about guilt: (a) Try not to repeat avoidable mistakes, but keep in mind that you will always make some mistakes; (b) If you can, rectify what you did wrong (replace what you broke or apologize for what you said); (c) Get more information to help solve the problem or to avoid future ones (this is what Allison did in her case).

Guilt is a great motivator. People frequently use it to control others. They imply that you have some character flaw if you don't do what they want. Just because someone offers you guilt doesn't mean you have to take it.

Make sure you don't fall into the trap of automatically taking all the blame. Jan, a secretary, did this chronically—but she learned how to overcome it by using the pie technique. Whenever others tried to make her feel guilty, she brought out a pad and drew a pie to see what percentage she was responsible for.

Once an important document in the office was misfiled but found before any problem could develop. The senior executive called her in and asked whose fault it was. She had anticipated this question and answered, "I was twenty-five percent responsible for not doublechecking with Tom; but Tom was twenty-five percent responsible for not giving clear instructions; Judy (who did the actual filing) was twenty-five percent responsible because she should have caught the mistake; and *you're* twenty-five percent responsible because you're the boss and hired the rest of us."

Her boss didn't have a retort to this. He just said, "Okay, I just wanted to know."

By overcoming guilt, her attitude toward herself improved and the people at her job started looking at her with more respect.

Negative behavior.   You may believe a sense of guilt prevents self-defeating and antisocial behavior. Yet guilt may actually lead to *more* self-defeating behavior. For example, you overeat, feel guilty, then overeat to cope with feeling guilty—so you pay twice. You have the natural consequence of gaining weight and you have the *additional* negative consequence of feeling bad. One of these is more than enough. Someone once said if you feel guilty for what you're doing, either stop doing it or stop feeling guilty—it's too much trouble to do both.

If you're engaging in some self-defeating behavior such as smoking, drinking, or procrastinating, and you feel guilty over this behavior, work toward controlling both the behavior and your guilt about it.

People cut corners and aren't always totally ethical. They don't return phone calls. They let store clerks undercharge them or give them too much change. They hand their creditors the universal lie, "The check's in the mail." One study found that Americans on the average tell 200 lies a day. Over fifty percent of Americans admit to stealing from their employers.

I'm not making a value judgment about this. But I am suggesting that if you're depressed, err on the side of being too ethical. I'm a little hesitant to mention this because depressed people often have an exaggerated sense of ethics. (One woman I saw felt guilty because she had accidently taken an extra paper from a newsrack.) But it is true that you can avoid guilt by keeping up your *normal* ethical standards.

Suppose you haven't done a report and feel guilty about it. You only make it worse by telling your boss that you've lost it. Better to say you haven't done it but you will, and then do it. If you're guilty about overdue library books, don't hide them so you won't have to think about them. Return them and pay the fine. This is more ethical and it's also a way to help you with your guilt.

SHAME

Have you been more ashamed lately? This can be one symptom of depression. Unlike guilt feelings that relate to a supposed breaking of your own moral or ethical code, shame comes from what you think others are thinking: the belief that others judge you as childish, weak, foolish, or inferior. If you expect to be or think you have been ridiculed by others, you feel ashamed.

Barbara Wiley, a twenty-seven-year-old telephone company representative, experienced a lot of shame during her depression. She believed fellow workers and customers thought she was a fool when she made a mistake, and concluded, "It's awful to act (or be) like this in front of others."

She, like most people, thought shame comes from others. It doesn't. *Shame is self-created.* Nothing is inherently shameful. The meaning *you* place on events leads to the shame you feel.

Barbara didn't believe this at first. But when she thought about it, she remembered many examples of her changing ideas about what is shameful. For instance, in high school she had been ashamed of her good grades and small breasts, but she no longer was. She also realized that what she is ashamed of doesn't correspond to what others are ashamed of. It must be self-created.

Antishame exercises. Dr. Albert Ellis, a clinical psychologist, has developed a novel way for overcoming shame. He sends people out to do outlandish activities in public—such as yelling out the time of day in a department store or calling out the names of the stops on the subway. People doing these antishame exercises find that the world doesn't come to an end—and they can choose to be ashamed or not.

You don't have to be that radical, but if you adopt an antishame philosophy, you can avoid a lot of pain and discomfort. When something happens that you believe is shameful, turn it into an antishame exercise by not hiding from it.

I always drive a beat-up old car. I used to be ashamed of it and park it out of sight. Some years ago I decided to turn this into an antishame exercise, so now I park my shame-mobile right in front of wherever I go and offer everyone a ride in it.

Barbara adopted this antishame philosophy. She did small acts at first, like forcing herself to sit out by the pool even though she was ashamed of her body. By following this open-door policy long enough, her tolerance for shame increased. Paradoxically, the more shame she could tolerate the less she felt.

Visual images. Some of your thoughts that precede shame are in the form of mental pictures. You see yourself looking foolish in some situation. This shameful mental picture may make you react with a physical shudder over how foolishly or badly you acted in the situation.

Here are some ways to control these images and the resulting emotional reactions:

• Next time you start to feel shame ("I'm too fat" . . . "They know I'm divorced"), ask yourself, "Am I having an image? If so: What color is it? Is there movement? Is it vivid? Do I hear anything? What emotions do I have in the image?" By asking yourself these questions you can *better focus on the images.* Once you're aware of them, you can control them.

- If you can't get rid of the images, *turn them off by distracting yourself:* Clap your hands or shout "Stop it" to yourself. One patient would ring a cow bell. Or you can concentrate on your surroundings and describe them in detail to yourself. Each time you turn off the fantasy, your shame and other negative feelings are reduced and the image loses power.
- *Repeat the image over and over again* to force yourself to face the particular problem. Solutions will start appearing. One woman was ashamed of her husband's drinking. She repeated the image of his getting drunk at parties over and over. This helped her come up with a solution—she told him if he started to drink too much in a social situation, she was going to get up immediately and go home.

  You may eliminate or reduce shame merely by repeating your fantasy and increasing your tolerance of it. The elimination of shame then carries over into real life.
- If you feel shameful about a particular situation or event, *imagine it in six months, a year, or several years from now.* One woman was ashamed about being divorced. She projected herself five years into the future. After repeatedly doing this she felt better about the divorce.
- *Search for a more realistic explanation of the situation.* Images about shame are consistently worse than reality because the positive factors of the situation aren't included in the image. Remember those children's pictures—ones that say "Find twelve things wrong with this picture"? Do the same with your shameful mental pictures—look for the errors.
- *Develop positive images to counter negative ones.* For example, suppose you have an image of yourself being humiliated because of your weight. Imagine yourself sitting around the pool getting a tan, looking more healthy and less self-conscious. Rehearse activities in your head that you believe are potentially shameful ("I see myself walking right out by the pool, taking my robe off, and stretching out on a chair with a book").
- *Gradually change the negative image into a neutral or positive one* ("In the image I am not thin but nobody is looking at me and thinking I'm fat"). If this is too difficult, gradually change certain negative aspects of the image ("In the image I won't walk around

in front of people, but I will take my robe off and stretch out on a deck chair").
- *Direct the image.* Imagine changing channels on a TV set and making adjustments to the picture. Redirect the action—even down to the technical steps of each movement. You can see the imagery as a painting. Blot out certain portions and bring others into sharper focus ("In my fantasy my thighs are fat but my shoulders and face are tanned and great-looking"). Change the content of the fantasy so it's more adaptive ("I see myself lying there getting tanned and reading my book").

ANGER

Depressed people don't commonly feel anger. In fact, many don't experience anger until they start to improve. (When this happens, it usually doesn't last long.) However, for some, anger—often accompanied by physical pain, such as backache—is an early and persistent symptom.

If you're bothered by anger, you can use many of the procedures I've outlined to cope with other negative emotions—such as distraction and increasing your tolerance of bad situations.

Karen Rice's increased feelings of anger and irritation were the prime emotional symptoms of her depression. These feelings were diffused. She would be angry at her mother, her husband, neighbors, and at times the whole world.

She learned to control these feelings partially by changing what she was telling herself. When she was angry, she flooded herself with irrelevant thoughts of intolerance for others ("I hate everyone") and thoughts of the necessity of retaliation ("I'll teach them"). After becoming aware of these thoughts, she worked on becoming task-oriented and telling herself, "What do I want? Will getting mad really help me get what I want?" She began to use self-talk to cool herself down instead of talk that heated her up.

By putting herself into the other person's place, she learned to control her anger better. One day her mother-in-law called to complain about how everyone (including Karen) treated her badly. Karen found herself becoming angry: She and her husband spent a lot of time with his mother. Before she got too angry, she sat down and wrote out all of the reasons why her mother-in-law might act this way. She found her anger leaving her. By empathizing with her mother-in-law, she shifted to *acceptance*. Acceptance is incompatible with anger.

She found that she couldn't always control her anger this way, so she developed other coping skills. She learned to distract herself from anger and to increase her tolerance of what made her angry.

Increase your tolerance for negative emotions and you'll improve the quality of your life. Instead of thinking, "I can't stand this," tell yourself, "I'm strong enough to take this," or "I'll time how long I can tolerate this without getting upset, and gradually increase it." With practice you can learn to increase your tolerance for nearly all forms of discomfort.

By developing tolerance, you're "inoculating" yourself against future bouts with negative emotions. You'll find you can tolerate higher levels of discomfort than you thought and increase your sense of control, which further slows down spiraling negative emotions.

VI

Controlling the Mental and Physical Symptoms of Depression

SO far I've talked about two symptom clusters—the symptoms that show themselves through actions and feelings. In this chapter I'll talk about two other symptom clusters—symptoms that show themselves in how you think and in how your body reacts.

DIFFICULTIES IN MAKING DECISIONS

Anita Moreland knew she had to make some decisions. Should she fix her car or buy a new one? Her lease on her apartment was up —should she stay or move? She told a friend, "I can't even decide what to wear to work. How can I possibly make big decisions about buying a car or moving?"

Since becoming depressed, Anita felt in a stupor. She couldn't concentrate on her work, she couldn't remember meetings she was supposed to attend, but the worst part was not being able to make decisions. The more she put off decisions, the more depressed she became.

She didn't realize how much she depended on decision-making skills until she lost them. She found that life is a series of big and small decisions—and not being able to choose severely handicapped her, much as losing an arm or leg would.

Depression throws your whole system off. Any part can be affected: how you talk, eat, sleep, feel, think, and even look. Anita simply lost her decision-making skills.

Why can't you make decisions? Maybe you're making the same mistakes Anita made. She *overvalued* their importance. She *escalated* (in her mind) *minor decisions* (what shampoo to buy, what gas station to stop at, what wedding gift to buy) into major ones. She *discounted her judgment* ("I don't know what's the best film to buy"). She *structured the decision into a no-win situation*—so no matter what she decided, she'd be wrong ("If I stay, the rent will be a lost investment, and if I buy a house I'll be tied down and probably won't be able to make the payments").

Making minor decisions. You may, like Anita, have trouble making even the smallest decisions. This has been called a handcuff depression because you can't decide whether to go right or left— so you stand still.

Fortunately, there's a simple and effective solution—*choose the option that comes first in the alphabet.* Anita was able to start making minor decisions after using this method for only one week. She couldn't decide whether to buy pork chops or lamb chops, so she bought the lamb chops. She couldn't decide whether to stop at McDonald's or Burger King, so she stopped at Burger King.

A twenty-five-year-old flight attendant I saw had great difficulty in deciding what clothes to wear. At times she wouldn't leave her apartment because she couldn't decide what to wear. In an early session she was agonizing over whether to wear her blue dress or her green dress to a party. I suggested she use the alphabet method, so in this case she would wear the blue dress.

She seemed relieved and said, "That's a good method. Now that I'm forced to choose the blue one I can see I *really* want to wear the green one."

I pointed out that this isn't the way to use this method. She must stick with her decision. If she didn't she would soon be back in the same position: vacillating from one choice to another.

She thought about what I said and seemed to get very sad. I asked her what she was thinking.

She said, "I was thinking I'll never get to wear my Wellington boots again."

I had to clarify this further. She only had to use the alphabet method when she couldn't make a decision. She could decide to wear her Wellingtons any time she wanted to.

The idea is to *make a decision* and take action on it. Don't ruminate over simple decisions. This leads to mental paralysis. Keep in mind that since *there's no absolute certainty in life,* there's no guarantee that any decision will be the best.

In minor matters, any decision is better than no decision. True, you may increase your chances of a good outcome if you research the alternatives, but most of the time your choices are neither right nor wrong; they're simply different. Each has different consequences. You may come up with only partial solutions, but they keep adding up until the whole problem is solved.

Be prepared to work on feelings of guilt or regret that usually come after making difficult decisions. Try not to set up your decisions as no-win propositions. If you do, you'll feel like you lose no matter what you decide.

For example, a fellow therapist called me one day. He wanted advice on what to tell a young woman waiting in his office. She couldn't decide whether to go to a small or large college. The large school offered a scholarship but the other was better academically.

She was really in a no-lose situation; either school was good. But in her indecisiveness, she changed it into a *no-win* situation.

If she chose the small one she would lose the scholarship; and if she chose the large one she'd miss the academic excellence. For two weeks she kept changing her mind back and forth. The day the therapist called me was the day she had to make her final decision. Unable to decide, she was experiencing waves of panic.

I'd seen similar problems when I worked in a college counseling center. At the start of each term, anxious students had to decide right away what courses to take. I developed a technique to help them decide immediately on *wants* (what they really wanted) and not on *shoulds.* I was glad to pass this technique on to my therapist friend.

I told him to take out a coin and flip it. He should tell his patient, "Heads is the small school and tails is the larger one." But *before showing her which side came up,* he should ask her what she hoped the coin showed. When she answered, he could put the coin in his pocket without showing it to her. She would have made her decision. At that point she should call the school and confirm her choice.

I found out later that she chose the small school. Flipping the coin forced her to voice her preference without taking time to ruminate. She made an immediate choice based on *wants* rather than fear of consequences.

When you think you can't make a decision, keep these points in mind:

1. The *act of making a decision* at this point (because of your indecisiveness) is more important than the actual decision.
2. Your problem is really obsessiveness. You're demanding absolute certainty that your choice will be right. Your anxiety stems from this demand. But *there is no absolute guarantee that any choice is right.*
3. No one can realistically expect absolute certainty or "correctness"; no one can predict the future. Unanticipated consequences, both positive and negative, occur no matter what you choose. A wrong decision is usually only the long way around to the same goal.
4. Ask yourself why you need absolute assurances. Make a decision and act on it. The spice of life comes from uncertainty.
5. No matter what you decide, you can expect to feel regret for a week or so. Sales people call this predictable regret "buyers' or sellers' remorse." Accept your sense of regret and deal with it as one of the normal inconveniences of life.

Making major decisions. When you're suffering from depression, you're constantly faced with small decisions that may confuse and overpower you. While you should act quickly and decisively on the small matters, you shouldn't move impetuously on major issues. Since depression distorts your view of your life and the people around you, it's a good idea to postpone major decisions until you're feeling better.

You may believe that a bad situation—your marriage, your job, your children, or where you live—is causing your depression. Outside events *may* play a big part in your depression, but most major decisions about them can wait until you're not depressed. You want to be able to make a rational decision. When you're depressed isn't the best time to decide to get a divorce or put your children up for adoption.

But sometimes important decisions just can't wait. If they can't, write out the advantages and disadvantages of each choice and the possible consequences of each. Then use this as the guide for your decision. This technique, though simple, can be very powerful.

Helen, a young mother and housewife, couldn't decide if she should take a part-time job. She came up with two main advantages: She would have a chance to get out of the house, and she could talk to someone besides children. The main disadvantage would be the cost of hiring a babysitter. After putting these down on paper she saw the advantages outweighed the disadvantages, so she decided to take the job.

Guilt feelings often play a role in making decisions. Helen's dilemma about the job was partly caused by guilt. She knew she'd like to get out for a few days a week, but she felt guilty about spending the money for a babysitter and leaving her children.

Be sure that when you list the disadvantages of either choice you're not distorting the situation. Helen at first listed her guilt feelings as a disadvantage. She came to realize that guilt isn't a real disadvantage since it is unfounded and self-created. She could choose to not feel guilty.

DIFFICULTIES IN CONCENTRATION AND MEMORY

Your problems in concentration and memory are often interrelated. If you can't remember, it's probably because you aren't focusing on what you're trying to remember. Like the other symptoms of depression, these problems are ones you're *supposed to have when you're depressed;* they aren't signs that you're losing your mind or that you're stupid.

Holly, a sophomore in college, had trouble concentrating on her studies. She couldn't focus on her lectures. Instead of concentrating on her teachers, she ruminated about her problems with her boyfriend.

She thought she'd lost her ability to concentrate. She didn't believe me when I told her this might be part of her depression, so I suggested an experiment. I would read a page from her school book and ask her questions. I did this and she was easily able to answer my questions. This proved to her that she could concentrate, at least for short periods of time.

If you have a problem with concentration, you might do what Holly did. She bought a kitchen timer and practiced concentrating for increased lengths of time. Starting with ten minutes, she gradually expanded the time to fifty minutes. Soon she was back to studying normally.

Steve Bishop, a psychologist doing research in cognitive therapy at the University of Edinburgh in Scotland, has noted that many of the depressed people he works with believe they're "going daft" or are "stupid" because of their loss of concentration.

He writes, "In nearly every case I've treated, the focusing techniques and subsequent practice sessions at home have been remarkably effective in reducing concentration and memory difficulties. Surprisingly, patients report regaining their 'powers of concentration' very quickly, sometimes after only a few homework assignments, e.g., six ten-minute practice sessions reading short newspaper articles or several pages of an interesting novel. Another benefit of the technique is that it provides a success experience for the patient (it doesn't hurt the therapist either!) at the beginning of therapy. This in turn shows patients the advantage of breaking down the depressive syndrome into concrete target problems. I find that this is particularly important for those who feel hopeless about overcoming their depression through psychological interventions." *

Like Steve Bishop, I've found that what appear to be simple techniques can be major tools for turning around depression.

Ruminations. Continually thinking about your problems can interfere with your concentration. Most people expect that thinking through their problems will help solve them. But continual thinking and thinking and thinking usually can't solve the problem. For example, if your husband leaves you, running this fact through

* Letter dated February 1, 1978.

your head thousands of times won't change things. While ruminating isn't dangerous, it can be uncomfortable.

If ruminations are interfering with your life, you can control them. First, plan a specific time for thinking—say thirty minutes each night. Use these thirty minutes to ruminate to your heart's content. But if you start ruminating at any other time, tell yourself, "Stop it!" Then, immediately focus on your surroundings. Think about where you are, what you're doing. You might have to do this a hundred times a day at first, but it'll become automatic with practice.

This technique works because you start to attend to the present. You cannot ruminate on the present, only on the future ("What if I get cancer") or on the past ("I shouldn't have told my father he looks old"). The more you can focus on what's happening *right now,* the fewer ruminations you'll have.

Watch for the behavior that keeps you ruminating. If you're thinking about your husband having an affair, continually checking up on him will increase the ruminations. Also, since many passive activities, such as watching TV, staying in bed, or staring out the window, increase ruminations, avoid them in favor of some absorbing activity.

You may feel the need for more dramatic methods. For example, Holly's ruminations about her boyfriend interfered with her concentration in class. She began wearing a rubber band on her wrist; every time she began thinking about him, she gave herself a sharp snap. (Sometimes patients use different colored rubber bands to snap different types of thoughts.) This interrupted her thoughts and reminded her to concentrate on the lectures.

These "stop it" methods are only temporary. Eventually you'll have to begin changing some of the beliefs fueling your ruminations ("I can't be happy without a man" . . . "I should be perfect"). Once Holly *fully* realized that she could be happy without her boyfriend, her ruminations about him completely stopped.

Memory difficulties. You may have trouble with your memory, which is another sign of depression. Generally, your memory will improve if you work on your concentration.

If you have to remember specific material on the job or at school, use the "SQ3R" method. This procedure, developed by an educational psychologist, incorporates much of what is known about remembering and forgetting. The steps in the process, which Holly used to improve her studies, are *Survey, Question, Read, Recite,* and *Review.* First, she *surveyed* the material (her notes) she wanted to remember. She looked it over. This gave her a blueprint to work from. Next, she asked herself specific *questions* about what she'd just surveyed. This helped her focus her attention and give meaning to the material. Then, she *read* (listening will work as well) the material. She followed this with an oral *recitation* (though making notes would also have worked). In the last step, she *reviewed* all of her notes.

If you follow the SQ3R method, you'll be better able to remember the material you're working on. Holly not only got help with her depression with the SQ3R method, but also improved her grades.

HOW TO CONTROL THOUGHTS OF SUICIDE

Thoughts of killing yourself—technically called suicide ideation—are symptomatic of depression. The threat of suicide is the biggest problem for therapists who work with depressed patients. If you ever think of killing yourself, you should work on this symptom first.

When your life is going badly, you may tell yourself, "Well, I'll just kill myself." Usually you don't believe this, but thinking about it may give you emotional relief. *This is a dangerous strategy.* If you're not careful, you *can* talk yourself into actually carrying it out. Nearly *everyone* who commits suicide begins by thinking like this.

Danger signals.   How serious are your thoughts of killing yourself? Thoughts themselves may not be dangerous (most people have thoughts of suicide from time to time), but yours may have reached the point where you need to see a professional to get some objectivity on your problems. Watch for these danger signals:

1. *Restraint.* Even when people have strong wishes to die, they usually have some reason to continue to live ("What would

happen to my kids?" . . . "It would hurt my mother" . . . "I wouldn't give people the satisfaction"). If your reasons to live begin to seem less important than they were, this can be a dangerous sign.

2. *Passive attempts.* Many suicides are the result of passive attempts such as walking slowly across a busy street or going into a dangerous neighborhood. Even a simple act like dropping knives while you work in the kitchen could be a sign of a passive attempt. Some elderly people kill themselves by not taking their medications.

3. *Plans.* Killing yourself requires some planning. You must design a method, judge how lethal it is, arrange for it, and tidy up loose ends such as making out a will and paying off bills. If you start making even tentative plans, this is dangerous business.

4. *Past attempts.* If you've tried to kill yourself in the past (or someone close to you has committed suicide), be on guard against suicide thoughts. Most people who kill themselves have tried before.

5. *Hopelessness.* The more your suicide thoughts are motivated by a desire to escape, the more dangerous they are. The Center for Cognitive Therapy has studied over 500 people who have attempted suicide. Our most important finding: *These people see suicide as the only way out of a hopeless situation.* Hopelessness is the key.

Problem solving. Who kill or attempt to kill themselves? Older people more than younger ones; widowed, divorced, or separated people more than those married; people with little financial and emotional support; and people undergoing a trauma such as a loss of job, the ending of a relationship, or a crippling accident. What you see is a picture of a person with problems who feels his or her abilities to solve them have dwindled away.

I find that people use suicide as a problem-solving strategy. I don't try to argue them out of suicide, rather I say, "Let's see if this is the best solution—perhaps there are other solutions you've overlooked."

Will suicide really solve your problems? Many women think of suicide because they don't want to be a burden to their children and husband. I remind them that they may be an even bigger burden after suicide. Close relatives have great difficulty getting over the suicide of a loved one. This is one of the reasons why suicides run in families.

Some patients also believe that they are a burden to their therapists. But, like family members, therapists are often devastated when one of their patients commits suicide. I know of several therapists who left the profession because of the sense of failure over the suicide of one of their patients.

It is possible that trying to kill yourself will leave you with more problems than you have now. It's not that easy to kill yourself, but it's relatively easy to *hurt* yourself badly. Many attempts at suicide have led to crippling conditions. Then you're really a burden.

Using suicide as a problem-solving strategy has its drawbacks. Remember, suicide is an irreversible decision—*you can't change your mind and go back.* A decision without an escape clause is usually a poor one.

Several patients said they decided against suicide after wondering what would happen to them if they *did* kill themselves. They had read books indicating that the afterlife for suicides may be found wanting. They thought they might be jumping from the frying pan into the fire.

Hopelessness. Jean Hayes wanted to kill herself because she didn't believe she could be happy after her fiancé, Paul, left her for another woman. The only way she saw out of her painful state was suicide. She was able to overcome this idea after cutting through her heavy level of pessimism. She came to realize that she'd been happy before meeting Paul and there was a good chance she'd be happy again without him.

Part of depression is a vision of your future as a combination of pain and suffering. Hopelessness is a big block to problem solving. Because you think there's no solution, you don't look for any, even though a solution will probably appear in time.

Have you ever misjudged problems and situations before? You may be doing so now and overlooking choices. Rather than giving in to hopelessness, you have to continue to experiment with solutions.

Ideas to keep in mind if you're thinking of suicide:

- *Don't have lethal means around.* Readily available pills and guns increase the chance of impulsive suicide attempts.
- *Don't make rash decisions.* You can always kill yourself later. This isn't the kind of decision to rush into.
- *If you're seriously thinking of killing yourself, tell someone.* The person can't force you not to, but he or she can help you come up with other problem-solving strategies.
- *If you're prone to thoughts of suicide, watch what drugs or drinks you take.* Many people decide to kill themselves while intoxicated.
- *Increase your tolerance for uncertainty.* Many of the solutions to your problems won't emerge for a while. As long as you're alive, there's hope.
- *List the reasons for living that you may have forgotten or discounted.* Writing them down can bring them back to mind.
- *List reasons against suicide.* One person decided against it because she thought it was a meaningless act—"a cosmic so what."
- *If your suicide urges begin to feel out of control, see a professional.* There are a number of suicide-prevention programs that can help. You can always call a suicide hotline any time of day or night.

If you endure your suffering and manage to overcome it, you'll be a *positive role model* to your loved ones. By committing suicide, you offer them the option of handling their problems the same way. As I mentioned before, suicides tend to run in families.

Over the years I've talked to many people who failed in their suicide attempts; they were glad they had failed.

PHYSICAL SYMPTOMS

If you're depressed, you may have some physical symptoms; most notably, changes in your appearance. Other common symptoms in this cluster include problems with your sleep, changes in your appetite, loss of your sexual drive, and at times increased aches and pains.

Changes in appearance. You probably are concerned about your appearance: Most depressed people are. You may be mildly worried that you've lost your looks—or you might be convinced that you're hideous and deformed.

Depressed people frequently have distorted self-images, usually caused by their underlying beliefs about the importance of appearance. But right now I want to talk about the real changes in appearance that often accompany depression.

Over the years I've become pretty good at spotting depressed people at parties and other places. Their sad expressions, stooped postures, slow, lowered voices, and eyes red from crying catch my attention. Over eighty percent of depressed people have symptoms like these. (There are exceptions, like the "smiling" depressive who hides behind a false cheerfulness.)

In the same way, I also can usually tell when a patient is getting over her depression. She walks into the office faster, she sits straighter in the chair, she has a new radiance as though her inner light has been turned up. Her face and eyes are clearer and she speaks in a stronger voice.

How you feel affects how you look. This isn't a new idea. When you're sad and unhappy, you won't look your best. Suppose what I say is true and you *can* control your emotions by changing your thinking. This in turn means that you have the ability, to some extent, to control how you look.

I recently ran across an article by psychiatrist Wallace Ellerbroek, M.D., in which he describes treating thirty-eight patients with chronic acne—a tough problem to treat, with a traditionally low rate of success. His treatment consisted of having patients become aware of their negative thoughts (itching was a cue for them to watch for thoughts) and then answer the thoughts. He found that over eighty percent of the patients were significantly helped by learning to change their thinking.

His report rings true for patients I see with skin problems. When they control their negative feelings (by controlling their negative thoughts), their skin problems clear up; and when they don't, the skin problems come back.

So one way to control physical symptoms of depression is to

work on your negative feelings. Another, more direct way is to *focus on your specific symptoms.* Choice exists. You can choose to change your posture (stand or sit straighter), your facial expressions (smile more and frown less), your voice (speak louder and more confidently), and your speed (walk and react faster). This takes effort, but you'll find that by *acting as if* you aren't depressed, you'll begin to feel (and actually be) less depressed.

Your grooming or lack of it adds to the "depression look." When you're depressed, you often don't feel like fixing yourself up or buying new clothes. You think, "I don't deserve it," or "It wouldn't help anything." Actually, this is a time when extra time spent on grooming pays off.

I have a personal rule about this. When I'm in a bad mood or when there's some place I don't particularly want to go, I spend extra time getting ready. I wear better clothes and try to look my best. This helps get rid of my bad mood and increases the chances I'll enjoy where I'm going.

Here's a common trap in depression: You don't like yourself so treat yourself shabbily, and this makes you like yourself even less. You can break out of this trap by spending more time on your appearance. Do something special for yourself—get a facial, buy a new outfit, go to a health spa for a weekend, or just schedule a long, relaxing bath.

Sleep problems. Many people who aren't depressed have trouble sleeping, but sleep difficulties (trouble falling asleep, restlessness during the night, early-morning waking, and inability to get back to sleep) are also one of the most common symptoms of depression.

If you're suffering from this symptom, you may be getting more sleep than you think. Researchers point out that people with insomnia consistently underestimate their amount of sleep. They've found that the person who says, "I was awake all night" actually dozed a good part of the night.

Fear of losing sleep keeps more people awake than anything else. One woman had the mistaken belief that she'd go crazy from lack of sleep. Many believe they're seriously endangering their health by not getting enough sleep. Lost sleep is not a catastrophe since it can easily be recouped, but worrying about it increases insomnia.

Sleep researchers have found people actually need less sleep than they think. In underdeveloped countries without electrical lights, people believe they need eleven or twelve hours of sleep each night and complain of feeling bad when they get less than this. As people find more to do at night, they need less sleep. One expert on sleep predicts that people will average three hours of sleep a night by the year 2000.

One patient tried to drink herself to sleep each night. Her insomnia was caused by the belief she *had* to sleep. She'd try to go to sleep at 8:30 at night ("If I sleep, I don't have to think"). Once she learned she could change her negative thinking, she lost her urge to escape it through sleep.

Improvement in other areas of your life leads to better sleep. For example, if you spend a large part of your day lying on a sofa or taking naps, you won't feel like sleeping at night. So you'll sleep better once you become more active.

Relaxation. The best way to overcome insomnia is to learn to relax. Try this:

1. While lying in bed, tense your hands for a few seconds. Then let the muscles relax. Do this with the rest of your body, part by part: arms, shoulders, face, eyes, chest (tense by breathing), stomach, legs, feet. Tense and relax . . . tense and relax. Do each part of the body twice, especially the muscles around the eyes.
2. Next, count backwards from ten. Let your muscles go and make yourself more relaxed as you go down the numbers. Make nine more relaxed than ten and so on. Do this twice.
3. Then, begin to visualize a pleasant scene such as the following: "It's a crisp spring day. You're walking into a forest you've been to before. The sky is blue. A few clouds are floating overhead. You find a path to walk down; you feel happy and relaxed. You continue to walk down it. Twigs and branches snap as you walk down the path. You see a small stream ahead and remove your shoes and socks to step into it. The water feels cool on your feet as you step over rocks and across the stream. At the other side is a lush, green meadow. You hear birds singing. The smell of grass is in the air. You can almost taste the

freshness of spring. You see a large oak tree and lean against the rough bark of the trunk. You feel the soft moss under you. Look up and see the blue sky with lazy white clouds floating by. You're breathing slowly and deeply. You're feeling perfectly calm and completely safe." Enjoy this scene and hold it until you fall asleep.

Additional techniques to help you sleep:

1. Try to discover what *your natural sleep cycle* is and go to bed only when you're tired. (I call this "getting on the bus"—if I miss the one at 11, I'll have to wait until 12:30 to catch the next one.) Some people sleep late and stay up late; others get up early and go to bed early.

2. A fixed routine right before going to bed, such as having a glass of milk or washing your face, can be helpful. Your body will associate these events with going to sleep.

3. Avoid stimulants. Don't drink coffee or tea too near bedtime. Don't watch stimulating TV or read exciting books before going to bed. Block out any light or noise that will keep you awake.

4. Don't lie in bed during the day or use the bed for anything other than sleep—you want to associate the bed only with sleeping.

5. Don't rely on sleeping pills. Aside from the problem of dependency, they often backfire (after continual use, they can actually keep you from sleeping). Many sleep researchers say a couple of aspirin are as good as anything.

6. And, finally, if you can't sleep, get out of bed and do something—read a boring book, take a warm bath. It's better to do this than to lie awake and experience unpleasant thoughts.

Disturbances in your appetite and sex drive. Loss of appetite and loss of interest in sex are common signs of depression. Both show you're losing your sense of pleasure. People usually don't complain too much about the loss of these appetites, so the symptoms are rarely directly worked on. When your depression lifts, your appetites for food and sex usually return.

VII

Dealing with Weight Gain

MANY depressed people suffer from more than the four symptom clusters—behavioral, emotional, mental, and physical—I've covered so far. Their other problems could be considered either symptoms or complications of depression. For example, many people gain weight when they get depressed. Descriptively, this could be considered a symptom of depression, but since most people over-eat to treat their depression, I consider it a complication of depression. Whether considered symptoms or complications, however, you must learn how to resolve these other problems and put them behind you. In this chapter I will talk about weight gain. In the next two I will discuss two other common complications of depression: alcohol/drug dependency and relationship problems.

Sally Goldman had been fighting her weight ever since high school. She'd tried just about every diet and had belonged to Weight Watchers—twice. During her junior year of college, she'd been depressed and gained twenty-five pounds that she'd never lost. But over the years she'd decided she could live with them—even though she was heavier than she wanted to be. Her weight became an inconvenience, but not a terrible problem.

After being divorced, she had a two-year affair with a married man. He broke it off and she became quite depressed. She started eating more and her weight shot up thirty pounds. The more she gained, the more depressed she became. After six months, she was referred to me.

I've working with many depressed people who are concerned about their weight. Not all are truly overweight. One woman took the motto, "A woman can't be too rich or too thin" to heart. Although she was twenty-five pounds underweight and looked like a skeleton, she thought she was fat. Others have severe obesity problems. Most, however, are like Sally Goldman and are between ten percent and twenty-five percent overweight.

Depression and self-control. I had been taught in graduate school that depressed people lose weight. But this didn't fit with what I was seeing in practice. After I found that many depressed people gain weight, a graduate student and I conducted a survey on weight gain and depression. We questioned 200 people.

What did we find? Most depressed people who didn't want to lose weight *did*—and those who wanted to lose *gained*. In both cases, depression wiped out the person's self-regulation: There was a breakdown in self-control.

I don't want to imply that all people with weight problems are depressed; they aren't. But I have found that when the overweight person becomes depressed, weight gain is often a major complication—particularly among women.

Priorities. Sally had a chronic weight problem that got worse when she was depressed. She gained weight, which made her feel more depressed. What should she work on first—depression or weight? Since Sally was quite depressed, her first goal was to feel better. She did this by working on her other symptoms and trying not to gain any more weight. After she felt better, she developed a plan to lose weight. If she'd been mildly depressed, I'd have suggested a weight reduction program right off.

I recommend the same to you. If you're very depressed, focus on *not gaining more* weight while working on your other symptoms. After you feel better, you can tackle *losing* weight. If your depression isn't too severe, you can start right away on losing weight.

Negative ideas about being overweight. The first step in either case is to change your negative thinking about being overweight. Sally bought many of the negative ideas being sold about overweight people: They are sinful, gluttonous, ugly, and without willpower. Sally bordered on being a weight fascist, a person who believes that anyone overweight is no damn good and who often even discriminates against the overweight.

You should remember that judgments about beauty are arbitrary. What's considered a good figure depends on cultural values. But even this isn't clear. Anthropologists have pointed out that leanness, so admired in our culture, is associated with meanness in others—the bad guys are usually thin, the devil is a toothpick. They ask: Have you ever seen a fat witch? Or do you know anyone who wants Santa Claus to lose weight?

Self-blame. I've found one striking characteristic shared by depressed people trying to lose weight—they badmouth themselves ("I'm a pig" . . . "I hate myself" . . . "I'm no damn good"). I hope they don't let other people talk to them like this.

Derogatory remarks like these are self-defeating. By putting yourself down, you're giving yourself license to overeat ("I'm no damn good, so what difference does it make if I overeat or not").

Sally believed, "If I give myself hell, I won't do it again." But she didn't realize that punishment isn't the best way to change behavior. You only have to look at all the repeat customers in prisons to realize this. You may be punishing yourself by calling yourself a "no account pig," but you aren't solving your problems.

It's also an overgeneralization to put yourself down for your weight. Your total life consists of countless acts, thoughts, and traits. It's illogical and counterproductive to judge yourself on one trait. Self-blame can make you depressed, discouraged, hopeless, and even self-righteous, but it can't help you lose weight.

Blaming yourself for being overweight is a version of *blaming the victim* for the crime. No one knows for sure why some people have weight problems and others don't. The causes of obesity are proving to be more complicated than originally thought. Scientists agree, however, that not *one,* but a multitude of causes (biological, social, cultural, developmental, psychological, and environmental) influence your weight.

Don't beat on yourself about your weight. It doesn't help and it can make you more depressed.

Sadness and eating. Many depressed people believe they eat sweets and sugar products to feel better. But do they feel better afterward?

I took part in a research project to find out the answer to this question. We examined the food records and mood charts of people in treatment; altogether, we looked at over 3500 meals. We found that eating sugary foods in response to sadness didn't make them feel any better. In fact, they often felt worse. Our conclusion was that depressed people frequently use the rationale, "I need to eat something to feel better," but they actually feel worse after eating sweets.

What does all this mean? First, it means you must check out your thinking: You may be tricking yourself. Second, it means trying not to react to your negative thoughts ("I'm so uptight, I need a candy bar to relax") by giving in to them. Tell yourself, "I can endure this unpleasant feeling without a candy bar." Part of being human is putting up with a certain number of bad days.

The next time you think, "I'm really down, I need something good to eat," try this experiment. Rate your mood from 0 to 100. Then, an hour after you've eaten, rerate your mood and notice the direction it takes.

Then try the experiment again. But this time *don't* eat when you're down and see if you feel better. Most people do.

Sally, once she started to lose weight, said, "I finally figured if I can't eat I'll feel bad and if I eat and get fat I'll feel bad. So I decided if I'm going to feel bad either way, I might as well be thin."

Self-talk and overeating. Since, as part of my doctoral dissertation, I wanted to know what goes through people's minds when they overeat, I asked forty people to write down what they were saying to themselves immediately before they overate. They did this for ten weeks.

Nearly everyone, after a short period, learned to become aware of her self-defeating thoughts. People were surprised to learn they were talking to themselves *before* overeating and even more surprised at *what* they were telling themselves. The thoughts ranged from the common, "I'll cut down tomorrow," to "I have to eat in order to face my teacher's beady eyes."

I discovered people often use the wrong strategy in trying to lose weight. Typically, they go on a severe diet. This inevitably leads to thinking, "I'm so hungry I have to have something good." Breaking your diet leads to the thought, "I blew my diet, so I might as well enjoy myself."

You probably failed to lose weight in the past because you used the wrong strategies to solve your problems. Your strategies turned into reasons for overeating. For example, Sally fought boredom by eating. One woman's strategy for a dry throat was to treat it with ice cream. Become aware of your own wrong strategies.

Eating habits. If you have a chronic weight problem, you'll have to change some basic eating habits. Most people don't think through what they eat and why. For example, I overheard this conversation at a restaurant.

"You said you weren't hungry. So why did you order the French fries with your coke?"

"I don't believe in drinking alone."

"What?"

"Well, if I'm going to have something to drink, I need some food with it."

When I suggested to a middle-aged businessman that he cut down on his large breakfast, he snapped back, "*I have to have a good breakfast.*" You would have thought I had insulted his mother. And in a way I had. While he was growing up his mother insisted that he have a big breakfast every day.

The belief that we're supposed to eat three meals a day is a cultural artifact, not a cosmic law. There is nothing holy about eating breakfast. Farmers who get up at four a.m. and work in the fields easily burn off the calories from a big breakfast. But you may have a difficult time doing so while sitting at your desk.

I've found many people start to gain weight once they begin to eat breakfast and others lose weight once they cut back on or cut out breakfast.

Once you start observing yourself, you'll probably see what habits have to be changed. It might be your food choices. Carmen, a college student, ate large quantities of ice cream when she was depressed. She'd eat a half gallon at one sitting. She thought, "It's my favorite food, I gotta have it."

Everyone has favorite foods and craves them at various times. Food preferences are learned early in life and rarely change. Because you can't totally eliminate them, you must learn to control them. You can limit your craving for a favorite food, be it chocolate, ice cream, or pizza. But first, decide if this is a true craving or merely the result of something you thought up, saw, smelled, or heard.

People think about their favorite foods in a limited context. Carmen associated ice cream with "purity, wholesomeness, fun, and the all-American food." Your food associations are learned from family and friends, but mostly from advertisements ("Wheaties, the breakfast of champions"). By thinking of a favorite food in a limited context, you set yourself up to eat too much of it. When Carmen was feeling "unwholesome," the idea of having a dish of ice cream quickly came to mind.

I often ask people to write down what their favorite food means to them and then to expand this range of meaning. Mrs. Novack's favorite food was rye and Russian breads. For her, bread meant the "staff of life" and reminded her of her childhood in Poland. When she was feeling lonely or vulnerable, she would eat a whole loaf of rye bread. She was able to break this association through hard work.

When she had the urge to eat bread, she would force herself to think of what bread really is (the factory making it, the packaging of it, waiting in line to buy it, the high calories, the price). Bread was still a favorite food to her, she still ate it and enjoyed it, but she learned to control her craving for it.

People often use the wrong strategy in trying to control their food cravings. For instance, Carmen came in to see me convinced she could never lose weight.

The day before, she had awakened with a vague craving for ice cream. She thought, "I'd better have a good breakfast to overcome this." She ate bacon, eggs, toast, and coffee (400 calories). Around 10:30 a.m., still craving ice cream, she ate a cup of yogurt (270).

Believing she'd better watch it, she only had a salad for lunch (120). An hour after lunch she felt deprived, and saying "The hell with it," she bought a half gallon of ice cream. Without planning to, she ate it all (3500 calories). Total calories: 4290.

What could she have done differently? When she realized she had this craving, she could have had a dish of ice cream and a cup of coffee for breakfast (300 calories). Then she could have had a moderate lunch of about 300 calories. This would have saved her from eating 3690 extra calories.

When you have a craving for a particular food, it's usually better to satisfy it in a moderate way and *build this food into your total daily calorie intake.* Overcome the belief, "It's my favorite food; *I need a lot of it.*" Satisfy your craving with a moderate amount of a favorite food.

Make the distinction in your mind between quality and quantity. For example, buy a good quality cake, but eat only a small amount of it. Try not to bring large quantities of your favorite foods into the house. If you can't buy small quantities, repackage the food. For example, when you buy a package of cookies, wrap them in packages of two or three cookies and freeze them.

Serve tempting foods on small plates or in small dishes, as good restaurants do with desserts. Make a special occasion out of eating your favorite food. Serve it on good china, eat it slowly, and really enjoy it.

Finally, try an experiment. First rate how much you crave a certain food. Then eat a small portion and two hours later rerate the craving. Do the same when you eat a large portion. Notice if there's any difference.

Drs. Kathryn and Michael Mahoney at Pennsylvania State University are leading authorities on weight reduction. They believe one of the best ways to lose weight is to practice what they call *cognitive ecology:* Clean up what you tell yourself. For example, instead of eating all of the food on your plate because you think, "I can't waste food," think "It's better to go to waste than to waist."

Right now, your eating habits seem natural and normal because they're what you've learned over the years. At first, new ways of acting and thinking will seem unnatural. However, if you stick with them, they'll eventually become natural to you.

Either/or thinking. Does this sound familiar? The first day of a new diet is tough, but you get through it. The second day is a little easier. On the third day you impulsively eat a candy bar or some other fattening food. You then think, "Damn it, I've blown it again," and eat like a madwoman for the rest of the day.

If it does, you aren't alone. This thought ("I've blown it") is a pervasive thinking mistake.

Researchers have studied this process in detail. In one experiment, half of a group of dieters were given milkshakes, the other half weren't. Then all were allowed to eat as much ice cream as they wanted. (They were told this was a taste experiment.)

The half that drank milkshakes ate almost a quart of ice cream each. The other half ate small amounts. In other words, those who thought they'd blown their diets by drinking milkshakes overate.

The same experiment was run with nondieters. Here, as you might expect, the results were the opposite of the experiment with dieters. Those drinking milkshakes had just a little ice cream afterward, and those not drinking milkshakes were hungrier so they ate more ice cream.

Looking at all of the studies, a pattern emerges. If you overeat, you see your transgression as more fattening than it is. You then think, "I've blown it," and really overeat. It doesn't matter if you *really* ate too much initially—it only matters that you *believe* you did.

Researchers found that once you overestimate how much you've eaten, you'll start to overeat and lose your awareness of how much you've eaten. But if you *underestimate* (and keep track of calories), you won't lose your awareness of how much you've eaten.

You have to eliminate the "I blew it" type of thinking in order to lose weight and keep it off. This thinking is based on the self-defeating notion, "I have to be either *on* or *off* a diet." Either/or thinking sets you up for failure. You can never be perfect in your food choices. You'll make mistakes. Try to look at your mistakes as friendly reminders to do better, not as reasons to go crazy in your eating.

Don't set up unrealistic goals ("I'll fast for two days" . . . "I'll never eat desserts again"). Unrealistic goals lead you right into a trap. I've found that those who set difficult but not outrageous goals do the best.

The next time you eat too much, regard it as a *critical incident* —a point where you can stick to your program or abandon it. Tell yourself, "Okay, I made a mistake. It's not the end of my attempt to lose weight. I'll just watch what I do for the rest of the day."

Problem situations. It's a good strategy to avoid situations and places that lead to overeating. Once you break your plan, self-defeating thoughts about overeating can be difficult to catch and answer. This can happen to you in a tempting environment.

I'll give you an example. Brenda James had trouble when she cooked. She told me, "I can't cook without tasting, and everyone in my family wants something different at odd times. So I do a lot of cooking and tasting."

Brenda differs from others who use this reason for overeating in that she admits to a lot of sampling. Many people believe food eaten while they're cooking doesn't count.

"I'm just tasting" is a deceptive thought. First, you are standing, and if you eat while standing it tends to be automatic and unaware —you end up eating more than you realize. Second, you are probably sampling more than just the food you're cooking. With this mental set, you can end up sampling everything from the soup to the nuts.

If you really want a taste of what you're cooking, sit down and have a small portion. Make eating a conscious decision, not an automatic response.

Answering your excuses is not always powerful enough to overcome your old habits. You have to *avoid* the *problem situations* that give birth to the excuses. Whatever your problem area, develop some ways to handle it. As an example, here are some ways to avoid the kitchen—a common problem area:

- Realize the kitchen is a hazardous area—spend as little time as possible there.
- Limit the use of the kitchen to cooking. Leave it immediately after you've finished cooking.

- Have someone else wash the dishes, or at least help.
- Eat in your dining room; if you don't have a dining room, partition a space in the kitchen that is only for eating.
- Don't use your kitchen as a social center, office, or retreat.
- Take the television out of the kitchen.
- Have the telephone moved out of the kitchen, or at least make your calls from another room.
- If your kitchen has a back door, use the front door to enter the house.
- Let the dog out the front door.
- Train your children and husband to get their own food and snacks.
- If a family member doesn't eat at a designated time, let him cook for himself. Or at least cook all of the food at one time and let others heat up their own food. This maneuver is difficult for some mothers, but the best thing you can do for your children is to teach them to be self-reliant.
- Put as much space as possible between where you spend your leisure time and the kitchen.

If your problem area is one other than the kitchen, develop similar ways to handle it.

Alcohol and food.　　Many people have trouble with alcohol and eating. A young executive, Sue Rogers, explained, "My problem is that I lose control over my eating whenever I drink. And I often go to business lunches and dinners where I have to drink."

Alcohol is a time-honored excuse for overeating, based on the myth that alcohol automatically leads to loss of control. Researchers have found that when dieters drink pure orange juice and are falsely told it contains alcohol, *they overeat.* And when they drink orange juice laced with alcohol and are not told it contains alcohol, *they actually eat less.* A person's thinking, not the alcohol, leads to the loss of control over eating.

I asked Sue to try an experiment: The next time she went drinking, she was to tell herself, "Alcohol is a sedative; it can't make me do anything I don't want to do."

She came back a week later and said, "It worked wonderfully—

except once at a dinner party. I drank too much and forgot to talk to myself.''

If you get drunk, you'll forget your strategies. I suggested to Sue that she control her drinking to keep this from happening again.

Guidelines to help you lose weight. After helping hundreds of people—children, adolescents, college students, and adults from a wide variety of backgrounds—lose weight, I've come to certain conclusions about how to lose weight and maintain the loss.

1. *Become aware of your eating.* Awareness is the first step to change. Buy a small notebook and write down *everything* you eat. Listen to what you tell yourself. How do you justify eating more calories than you need to lose weight? How do you justify getting less exercise than you need to lose weight? Write down what you're eating.

2. *Slow down your eating.* I recommend this for everyone. One of the most important changes you can make to lose weight, slowing down will make you more aware of eating, increase your pleasure, give you more control over your food choices, let your body know when you're full, and most importantly, make you aware of your excuses.

   There are different ways you can slow down your eating: put your fork down after each bite, chew your food twenty to thirty times before swallowing, or plan delays of one to three minutes between bites. Sally found pacing herself with slower-eating friends the best strategy.

3. *Count the calories of everything you eat.* Focus on your calorie count, not on your weight. The weight will take care of itself. You need calorie information to make decisions throughout the day. Buy a regular and a name-brand calorie-counter book. You can estimate the calorie count of foods you can't find in the book provided you are consistent about looking up the food you eat regularly. Force yourself to look up the calorie counts you don't know at the end of the day. You'll eventually learn the calorie counts and won't have to look them up.

4. *Determine how many calories you can eat and still lose*

weight. This amount varies for each individual. After several weeks of counting calories, you'll have a good idea of how many you burn up on an average day. You have to eat *500 calories less each day* or use up 500 extra calories, to lose a pound a week.

5. *Choose a realistic weight goal.* An unrealistic goal can backfire. It's a poor strategy to try to lose more than two pounds a week because the faster you take weight off, the greater your chances of regaining it. You probably don't believe this, but that's what study after study has found. There are two reasons for this: First, if you are losing weight at a rapid rate, you are using some method you can't live with in the long run. Second, your body is in balance even when you're overweight. If you offset this balance too quickly, your body will respond by increasing your urges to eat until you get back to your old weight.

6. *Plan your meals.* Each night, decide what you're going to eat the next day. Make your plans around the number of calories you can eat. Save calories from your daily total for special occasions. If you know you're going out for Chinese food at the end of the week, bank extra calories to use for this.

7. *Pinpoint your thinking mistakes.* When you eat more than you'd planned, write down your thoughts. What was happening to influence you? What did you eat? I've listed common types of mistakes in Table 8.

8. *Challenge your reasons for overeating.* Answer your negative thoughts ("My hostess expects me to ask for seconds") with a more balanced point of view ("I explained to her I'm trying to lose weight, and she understands"). I've listed some answers you can use in Tables 9, 10, and 11.

9. *Act on your new answers.* Say "No thanks" to the hostess. When you begin to recognize situations that give you excuses to overeat, avoid them—or develop new strategies other than eating to deal with them.

10. *Increase your physical activity.* If you include exercise in your weight loss program, you can lose weight without cutting out as many calories. Walking is probably the best overall exercise. You can do it alone and it doesn't take any special equip-

TABLE 8
Some Common Thinking Mistakes in Losing Weight

Self-Defeating Cognitions	Cognitive Errors
"I've just eaten some ice cream. I *never* have any control."	Overgeneralization
"I was *only* able to stick to my plan for three days. I completely messed it up by making a *pig* of myself last night."	Minimization of achievements, magnification of slips, and inexact labeling (i.e., calling self a pig)
"Well, I've eaten the chocolate bar. I'm off my plan for good, now."	Either/or reasoning and exaggeration.
"I couldn't tell them I didn't want a beer, they'd think I'm a party pooper."	Jumping to conclusion and overreliance on others' opinions
"I want to weigh a hundred and twelve so I'll look like a model."	Buying into society's appearance neurosis
"Eating this sandwich won't make any difference."	Magical thinking

TABLE 9
Answers to Common Unrealistic Goals

Maladaptive Thoughts	Answers
"I've dieted for three days and haven't lost anything."	"I'm trying to change my eating habits. The weight will take care of itself."
"I've only lost a pound this week. This isn't worth it."	"The ideal goal is a one- to two-pound-a-week loss. If I lose it faster, it will be harder to keep off."
"I've gained a pound so I might as well forget about my diet."	"My weight fluctuates for a lot of reasons (water content, menstrual periods). I didn't gain all this weight in a week and I know it will take time to lose it."
"I completely messed up when I ate that pizza. I'll have to wait until Monday to begin again."	"Right now is the best time to start my diet again."
"I'm never going to eat starches again."	"That statement is perfectionistic, and because I'm not perfect it is self-defeating."

TABLE 10
Answers to Some Typical Self-Defeating Thoughts

Self-Defeating Thoughts	Answers
"I just don't have the willpower."	"I have changed other habits and have lost weight before."
"I'm just naturally fat."	"It is difficult to change habits, but difficult doesn't mean impossible."
"This will never work for me."	"Where is the evidence that I can't do this? This is frustrating, but in the long run it will be worth it."
"I can't control myself when I'm at home."	"It is more difficult under these circumstances to diet, but not impossible."
"My friends made me overeat."	"No one really makes me overeat unless he is holding a gun to my head."
"I can't expect myself to follow the plan when I'm tired."	"I just have to remember what my main goal is and not be taken in by these side issues."
"I really need some chocolate."	"There is a lot of difference between *wanting* something and *needing* it."

TABLE 11
Answers to Some Common Self-Blaming Thoughts

Self-Blaming Thoughts	Answers
"What in the hell is wrong with me? Why can't I change?"	"No one is perfect. And it is grandiose to think I never should make any mistakes."
"There is something wrong with me for not being able to lose weight."	"My eating behavior is a tiny fraction of my total self, and it's an overgeneralization to rate myself on this."
"I shouldn't have eaten that. It was wrong."	"Blaming myself does little good in changing my habits, and often does harm."
"I'm a hopeless pig. Why did I eat that ice cream?"	"Calling myself names doesn't help. The important thing is to stay on my plan for the rest of the day."
"This is the third diet I've tried in three weeks. I'm a failure."	"I won't dwell on the past. Today is what counts, and I'm going to stay on my plan today."

ment. A point to keep in mind is that it's distance—not time spent—that accounts for burning calories. You burn up the same number of calories walking a mile as you do running a mile.

VIII

Overcoming Alcohol and Drug Dependency

REBECCA Jenson led two lives. In one, she was a model naval officer's wife, the mother of two happy, well-adjusted children, a perfect hostess on the Arlington party circuit, and a joy to her parents. In the other, she was depressed a good deal of the time, suffered from periods of irritability and confusion, and was consumed with self-hatred.

She came to the Center for Cognitive Therapy to be treated for her depression, but when I was talking to her during our first session, it became obvious that she had a more urgent problem—a dependency on alcohol and sleeping pills.

Many women with alcohol and drug problems suffer from depression. Some start their slide into drug dependency *after* they become depressed. Others become depressed after they're already mired down in heavy drug and alcohol use. Depression and drug dependency are so intertwined it's often impossible to tell which came first. The symptoms of both problems are remarkably similar. The pattern is the same: *Depression leads to excessive drug use and excessive drug use leads to more depression.* If you're depressed and dependent on alcohol or drugs or both, you must work on both problems.

Recent publicity has caused many women to fear that they have an alcohol or drug problem. You may have a history of alcohol or drug abuse in your family; you may wonder if you have a problem or the potential for it.

You can ask yourself three general questions to tell whether or not you have an alcohol or drug problem:

1. *Have alcohol or drugs caused you difficulties in your life?* Have you had a problem on the job (or lost a job) because of them? Have they led to a divorce or separation? Do they interfere with your everyday activities, such as fixing meals or taking care of the children?

2. *Has your use of alcohol or drugs come to the attention of others?* Have any of your family members talked to you about it? How about your friends? Has it ever come to the attention of public officials; have you gotten any traffic tickets or had any accidents?

3. *Have you lost control over your use of drugs or alcohol?* Have you ever wanted to stop but not been able to? Do you frequently use alcohol or drugs before breakfast? Have you gone on benders (more than three days of steady intoxication)? A *yes* to any of these questions could well indicate a problem.

Even if you don't have an alcohol or drug problem, you still must be on guard against developing one, particularly if you're depressed. Many people develop alcohol or drug problems late in life. Alcohol and drugs are so prevalent in our society that they can become a convenient way to feel better. The lesson is clear: *Don't use alcohol or drugs to self-treat your depression.* This is how the mixed problem of depression and substance dependency often begins.

Using drugs and alcohol to fight off your black moods is guaranteed to backfire. A Valium and a cocktail can temporarily make you feel better, but the depression always returns—usually in spades.

Recently, a year-long government study revealed that alcohol and drug problems among women have reached epidemic proportions. Twenty million women in this country are dependent on drugs or alcohol, and the number of women with the double problem of drugs *and* alcohol has shown the largest increase.

When Betty Ford announced that she was addicted to alcohol and Valium and was entering a hospital for treatment, millions of Americans were shocked. How could the wife of a former president be hooked on drugs and alcohol? And how could she admit it publicly? The attitude of the country has always been that "nice" women just don't have alcohol and drug problems; and if by some chance they do, they should at least have the decency to keep quiet about it.

Millions of American women suffer in silence, only ten percent seek treatment. Many of Betty Ford's friends and staff were unaware that she had the problem at all. You may be hard-pressed to name a woman you know who misuses drugs and alcohol. Yet millions of women are dependent on such drugs as Valium, Librium, Dexadrine, Darvon, Demoral, Seconal, and alcohol. Many are hidden drug users, perhaps your sister-in-law, your best friend from college, your children's teacher, or yourself.

You seriously harm yourself by hiding the problem. Rebecca's friends and relatives—except for her immediate family—were totally unaware of the problem. Because they didn't know, they weren't there to say, "Wait a minute, Rebecca, you're drinking more than is good for you." Without the support of friends and relatives, her problem steadily grew worse. Rebecca, like many women, didn't seek help until the problem was out of control.

Women such as Rebecca drink and take pills when they are alone at home, so they are less likely to be seen "under the influence." The listed occupation of the largest number of women with alcohol and drug problems is "unemployed housewife"; they can go a long time without detection. This really isn't anything new. Before opiates were outlawed in 1914, the American housewife was their biggest user.

Rebecca would see her husband off in the morning. She then would drink wine throughout the day. Before he came home she would take a nap. She would have drinks with him in the evening. But she would stay up drinking after he went to sleep and then would often take sleeping pills to get to sleep. Her husband was preoccupied with his career and didn't see what was happening to her.

This doesn't mean that career women with part- or full-time jobs are immune. They also drink or take pills, but because society frowns on female intoxication, they confine their use of drugs and alcohol to evenings and weekends. When their problem reaches the stage where they are unable to control it at work, they are often fired.

The path to alcohol and drug dependency starts innocently enough—usually with a problem you have. The problem may be pain, as in Betty Ford's case. With Rebecca, it was boredom and sleeping problems. Some women use drugs and alcohol to control depression, anxiety, or anger. Or you may drink or take pills to overcome a general feeling of helplessness about your children, marriage, or work difficulties. In each of these instances, you've bought the same bill of goods: Drugs or alcohol can solve your problems. But before you know it, you're likely to have a new set of problems much worse than the original.

Fortunately, a *nondrug* way to deal with your problems lies within yourself. By changing your thinking and behavior patterns, you can learn to control your emotional and social upsets and even many of your physical problems—without drugs or alcohol.

If you're physically dependent on drugs or alcohol, you may need to go through a period of detoxification under medical care, as Betty Ford did. This can take from one to four weeks. Detoxifying is a serious business that may have physical ramifications. If you've reached this stage, see a doctor who is experienced in detoxification. However, *after detoxification you'll still have to learn nondrug ways to solve your problems.*

Goal setting. Rebecca's problem was primarily alcohol. She used sleeping pills as substitutes when there wasn't enough alcohol around or when she wanted an extra effect. First, she had to decide what she wanted to do with her alcohol problem. I left the goal up to her. Being realistic in your goals is an important part of treatment.

I asked Rebecca if she wanted to try controlled drinking or to stop drinking altogether. This is an important decision. I've found many people won't come for treatment if the only goal is never to drink again. So I usually give them this option.

Rather than give up alcohol altogether, some people learn to drink moderately. Rebecca was surprised to hear about this alternative—she thought the only treatment was to stop drinking forever. She wanted to try controlled drinking first.

However, learning to drink moderately is considerably more difficult than not drinking at all, so controlled drinking isn't for everyone. For this reason, many decide to give up drinking altogether.

No matter which goal you choose, you do need to go through a period of not drinking—at least a month—to get the alcohol out of your system.

Rebecca agreed to do this. The detoxification period wasn't too bad for her, though many people go back to drinking because the symptoms of getting the alcohol out of their systems are too uncomfortable. She sweated a lot and was shaky at first. She took a lot of vitamin C and had her husband's help throughout the process. After a month, she said she was ready to try controlled drinking.

Controlled drinking. Controlled drinking is a controversial topic. A recent government-sponsored Rand Report of a large number of studies found that some alcoholics can learn to control their drinking. Many people take exception to this and say it's impossible. They feel it's a dangerous idea because it encourages recovered alcoholics to start drinking again.

Controlled drinking is never recommended for people who have successfully stopped drinking. I also discourage a controlled drinking program if a person has a long-standing alcohol problem, or if a related health problem, such as pancreatitis, exists. A controlled drinking plan works best before the alcohol problem becomes too severe. The program is time limited. If after six to eight weeks the person isn't able to control her alcohol consumption, I recommend she give up alcohol altogether. In general, it's much easier to give up alcohol completely than it is to control it.

The instructions in controlled drinking are simple, but can be difficult to carry out. Here's the general list:

1. Sip your drinks. Don't drink more than an ounce of alcohol an hour (one beer, one mixed drink, or one glass of wine); this will prevent you from becoming intoxicated.
2. If you finish before the hour is up, add mix or ice to your present drink.
3. Tell those offering a refill, "Thanks, but I haven't finished this one yet."
4. Plan how much you want to drink before you start, and stick to the plan.

5. Don't offer to get drinks for others.
6. Stay away from the bar or the area where drinks are being served.
7. Dilute your drink, add an extra amount of ice, and tinkle it frequently. The sound becomes a substitute for the substance.
8. Keep accurate records of how much alcohol you drink. The amount you can drink without becoming intoxicated depends mainly on your weight.
9. Become aware of the alcohol content of what you drink. Wine has more alcohol than most people think. With beer, brands differ (Coors, for example, has 3.5 percent alcohol; most other beers have 5 percent).
10. You might find buying a breath analyzer, which measures the alcohol in your system, helpful.

Controlled drinking has the best chance of being successful when you work with a professional who has experience in it.

Rebecca had problems at first with controlled drinking; she found that when she was bored and restless, she started to drink too much again. Her husband was very busy and she had a lot of time on her hands. I told her that the solution to problem drinking and drugs is the same as for other problems—listen to yourself before you engage in the problem activity, answer your thoughts, and act on your new thought.

Drinking when alone. Rebecca's main problem was drinking when she was alone. She had a bad habit of thinking, "I'm alone, so I can drink whatever I want to." This was based on the half-formed, almost magical notion, "When no one sees me drink, it doesn't count." She hadn't been aware of this thought before she started looking for it. In the past, she had been alone so she drank. Stimulus—response. By working on this thought, she was able to control much of her drinking.

But she would still have three stiff drinks before going to bed, and she didn't know why. I asked her to pay attention to what was happening immediately before her drinking and in particular to what she was telling herself.

She discovered that right before she took the drinks, her husband would leave to walk the dog and she would think, "Now's my chance." She solved this problem very simply—she began to go with her husband to walk the dog.

Here are some suggestions if you drink when you're alone:

1. *Remove temptations.* Don't bring large quantities of liquor into the house to keep you company when you're going to be alone.
2. *Make tempting alcohol difficult to get.* One woman who would stop at a bar when she was out driving overcame this by not taking any money with her.
3. *Question yourself.* When you find yourself giving in to this thinking, ask, "Who am I really fooling? Am I doing what I really want to do, or am I giving in to a silly habit?" And, "Who is in charge here, me or my habits?"
4. *Challenge the idea that you're getting away with something.* There is a certain thrill in breaking a rule that says you can't drink when you're alone. You can, but you'll be sabotaging your goal—not getting away with something. If you want to get away with something, cheat at solitaire.
5. *Question and challenge your self-defeating thoughts as soon as they appear.* If your husband won't be home and you find yourself thinking, "Oh good. This is my chance to drink," argue with yourself *then,* not after you're alone and facing alcohol.
6. *Make a rule to drink only in front of others.* Solitary drinkers usually don't drink at all, or else only drink appropriately, when in front of others. (Talking on the telephone doesn't count.)

Boredom drinking. Boredom is another common excuse for drinking. When Rebecca became bored with her housework, she would go to the kitchen and fix herself a drink. She would then return to her work and soon be bored again. This routine continued throughout the day.

She overcame this problem by convincing herself that she didn't always have to be doing something productive. If she needed a work break, she could just sit back and relax, rather than fixing a drink.

The following suggestions may help you with the problem of boredom drinking:

1. *Increase your tolerance for boredom.* It won't kill you. Instead of thinking, "I can't stand this," tell yourself, "I can take this boredom, I just don't have to like it." Gradually increase the time between when you start to get bored and when you do something to relieve it. With practice, you can learn to increase your tolerance for all kinds of discomfort, thereby strengthening yourself and inoculating yourself against future periods of boredom. This in itself will give you a greater sense of control.

2. *Develop a time-consuming interest or hobby.* One woman became interested in CB radio. Whenever she became bored and felt like drinking, she would talk on the radio. Look for interests that you have pursued in the past such as writing, painting, sewing; these are the ones you could become seriously involved with again. You usually have to force yourself to overcome inertia and to undergo a learning period before an interest becomes enjoyable in itself.

3. *Use distractions.* When you become bored, don't ask "What can I drink," but rather "What can I do?" Draw up a list containing activities you enjoy doing (reading, calling a friend, listening to a record) and activities you *must* do (pay bills, write letters, sort slides). When you're bored, reach for the list.

4. *Avoid boring situations.* If you know a party is going to be boring and you're likely to overdrink, don't go. Avoid TV reruns and unplanned time. Don't rely on alcohol for entertainment.

Self-defeating thoughts. I asked Rebecca to keep track of her thoughts and to bring them in. Table 12 gives a sample of what she wrote and how she answered her self-defeating thoughts.

She began to get on top of her problem by keeping track of her self-defeating thoughts, answering and acting on them, and realizing that excuses easily become reasons. For example, one woman thought, "I need a Valium to handle the kids." Excuses can determine how you feel. This excuse made her feel inadequate and second-class. Excuses also determine what you do about a problem. Because her excuse was, "I can't handle problems without drugs," she never tried.

Short-term effects often obscure the actual consequences of drugs or alcohol. Table 13 shows how one woman focused on the consequences of her alcohol problem.

Prescription drugs. People expect doctors to alert them to serious health problems, yet medical professionals have largely ignored or downplayed the growing epidemic of drug dependency among women. This may be due to their own role in the problem. For example, physicians write over 250 million prescriptions for mood-altering drugs yearly.

Muriel Nellis directed a HEW study on drugs, alcohol, and women. She reports: "Some doctors have made a great deal of money providing these quick panaceas for their patients. Women see a physician many more times throughout their lives than man do. One reason is that they are usually the ones to take the children

TABLE 12
Examples of Rebecca's Self-Defeating Thoughts

Self-Defeating Thoughts	Answers to Herself
I don't care.	That's not true. You do care. You're just lying to yourself because it's a little difficult.
What difference does it make?	It makes a lot of difference. Controlling your drinking is one of your highest priorities. Don't forget it.
I don't care about controlling my drinking if it means I can't drink what I want to.	Listen to yourself for a moment. Of course controlling your drinking means you *can't* drink everything you want to. Just because you want something doesn't mean you *have* to have it.
The hell with it. I'm going to have a drink.	Oh, that's mature! If you are going to use excuses you'll have to be more creative than "the hell with it." Any three-year-old could come up with better excuses.
It's not worth the effort.	Whoever said it would be easy? Anything you've ever done that you've been proud of has been hard work.

TABLE 13
Example of Assessing the Consequences of Drinking

Reason for Using Alcohol	Specific Thought	Actual Consequences of Alcohol Use
To get over depression resulting from argument with husband.	I can't stand feeling so bad. I have nothing to look forward to in marriage . . . in life. A drink will make it all go away.	1. Temporary feeling of euphoria, relaxation—lasting ten minutes to a few hours.
		2. Feeling more depressed as the drink wears off.
		3. Feeling guilt, self-blame, and giving myself hell when alcohol wears off.
		4. Negative physical consequences of using excessive alcohol.
		5. Adding more fuel to trouble with my husband.
		6. Original depression unchanged or worse.
		7. Original marriage problem unchanged or worse.

to the doctor. It sounds like a dreadful thing to say, but that puts women in much greater jeopardy."

It's not just the medical profession. Drug companies make millions from selling mood-altering drugs to women. Their hard-sell advertisements are largely geared for female patients. Medical journals are full of ads (with pictures of distraught women) urging doctors to prescribe mood-altering drugs. The advertisements are having their intended effect. Women are the largest consumers of these drugs. They use eighty percent of all prescribed amphetamines (diet pills) and they use so much Valium that it has been called "the woman's drug."

For example, Mary Spencer was taking amphetamines to lose weight. She soon discovered that diet pills kept her awake, so she started taking sleeping pills (barbiturates) at night. The effectiveness of the sleeping pills gradually wore off. She then discovered that the sleeping pills worked fine if she had a few drinks with them. She never did solve her original weight problem, and in the process of working on it she developed a dependency on alcohol and barbiturates.

After she got her drug and alcohol problems in order, she was able to start effectively losing weight on her own—she switched from *drug* management of her problems to *self*-management.

Adolescents and drugs. Although there isn't one particular type of person that is especially vulnerable to alcohol and drug dependency, there are stages in any woman's life when she is more apt to resort to alcohol and drugs. Adolescence is one such period. In many ways teenage girls have a tougher time of it than boys. A recent study reported that young girls are drinking much more than young boys, and an even bigger problem is poly-drug abuse (mixing various drugs) among female adolescents.

Karen was a bright seventeen-year-old—and a poly-drug user. She smoked marijuana, took uppers and downers, and would drink if nothing else was around. She was primarily depressed, but she would start taking drugs mainly when she was angry at her mother.

One week she came in and said, "I had a bad week. My mother unfairly grounded me so I said the hell with it. I stayed up in my room stoned all weekend."

I told her I could see that she was angry with her mother, but how did that affect her goal to get off drugs?

"Well, she made me mad and I wanted to get back at her."

I asked her, "Whom did you hurt more—your mother or yourself?"

"Me, I guess, but I also got to her—she hates it when I get stoned."

I pointed out to her that she probably *did* get to her mother, but that just meant that her mother was probably going to want to get back at her. There's no end to it. I suggested, "Get back at your mother if you want; but do it in a way that's not so blatantly self-defeating."

She said she knew what I was saying was true, but she didn't want her mother to think she could control her.

I said, "Perhaps you could say something like this, 'Mom, by forcing me to stay in the house all weekend, you're making it extremely hard for me to get off drugs. But no matter what you do or say, you aren't going to force me to take drugs. I'm going to stay off drugs in spite of you.' "

She said that might work, "But sometimes when I'm angry, I don't think about getting back at anyone. I just start getting loaded."

I pointed out several other ways to get over anger. One strategy is to start some strenuous physical activity, such as cleaning out the closet or jumping rope. Another is to count the number of angry thoughts you have.

What you want to do is gain some control over the situation, not get lost in thoughts of revenge or how bad the other person is. Talk to yourself to keep yourself cool.

Karen, after a great deal of practice, learned to control the number and duration of these angry drug binges.

Social problems. Often the drug or alcohol problem is brought on by lack of social skills. For instance, Claire Ulright came for treatment of her depression and poly-drug abuse, including alcohol dependency, for which she'd been hospitalized twice. Her drug problems began after she ended an affair with a married man six years earlier. She believed, "If I become too close to others, they'll find out about my terrible past [the affair and drug problem]." Largely because of this belief, she led a relatively isolated life. She was a teacher and her social experiences were limited to her work.

She wanted to improve her social life and began by taking a night course and gradually expanded on this. She found that she could control the information she wanted others to know—and if she did disclose her past, people didn't automatically condemn her. At the three-year followup she reported that she had been dating regularly; she also reported that she had no further problems with depression, alcohol, or other drugs.

People often rely on alcohol and drugs to get through a party or other social encounter. But you can learn to increase what you can do on your own without the help of drugs or alcohol. This includes talking and being with others. You may have to force yourself at first, but it gets easier.

Magical thinking. Some people's drug and alcohol problems are caused by their own myths about alcohol and drugs. One man, for example, thought alcohol made him socially charming and a great lover. He was convinced of this. I videotaped him talking to people before drinking and after drinking. He readily saw that he was much more interesting and charming before drinking. The more he drank, the less he listened to others and the more repetitious he became.

He then decided to ask his wife about his lovemaking. When he told her his theory that alcohol improved his lovemaking, she said, "Are you kidding me?" She told him not only was his lovemaking not enjoyable when he was drinking, it was actually aversive. He began to see that many of his beliefs about the effects of alcohol were wrong.

Maintenance. It can be difficult to maintain your progress in the fight against drug and alcohol abuse. Try the following suggestions:

1. *Develop a comprehensive plan.* You must develop an overall strategy for solving an alcohol or drug problem. This strategy must include solving the problems that led to the alcoholism or drug dependency in the first place. If you suffer from insomnia,

for example, you might want to learn relaxation techniques. Also, plan ways to avoid situations that lead to the problem— and ways you can think and act differently if you find yourself in a difficult situation.

2. *Watch your thinking errors.* Some common beliefs about drinking are not true and can cause problems in overcoming it ("Once a drunk, always a drunk" . . . "I'm one drink away from a drunk"). In Table 14, I list some other thinking errors.

3. *Watch for critical incidents.* A critical incident is a moment that requires you to make a decision affecting your progress in overcoming drug and alcohol dependency. Rebecca, for example, had a drink at lunch with friends. When she got home, she continued drinking. However, she caught herself after one drink and decided, "This isn't what I want to do." She took charge.

4. *Beware of AIDS.* Dr. Alan Marlett, a psychologist at the Univer-

---

TABLE 14
Common Thinking Errors That Lead to Using Alcohol and Drugs

ESCAPE FROM FEELING BAD
1. Having a drink is the best way to escape from depression, anxiety, boredom, anger.
2. Once I'm high, I don't have to deal with anything bad.
3. I can't stand feeling bad.
4. The doctor gave me the drugs in the first place, so it must be all right.

DEALING WITH HOPELESSNESS
5. There's nothing else for me.
6. Nothing else can make me feel good.
7. Life isn't worth living if I can't drink.
8. I'm a loser anyway.
9. I don't have any future, so what's the difference.

REPLACING SOCIAL SKILLS
10. I can deal better with people after a few drinks.
11. I feel tense, awkward, inferior with people unless I have a tranquilizer.
12. I'm afraid they'll see how nervous I am.
13. I don't know what to say.
14. I'm more outgoing when I'm high, more charming.

ESCAPE FROM STRESS
15. I won't have to deal with my children, husband.
16. I'll be able to handle my duties better.
17. The arguing, yelling, lack of money won't bother me.

sity of Washington, has done a great deal of work to help people remain free from alcohol dependency. One of Dr. Marlett's techniques is to teach people to become aware of decisions that don't appear to take away from their control, but in fact do. He calls them Apparently Irrelevant Decisions (AIDS). These are decisions that set the stage for relapse.

One of Rebecca's recurring AIDS before she controlled her drinking was to bring home large bottles of liquor in case someone else might want a drink. She stopped doing this.

Another woman hadn't had a drink for two months. She decided to pack a bottle of whiskey for a vacation she was taking. However, once she reflected on it, she realized that this was an AID, so she unpacked the bottle.

5. *Seek professional support.* I want to stress a final point about drug and alcohol problems. Of all the complications of depression, I would most strongly recommend you seek professional help for this one, not because it's so difficult to overcome, but because of the physical complications. Most hospitals and social agencies can put you in touch with help.

There is an unfounded general pessimism about people's ability to solve drug and alcohol problems. In fact, I've found it easier to treat these problems successfully than to treat much less serious ones.

IX

Overcoming Problems in Relationships

GLORIA Newman decided that she couldn't live without Rob. So when he said he wanted a divorce to marry another woman, she decided to kill herself by taking over 100 pills. This decision was the end result of a series of problems for Gloria. Many of them centered around Rob.

Gloria's situation illustrates what often happens with depressed people's relationships. She was a secretary at a food-processing firm when she met and married Rob, an engineer at the same firm. Her depression began after they'd been married two years and she found she couldn't have children. At first, Rob was sympathetic toward her. But when she didn't snap out of her depression, he began to ignore her. The sadder and more depressed she became, the more he withdrew.

When Rob wasn't ignoring her, he was frequently angry. He said he was "fed up with her pissing and moaning." So she kept quiet about how she felt. Their marriage continued to deteriorate; they almost completely stopped having sex and even touching became rare. Rob began doing more on his own, such as going to parties and on camping trips. Gloria didn't want to go out anyway, but she felt worse knowing he was out having a good time with his friends.

Several times Gloria seemed to be coming out of her depression. Rob reacted positively to these periods—at first. But when they didn't last he became discouraged and began to ignore her flickers of improvement. Without his encouragement, she slipped back even more quickly into depression.

Rob eventually started seeing the younger sister of one of the men with whom he worked. After two years of dating and a lot of pressure from his girlfriend he finally told Gloria that he didn't love her anymore and wanted a divorce.

After she took the bottle of pills, Gloria was taken to the hospital and survived her suicide attempt. I first saw her after she was released from the hospital.

Among women the most common complication of depression is problems in their relationships with the important people in their lives—parents, children, husbands, friends, lovers, bosses, employees. Relationships with husbands and boyfriends seem to be the most troublesome for depressed women; however, the ideas and techniques I talk about here can be applied to any of your relationships.

The central element of depression is *vicious cycling:* Depression worsens a relationship and the deteriorating relationship worsens the depression. As I've shown in Table 15, the cycle may be more elaborate, strengthening itself and picking up speed at different points. Your depression may follow the ending of a relationship or the worsening of an ongoing one. It may even stop you from starting a new relationship—and the social isolation you experience then makes your depression worse.

IMPROVING ONGOING RELATIONSHIPS

Changing any part of depression for the better can start to turn the vicious cycle around. Because most relationship problems need time to be sorted out, your best strategy usually is to get your symptoms under control. Then you can go after the stickier relationship problems in full force.

However, you may need to work on a relationship immediately if it seems to be hindering your recovery. This is what I had in mind when I called Gloria's husband and asked him to come in. Rob said that there was no chance that he and Gloria could get back together. He was determined to get a divorce and marry the other woman. He made it clear that there was no relationship to improve. Gloria, instead, had to focus on getting over the breakup and moving on with her own life.

People make two common mistakes with their relationships: (1) breaking up too soon, and (2) staying on too long. In the first instance, couples give up without making real attempts at solving their problems. In the second, people stay on in a miserable relationship after repeatedly failing to solve their problems.

My belief about most marriages and other long-term relationships is that if two people saw something important in each other in

TABLE 15
Vicious Cycling of Depression and Relationships

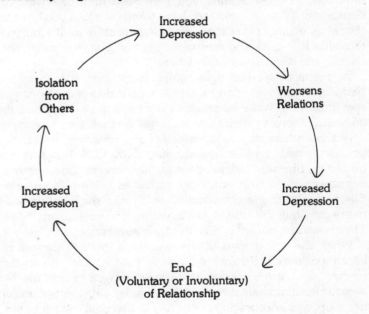

the beginning—the same values, interests, potential for enjoyment —there's good reason to believe that the common basics are still there if the negative parts can be resolved. Most relationships that are on the downturn can be saved, provided both parties are willing to try.

Researchers have found that when a person remarries, the new husband or wife is often almost exactly like the last one—similar in age, appearance, and personality. So in terms of psychological and emotional costs (not to mention economics), it makes sense to try to save your existing relationship.

Role of others in depression. You might not realize how your depression affects those around you. People get used to many situations, so those around you may have done this with your depression. Your husband may have taken over jobs you once did: shopping, planning vacations, or rearing the children. It's important to realize that once you start getting better, you may cause some change and disruption in your family.

Be prepared for less than complete enthusiasm (although on balance, others want you to get over your depression) once you start improving. While others don't want you to be depressed, they *do* get used to your symptoms and organize their lives accordingly.

At times others may, through lack of understanding, help to keep you depressed. I recall one woman, Judy O'Neil, a successful physician. She was independent to the extreme. She was a nononsense person who struck you at first as being cold and aloof. She had a boyfriend considerably older than she who wanted to marry her, but she valued her freedom too much to marry him. Their relationship went on like this for a number of years.

When she was depressed she was like a different person. She became extremely helpless and believed she couldn't do anything on her own. At these times, she usually moved in with her boyfriend. He strengthened her helplessness by babying her, making her soup, and encouraging her to stay in bed until she felt better.

After she got over her depression and moved back to her apartment, her boyfriend called me and said *he* was getting depressed. When depressed she wanted to be held, enjoyed lovemaking, and told him she loved him and couldn't live without him. It seemed what he liked most about her when she was depressed was that she was much more affectionate.

I told him that while I could understand how he felt, encouraging her helplessness could only hurt their relationship in the long run. He agreed and I referred them to a family counselor to see if they could develop a healthier relationship.

This is an extreme and a rather uncommon example of a man's reaction to a woman's depression. Usually the husband or boyfriend ignores or berates the woman for becoming depressed. So the question becomes: What is the best way others can help you overcome your depression? The following are some positive suggestions for ways others can help, along with advice about what they should *not* do:

1. Don't blame the person for being depressed; rather, see the depression as a series of problems to be solved.
2. Don't attribute the depression to motivation ("You want to be depressed"); rather, see depression as the natural result of faulty thinking.
3. Don't feel guilty about the person's depression; rather, realize it's the other person's problem, not yours. Develop your tolerance for her depression.
4. Don't demand that the other person pull herself up by her bootstraps; rather, encourage her to experiment with new ways of thinking and acting.
5. Don't do jobs she can do for herself; rather, encourage her to be self-reliant in a gradual, consistent way.
6. Don't discount her small achievements; rather, point out that getting out of depression is a series of small steps.
7. Don't bring up past failures; rather, focus on present challenges.
8. Don't engage in neurotic agreements ("I agree that you can't do anything right"); rather, present the clear facts ("You make some mistakes, but you also do a lot of things right").
9. Don't ignore her symptoms; rather, let her know you understand that she feels bad.
10. Don't patronize and condescend to her; rather, let her help you with one of your problems in return for helping her.

Changing the other person. Many depressed patients ask, "How can I change the other person?" Their focus is wrong. To try directly to change another person is frustrating and nearly always futile. It's hard enough to change yourself, let alone change others. But by learning to change how *you* act, you can often bring about changes in others and in the relationship. It doesn't always follow, but this strategy has a better chance than trying to change another person directly.

Empathy. What can you do to improve the relationship? First, aim for accurate empathy. Try to put yourself in the other person's shoes. See the world from his eyes. How do you do this? Ask specific questions and then reflect back on what the person answers. Do this until you reach agreement on what you're both talking about. The first step toward direct communication and problem solving is accurately understanding how the other person feels. Don't react to what he says ("How can you say I don't keep the house neat enough?"); just reflect and try to understand his point of view.

If you go to the trouble of finding out what the other person is really thinking, he'll be more likely to return the favor. Also, you can find out how he sees your actions.

The opposite of accurate empathy is telling the other person what he's thinking and feeling. Consider how awful you feel when he does this to you; he probably feels the same way when you do it.

Avoiding distortions. What happens when you argue with someone is similar to what happens when you get depressed: You develop a conclusion about the other person ("He's wrong!") and then you distort the evidence to fit the guilty conclusions.

If you think, "I'm stupid and can't do anything right," you're likely to feel bad or depressed. The same thing happens in an argument—only you tell the other person, "You're stupid and can't do anything right." Then he's likely to feel bad and retaliate with the same type of distorted charges.

Pointing out that he's making these mistakes ("You're always making overgeneralizations") will just make him more defensive. But you can become aware of your own errors and replace them with more specific factual information. When you're both more relaxed and able to be more rational, talk to him about how distorting facts escalates arguments and blocks problem solving.

Often in arguments you want to get revenge. The trouble with revenge is that it almost always backfires. For example, if you bring up something that you know is going to hurt the other person, the other person will usually retaliate with something that will hurt you.

Avoidance.   Don't get overwhelmed by your problems and carried away with hopelessness. Orient yourself to solution, not hopelessness. One way to do this is to schedule time to discuss and work on your problems. A major reason that relationships break down is that people stop discussing the issues; when problems aren't resolved, they become worse.

Avoidance is at the heart of most problems. In one troubled family the husband and wife would both escape when an argument started—he would go to the neighborhood bar and she would go to her mother's. Their problems grew steadily worse because they didn't face them. When you avoid thinking through and discussing problems, you nearly always make your problems worse.

When you schedule time to discuss your problems, allow enough time to discuss them fully. An aborted discussion can be worse than none. Expect to feel bad during the discussion. When one problem is solved, other ones will appear. Expect to be overwhelmed at first. This indicates the start of a productive discussion.

Often you must settle for a compromise no matter what your problem—be it sexual activity or child rearing. One woman's husband stopped having sex with her. They reached the compromise that he would go and seek help if she would stop placing sexual demands on him.

Focus on the positive.   Everyone has a certain number of flaws. When relationships go bad, people frequently start focusing on flaws and forget why they got together in the first place. In getting along and living with others a certain amount of good-hearted dishonesty is helpful. If your husband thinks his sloppy paint job is great, why bother telling him the truth?

One woman's husband used to criticize her appearance right before they went out—when there was nothing she could do about it. She pointed this out to him and he agreed to stop doing it. He did stop for a while, but then started again. She then suggested a contract. Every time he did this he had to give her ten dollars. He agreed to this contract and that put a stop to it.

One unusual technique to help you focus on another's positive qualities, though it might take some doing, is worth the effort if you can get the other person to agree. Take a bunch of adhesive labels, such as the ones that go on file folders, and stick them all over yourselves. Do this in the evening or on a Saturday or Sunday. Over the next few hours, pull off a label when the other person does something you like. He does the same.

What's the purpose of this bizarre technique? Each time you pull off a label you let the person know that you're aware he's doing something you like. In other words, you reward his behavior so he's likely to repeat it. This also teaches you both to start looking for positive aspects rather than negative ones. Plus there's a bonus —you start touching again.

The critical incident technique. At other times, you can decide to turn disadvantages to advantages by acting in an adaptive rather than a maladaptive way. Your best bet may be to do the opposite of what you feel like doing.

Denying your feelings can often worsen a relationship. But sometimes it's difficult to tell what your true feelings are. My wife Pat and I used to go through this ritual when we were first married. One of us would ask if the other was in a bad mood. Then there would be the standard reply, "No, I'm not . . . but if you keep asking me I will be!" When Pat asked me several times if I was in a bad mood, my instinct was to answer with an annoyed "No!" But I decided to try the critical-incident technique and do the opposite of what I felt like doing.

I thought I was lying when I said, "Yes, I'm in a bad mood." But immediately I started to feel better. And then I realized that I *had* been in a bad mood and that only by accepting it was I able to change it. We're both much more inclined now to admit our bad moods and avoid the secondary problems of denying them.

Acting the opposite of how you feel toward someone can be a powerful way of changing your relationship. Sticking to your old way of responding lets your past control you and keeps the problem going, but acting the opposite gives you control.

For instance, if someone does something you don't like, your immediate inclination may be to get mad and get even. But it's usually more advantageous to respond positively (unless you normally do this)—particularly if you value the relationship.

I saw evidence of this when I worked in Japan. When an employee stopped producing or goofed off, his fellow workers and boss would bring him presents and show him extra kindnesses. The person soon stopped goofing off.

Limit discussions of your depression. While open and honest communication is crucial in a relationship, excessive discussion of and focusing on your depression is not. People suffering from psychological pain, like those suffering from physical pain, often try to get relief by telling others about their suffering. But people may misinterpret your complaints about feeling sad as self-pity, or they may think that you're blaming them.

Prolonged discussion of your feelings intensifies them. When you tell friends and relatives about your suffering, you often strain your relationships with them by becoming excessively involved with your own feelings. Try to limit how much you talk about your unhappiness. You know you've gone beyond merely seeking advice when you keep going over and over the same material.

HOW TO END A RELATIONSHIP

You can't always keep a relationship going. There are times when it's best to end it—sometimes it's your choosing, sometimes it's not. But in either case, you can take constructive steps to deal with endings.

When should you end a relationship? When is it past the point of being saved? How can you tell it's at this point? Here are some general guidelines to help you answer these questions:

1. *When you're depressed isn't usually the best time to decide to end a relationship.* Give yourself some time to get your thinking and feeling in order before you make rash judgments. You might not always be able to do this, but it's the better strategy. Make the decision when you aren't distorting the situation.

2. *Ask yourself if you have a choice in the matter.* Many times the choice isn't yours. If the other person doesn't want to keep the relationship going, as in Gloria's case, you don't have to worry about whether or not to end it, but rather how best to handle the ending.

   Sometimes the other person may say he wants to keep the relationship up, but his actions don't jibe with this. One woman's boyfriend said he was in love with her, but he only came around once or twice a month to have sex. Pay attention to what he *does* rather than what he says.

3. *Hope is a poor basis for a relationship.* If you've seriously tried to work out problems with no luck but you keep hoping things will change, reconsider the situation. One woman said, "I stay with my husband because I keep hoping he'll stop drinking and abusing the children." Her hope was just a way of avoiding the situation at hand and trying to block out the present. Your best guess usually is that the other person isn't going to change. He's going to act the way he does despite your wishful thinking. If you can live with the current behavior you can perhaps save the relationship. If not, it might be a good time to get out.

4. *Good relationships aren't held together by fear or guilt.* Many women put up with a bad situation because they fear being on their own. They settle for less in life. The idea that you can't live on your own is a *prediction,* not necessarily a *fact.*

   One woman stayed with her husband out of guilt. Her mother thought he was great; he supported the family and was sympathetic to her. All her friends said he was a nice guy. But she found him emotionally cold and didn't love him. You don't have to stay in a relationship just because you don't want to hurt a person.

Relationships based on guilt rarely have a good outcome. Many women eventually end bad relationships. They could have done so earlier and saved a lot of suffering if they had had more courage.

5. *Are you staying in the relationship because he "has the whammy on you"?* I've seen many cases where a woman is with a man she doesn't like or respect; he seems to have a power over her.

One woman, Joan, had been going with a man for several years even though he seemed to bring out the worst in her. He had other girlfriends and would only come around when he felt like it, yet she would drop everything (including other men) when he called. She would then get over her depression, but as soon as they fought or he left she would sink back.

I've noticed a pattern in many cases where the man has the whammy on the woman. The woman seems to be vulnerable to a certain type of man. He's usually somewhat sociopathic; that is, he is charming, able to give his full attention to her, good sexually, and usually attractive, but has extreme difficulty in forming lasting love relationships. He's often ambivalent toward women and can be quite cruel. The chances of a lasting relationship with this type of man are poor.

Ending such a relationship can be difficult and painful, as it was for Joan, but in the long run it's less difficult than repeated anguish. But remember, after you end this sort of relationship you have to guard against falling into another just like it.

6. *Try to avoid the no-win bind.* One woman was depressed because she was in love with a married man who had no intention of getting a divorce. She felt guilty and saw little future in the relationship. She had three options: (1) change her attitude about the affair, (2) stay depressed, or (3) break off the relationship. She eventually broke it off.

Women often get themselves into another kind of bind—engaging in or tolerating some type of behavior they disapprove of in order to keep a relationship going. If you have to put up with his other girlfriends in order to keep him, as Joan did, or if you can only keep the relationship going by being perfect and not complaining about anything, think of it as over.

The irony of this is that what you're doing to keep the relationship going in the short run is also almost guaranteeing that it won't last in the long run. Do what you think is right for you rather than giving in on basic points. People don't respect and value you if you give in easily. In the long run, you're hurting yourself.

7. *Don't overexpose the relationship problem.* As a general rule, by the time all your friends and relatives know you're having problems, it's difficult to save the relationship. And their knowing can escalate your problems. Work on the relationship in private. Don't bring everyone else in on it.

Sticking to it.   Once you've made the decision to end a relationship, it's crucial that you don't change your mind. Remember, you thought it through and made your decision. Now your job is accepting it. Self-doubt will cause problems. For example, repeatedly Sara Hart would decide she'd had enough of her husband and leave him. Then he would come around and show his nice side—bringing presents and promises. Before she knew it, she was back in the old situation and he was his old self again.

Once you decide to end the relationship, you have to keep from slipping back. If you start to see the other person again, like a heroin addict taking a fix here and a fix there, you could easily get hooked again.

Once you decide to end the relationship, there are some strategies you can use to make it less painful. First, after you've carefully looked at the situation and decided what's best for you, you have to go cold turkey, at least for a period of time. You just have to stop it.

Secondly, if you want your decision to end the relationship to last, it's important that you don't do anything to undermine it. People with strong compulsions must devise an environment free from temptation—even if it means locking themselves in a room.

The same applies to breaking off a relationhip. Design your life so that you don't slip back into it. Make a simple rule that you won't see the other person for a specific period of time. Once you're emotionally free of him you can reestablish contact—if you want. Some couples can remain friends after a divorce or breakup, but this has to come later.

The pain of separation. Expect negative feelings when a relationship breaks up—even (and sometimes especially) bad ones. Become aware of what you're thinking and doing to keep the pain of separation going. Are you telling yourself that you can't live without him? That life has no meaning and you're nothing without him? Are you spending a lot of time brooding over it? If you have thoughts like these, then answer them ("Yes, I *can* stand it. I don't know what can happen in the future—that's a prediction, not a fact").

Are your actions keeping him in mind—are you looking at old photos, listening to old songs? If you are, change your behavior. Don't call his house to see who'll answer, or ask about him, or drive by his house. This will only keep the pain going and strengthen the *unfounded belief* that you can't be happy without him.

Avoid feelings of rejection. A common problem in ending a relationship is the belief that since you've been rejected, you are unlovable, which in turn often leads to depression. I discussed this with Gloria.

She believed, "Anyone would be depressed if they were put down by someone they love."

I told her that you can't be put down unless you're asking or demanding that someone hold you up. Depending on someone else for approval is trying to accept yourself through someone else ("If that person loves me I'm great and if he doesn't, I'm worthless"). If you accept yourself, you won't be depressed if someone chooses not to be with you.

No one can totally reject you—he just can make a choice. Some people like classical music, others like jazz. If someone doesn't like classical music, that reflects on him, not on the intrinsic value of the music. He may not know enough about it to appreciate it, and for a variety of reasons, he may not be willing to spend the time learning to enjoy it. But he doesn't have the power to make classical music second-class for all time for all people. Similarly, no one has the power to make a reject out of you.

"I still think it's something I did," persisted Gloria.

I told her that, although that was possible, there were a number of other ways of looking at the experience. For example: (1) "I feel sorry for him, he's missing out on me!" (2) "Well, someone else will come along," (3) "This is really for the best," or (4) "It's better to break up now than later when I'd have more time invested."

Gloria was eventually able to change her belief that she was unlovable and put the breakup behind her.

Closure. You too, will have to change some beliefs in order to get over your relationship. I don't know what your particular beliefs are: They could have to do with rejection or with being played for a fool. But when you change these beliefs, you'll be able to get over negative feelings and get on with your life.

A basic psychological principle about finishing business is that you'll keep remembering unfinished business until you get closure on it. For example, waiters in beer halls keep in mind what every customer drinks until they pay the tab. When the customer pays, the waiter reaches closure and forgets about it.

The same applies to accepting the end of your relationship and getting closure on it. You keep the pain up by continually going over the tab or balance sheet of the relationship. You may not get closure because you believe a perfect, magical solution will occur (he'll return and love you, or will change his ways somehow). When you accept the end of the relationship and give up magical wishes, you'll finally achieve closure.

A warning: Just because you change irrational beliefs and reach closure doesn't guarantee that your new beliefs will be in your best interests. One woman believed she couldn't live without a man. After ending a bad relationship she changed this irrational belief to "I hate all men," and then acted on this by avoiding all men. While she got over the breakup, she gave up the possibility of greater happiness.

Handling divorce. Often practical as well as psychological problems affect depressed women going through divorces: children to consider, houses to sell, financial problems to solve, new logistics to work out. Over a million couples divorce each year—triple the number of twenty years ago. No-fault divorce has corrected many problems, but has created others.

Many women aren't getting an equitable share of what has been built up during the marriage. Plus, they are often left with the responsibility for the children while the husband reluctantly gives minimal child support. Many women gave up their careers to help with their husbands' careers; after a divorce they find themselves at middle age without the income to maintain their lifestyles.

Solving the practical problems of a divorce can help solve the psychological ones. For instance, many women feel bad about arguing over money. You can better handle the practical problems if you look at the divorce as a legal adversary proceeding.

Separate the personal from the practical. Try to see the marriage as a business enterprise that you're dissolving; as a partner, you want your fair share. There's nothing demeaning about this.

While recent movies might have us believe that divorced women always end up with handsome, understanding men, most people realize that this is unrealistic. However, nearly everyone who goes through a divorce eventually gets over the trauma of it and many begin positive new relationships. At first most have regrets, but eventually they're glad about their decisions.

Self-reliance. The breaking off of a relationship offers an excellent opportunity to develop self-reliance. You have a chance to disprove ideas about being dependent on other people for happiness and support. Many women never have this opportunity. They go from their father's house to their husband's house. Gloria later viewed her divorce as a good chance to move out of adolescence.

Many women miss this opportunity by rushing into new relationships. It's much better to endure loneliness while strengthening yourself against future problems. After you've proven to yourself that you can be self-sufficient, then you may want to start a new relationship.

Isolation. After a divorce or separation, many women find themselves isolated from others. Some are isolated because they don't want to be bothered with other people; others are isolated because they had counted on their husbands to provide all of their social support.

Isolation can compound your depression. Since no one challenges your erroneous beliefs, you hold on to them. People can provide you with alternative ways of seeing the world. They give good advice along with some bad. If you're isolated from others, you don't have a chance to have your thinking tested out. You may also be out of touch with the common sense that prevails in society.

When you're depressed, people may avoid you and you in turn avoid others. You become more isolated and have fewer opportunities to check out your thoughts. Your social interactions become fewer and shorter. So even if you don't want to have another long-term relationship with a man, it's a good idea to be with people in general.

STARTING NEW RELATIONSHIPS

You *can* be happy without a romantic relationship. I can't stress this enough. Many depressed women don't believe this, even when I point to happy times in the past when they were without a man. They counter with, "That's like telling a poor person money won't make you happy!" I suppose it is, but it's still true: *Happiness is not dependent on being loved.* If you believe you can't be happy without a man and tend to rush from one relationship to another, I would strongly urge you to go for a period without a man. Test out your belief.

This doesn't mean that you can't start a relationship later on. When you're ready, however, you should know how to begin.

I once ran a job-finding club for long-term unemployed people. People who'd gone months without finding a job were able to find one in a few weeks once they began to look systematically. I've used much of what I learned in that program to help people find new relationships. Your relationship to others is, in fact, similar to your relationship to your job. Depression plays the same role: It can lead to the end of a job, or a relationship, or worsen a present one. A lack of skills in finding a relationship can handicap you as severely as a lack of skills in finding a job. And the fear that accompanies this lack of skills can keep you in relationships and jobs you don't want to be in.

Once Gloria was over her depression and accepted the fact that Rob wasn't coming back, she decided to see if she could meet someone new using some of the strategies that I'd developed in the job-finding club.

1. *Avoid hopelessness.* Gloria's first reaction after her husband left her was, "No one would want me." Later she realized she had some assets, but still doubted she could find another man. Pessimism is common if you're without a job or a relationship. This hopelessness hindered Gloria until she started to question it by asking herself, "Where is the proof I'll never find someone?" and then acted on this answer by doing something to change the situation.

2. *Take realistic stock of yourself and your situation.* Know your strengths. What are you doing now that's stopping you from meeting someone? Ask yourself, "Are there some aspects about myself that I can improve?"

   Gloria remembered that in the past she'd been able to get dates, so she compared what she was doing now to then. She saw that she was now waiting for people to come to her rather than going out to them. She also realized that although she'd bought new clothes, she wasn't wearing them. She was waiting for the right occasion rather than creating the right occasion.

   Remember, the basic problem with depression is that your system of predictions isn't working so you can't rely on it. Be careful that you don't confuse the facts with predictions. Not being in a relationship is a fact. Not being able to enjoy or find one is a prediction that has to be tested out.

3. *Improve your social skills.* In taking stock, Gloria looked at ways she could improve how she got along with others. There are three common mistakes people make in starting relationships: *underestimating the importance of small talk, being too negative in their conversations,* and *being inconsistent in how they relate to others.*

   Small talk is important when you first meet people. It gives you a chance to relax and get your bearings. You can improve your small talk by using standard leads or asking questions. (One woman read scandal newspapers sold in grocery stores to give her material!) Whatever your method, know that while small talk is artificial, it's a crucial part of meeting people.

According to a recent study, the most important trait in determining a person's attractiveness is the degree of his or her negativism. *The more negative the person, the less others want to spend time with him.* Negativism can even prevent relationships from starting.

When you're talking to someone you can respond in one of three ways: You can *agree, disagree,* or *change the topic.* Gloria would mostly disagree. She'd point out exceptions and express the opposite point of view. For example, if someone said, "I enjoy going to Florida in the winter," she would say, "I don't like Florida. I think it's too commercial." Or she would correct him or her, "Part of Florida is okay, I guess, but it's hot and there are a lot of mosquitoes." She didn't realize that *absolute truth ruins good conversation.* When you contradict a person, you inhibit him; the other person is less likely to come up with something interesting to say; and he's not likely to lose himself in the conversation.

Gloria began to practice agreeing more and disagreeing less. (After she was more comfortable with agreeing, she learned to disagree more appropriately.) She noticed that when she'd agree, she could add more to what the other person said: "Yes, I know a lot of people that enjoy going to Florida."

If you don't agree and don't want to be negative, you can change the topic. For example, you can change the focus: "How long do you have for vacation?" Or you can disclose something about yourself: "I'm planning to go to California in several months."

When Gloria didn't return phone calls or was quiet with others, she thought they knew it was because she wasn't feeling well. But people can't read your mind. Gloria began to account for her inconsistency ("I'm being a little quiet today because I have my mind elsewhere"). Too much consistency can be boring but too much inconsistency drives people away.

4. *Try to meet a lot of people even if you don't want to have long-term relationships with them.* The key to finding a person you can relate to lies in generating a lot of contacts. It's a percentage undertaking. If you're meeting a lot of people who don't fit your bill, you're probably on the right track. The key to finding a job is collecting a lot of *No*'s. It's the same with people.

Gloria used the "spiderweb approach." She let others know she would like to meet more people. She realized the percentages were against her so she'd have to use all the approaches available. She developed a referral system. If she went out with someone she didn't like, she would refer him to other girlfriends. And they responded similarly.

You'll need to generate a large number of contacts and then filter these down to the person with whom you want to have a relationship. Expanding your social relations takes planning and action. Use whatever resources you have. Many people find jobs by going back to employers of a few years back. Even if your old high school boyfriend is married, he may know someone with whom you may have something in common.

5. *Get over the shame of being alone.* You might be thinking, "I could never let my old boyfriend know I'm alone." You may be ashamed to let others know you'd like to meet some men. But if you don't tell them, how will they know? Maybe you need to go to a party to meet someone but don't want to go alone. Shame is often a *Catch-22.*

One woman overcame her shame by picking up a man on the train and telling him that she was trying to meet more people. She dated this particular man for quite a while.

If you've ruled out joining a singles club or using a computer dating service because of shame, think of them simply as ways to meet people; there's nothing inherently shameful about them. Similarly, if shame stops you from meeting people you don't know, but want to, remember that you reduce your potential contacts if you wait to be introduced. Many good relationships start with a "pick up." Although it takes courage to overcome shame, you can force yourself to strike up a conversation with someone you want to meet. Introduce yourself. It's one of the best ways to meet people.

6. *Be task oriented.* People seeking employment often make two mistakes after an interview: (1) When the interview goes well they believe they'll be hired and stop looking, or (2) when the interview goes badly they become discouraged and stop looking. The same often happens when you want to start a long-term relationship. Try to keep in mind that any one date or contract is irrelevant to your final goal. Focus on generating leads and being open to opportunities as they appear.

Gloria started to go places that interested her. She went back to her church and joined a ski club. She knew she'd be more likely to meet people with similar interests there—plus she'd be doing something she enjoyed. If she felt self-conscious going some place such as a museum alone she'd find something to occupy herself, such as looking at a guidebook.

7. *Developing alternatives.* Many people arbitrarily restrict the types of jobs they seek. They must develop lists of alternative jobs they would take, including jobs they previously believed they were unqualified for. They also must consider other forms of transportation, such as car pools, for jobs outside their areas.

Keep this in mind when you're looking for people. You may be ruling men out because of some arbitrary standard—too young, too old, wrong profession. Test it out. You may have changed and no longer want the same type of man you wanted years before.

My wife's philosophy when she was single was that she'd go to dinner with anyone who didn't spoil her appetite; she now has many varied and enjoyable dates to remember.

8. *Look without desire.* You might be asking, "But where specifically do I meet people?" Anywhere and everywhere. Keep your eyes open. I used to go to a neighborhood bar in West Philadelphia. An old man who often came in supplemented his social security by finding things—watches, rings, and even money—in the streets. He said his secret was "looking without desire."

He didn't expect or demand to find these things, but he always had his eyes open. I think the same applies to relationships. You might meet someone in a park or at the Laundromat. Just keep your eyes open.

Gloria dated many more men after divorce than she had before she was married. She finally started a long-term relationship with a man she met at a new job she took in order to meet new people. In fact, she began the relationship by taking a risk and asking *him* out!

Changing Beliefs That Lead to Depression

SUPPOSE you heard that a friend was fired from her job. What would your reaction be? Would you automatically think, "I wonder what she did wrong" because of an underlying belief that people deserve the bad things that happen to them? Would you suppose that when bad things happen, it's other people's fault, and think, "Someone must have treated her unfairly"? Maybe you'd think, "It could be worse . . . it could be me," because of your belief that when something bad happens to others, it's better than if it happens to you.

Everyone needs rules to survive. You use them to make sense of your experiences, to set and reach goals, to evaluate and change behavior. Personal rules give meaning and value to life by providing consistency.

Unfortunately, some rules such as self-defeating beliefs or assumptions provide harsh standards for judging yourself and others. They lead to depression. They differ from other beliefs in that they're *absolute, excessive,* and *maladaptive.* They allow for no grays, only blacks and whites. They're overgeneralized ("All successful women are beautiful") and extreme ("If I'm not the best, I might as well be dead"). They take the form of syllogisms. For example, Sandy Harrison, a thirty-three-year-old computer programmer, believed, "Anyone who isn't loved is worthless. I'm not loved, therefore I'm worthless."

How do self-defeating assumptions come about? Generally you learn these formulas for behavior early in your life, probably from some well-meaning relative who tells you, "Always be nice—something bad could happen. Don't complain." You were given example after example of the benefit of believing these rules: "You're so sweet, here's a cookie!" . . . "Be careful! You'll get dirty!" . . . "Grandma won't want to keep you if you cry." You weren't warned about the drawbacks of these beliefs.

Your negative beliefs stay underground most of the time. You generally use more adaptive beliefs—that is, until you run into situations that are relevant to beliefs about *rejection, love, achievement, attractiveness, health, intelligence, social success,* and *morality.* Then your negative beliefs are automatically activated. In Sandy's case, her self-defeating beliefs were activated when Roger, the man she lived with, left her.

If you've been depressed for a long time, you've been operating on some self-defeating beliefs. You, like Sandy, probably haven't questioned them. She rarely examined or doubted her views on love. They were as much a part of her identity as being female.

It's important to change your negative beliefs. The stronger you hold on to dysfunctional beliefs ("I have to be the best at everything I try"), the more vulnerable you are to depression ("I only got a B on the final" . . . "I only came in fourth in the dance contest" . . . "My daughter refuses to go to college"). I've listed some common dysfunctional beliefs in Table 16.

It's important to take your fight against depression to a deeper level. If, after reading the previous chapters, you've been working on your symptoms, you're probably feeling better. But *feeling* better isn't enough. Unless you *change your basic maladaptive beliefs* about life, you won't be free from the threat of future depression.

Sandy worked on her depression symptoms—the major one for her was sadness—by becoming aware of and changing the automatic thoughts that led to them. By doing this, she began to feel better. She also discovered and changed the underlying beliefs that led to the automatic thoughts; this greatly lowered her risk of becoming depressed again. Up until then, her beliefs about how life *should be* and how life *really is* didn't fit. This led to her depression. Her assumptions about herself and her abilities didn't add up—mainly because long ago she'd let others do her arithmetic.

As you might guess, the way to change these beliefs is to become aware of them, answer or replace them with more flexible ones and act on the new ones.

HOW TO IDENTIFY YOUR BASIC NEGATIVE BELIEFS

1. *Become aware of your automatic thoughts.* (Chapter II describes how to do this.) Your automatic thoughts rest on implicit beliefs. Although these beliefs may be silent, they can be inferred from the thoughts that lead to bad feelings. When Sandy's boss ignored her, she thought, "He doesn't like me." This was based on her belief, "Everyone has to like me all the time."
2. *Look for themes.* Look over your automatic thoughts. See how many are of a particular type. You'll see a pattern forming in

TABLE 16
Twenty Common Dysfunctional Beliefs

1. I have to be loved to be happy.
2. It's best to give up my interests to please other people.
3. I can't be respected unless I've achieved something (have a good education or occupation) or am especially talented.
4. If other people dislike me, I can't be happy.
5. If I'm alone, I'll be lonely.
6. I have to do more than other people to be as good as them.
7. I can't trust other people because they'll hurt me.
8. If people know what I'm really like, they won't like me.
9. My happiness depends more on other people than on me.
10. If a person I want to love me doesn't, that means I'm unlovable.
11. To be nice, I have to help anyone in need.
12. I can't cope on my own.
13. My group (women, Blacks, Jews, poor, old, uneducated, etc.) is inferior to other groups.
14. It's my fault if those I love (husband, friend, children) are in trouble.
15. I should think of other people first, even if I have difficulties.
16. I should always be modest about my abilities.
17. I have no right to ask other people to help me.
18. I should never hurt anyone's feelings.
19. I'm basically bad (stupid, ugly, phony, immoral, lazy, a bitch, demanding).
20. I must have total control.

your thinking ("I'm dumb" . . . "I'm ugly" . . . "Nobody loves me" . . . "I'm too old"). Note situations in which you frequently feel bad. For Sandy, these situations often revolved around rejection and standards of personal appearance: "Everyone has to accept (love) me," and "People have to think I'm attractive." These general themes were part of one of her basic underlying beliefs: "People won't love you if you're ugly." *Ugly* to her applied not only to appearance but also to personality. Her belief could go in a number of different directions ("I'm unhappy, that means I must be an ugly person" . . . "I have to fool people to make them think I'm attractive" . . . "I'll be ugly when I get old so I'll be unhappy").

3. *Note key words.* You may find that you use the same words over and over again in your automatic thoughts—words such as *rotten, weird, ugly.* These are clues to your underlying beliefs; since most of your beliefs were learned when you were a child, they contain words that children use (such as *stupid* and *dumb*).

Once these words have been identified, uncover the meanings behind them. This is the time to sit back and reflect on your childhood. Certain family sayings and bedtime stories may contain further clues.

Sandy often used the word *ugly* in her negative thoughts. Thinking back to her childhood, she remembered her relatives saying her sister was the pretty one and she was the one with the brains. She identified with the ugly-duckling story.

4. *See how you view others.* Another clue to your underlying beliefs is the way you see others. This requires tuning in to your thinking even more. For example, Sandy thought, "Shannon has lots of dates because she's beautiful." Also, look for people with whom you feel the most uncomfortable. What is it about them that gets to you? Sandy didn't like extremely attractive women.

5. *Underline thinking errors.* Look over your automatic thoughts and see what kinds of errors you make the most. Overgeneralizing? Jumping to conclusions? Ignoring the positive? Thinking in either/or terms? This last was Sandy's mistake; either she was great or she was nothing.

6. *Examine your happiness.* When you're unusually happy about

some event, ask yourself, "Why am I so happy?" Many underlying beliefs have a payoff when they appear to be working. For example, when a man paid attention to Sandy, she became exuberant. Conversely, she became depressed when she thought men weren't paying attention to her.

To find your own dysfunctional belief system, draw up a chart similar that in Table 17; work from your thoughts back to basic beliefs.

After you've listed your dysfunctional beliefs, rate each on a scale of 0 to 100 according to how much you believe it. This belief scale will allow you to measure your progress in changing basic beliefs.

HOW TO CHANGE NEGATIVE BELIEFS

Identifying your rules is the first step toward changing them. Don't be surprised if you immediately see how wrong your beliefs are once they are out in the open. You'll probably be amazed that you held them for so long as certainties beyond question.

What causes you to change your beliefs? One or two new ways of looking at a situation can make the difference. Usually, you won't question your beliefs merely because you come up with a batch of counterarguments, but rather because you come up with one or two that make particular sense to you.

Many of the methods you used to change automatic thoughts can be used to change your beliefs and assumptions. However, the targets are different, as the following shows.

Sandy had automatic thoughts about being ugly and undesirable. I asked her, "Other than your subjective opinion, what evidence do you have that you're ugly?"

"Well, my ex-husband always said I was ugly."

I asked if her husband was always right in these matters.

"No, actually, he had his own reasons for telling me this. But the real reason I know I'm ugly is that men don't ask me out. If I weren't ugly, I'd be dating now."

I told her, "Maybe that is why you aren't dating, but maybe there are other explanations. You said you work in an office by yourself

TABLE 17
Examples of Underlying Beliefs

	Sue Berlie	Rebecca Jensen
PRIMARY BELIEF (USUALLY SILENT)	Life should be fair.	If I'm not nice, bad things will happen.
SECONDARY BELIEF (GENERAL THEME)	If bad things happen, it must be my fault.	It's my fault when bad things happen (because I wasn't good).
AUTOMATIC THOUGHT	I'll always be unhappy.	I'll never enjoy anything because there's something wrong with me.
FEELING	Sadness	Sadness
	Pat Claudy	Nancy Ong
PRIMARY BELIEF (USUALLY SILENT)	I have to be the best or I'm nothing.	I have to be loved or I'm nothing.
SECONDARY BELIEF (GENERAL THEME)	I have to be the best graduate student in the program.	My husband, Jim, has to show me he loves me all the time.
AUTOMATIC THOUGHT	I know I'll fail the next test.	Jim didn't call because he doesn't love me anymore.
FEELING	Anxiety	Sadness

all day and spend your nights alone at home. It doesn't seem as if you're giving yourself opportunities to meet men."

"I can see what you're saying, but still, if I weren't ugly, men would ask me out."

I suggested she run an experiment: become more socially active, stop turning down invitations to parties and social events, and see what happened.

After she became more active and had more opportunities to meet men, she started to date and feel better. At this point she was no longer absolutely convinced she was ugly.

But we didn't stop there. She still believed that her worth was determined by her appearance. She knew this didn't make sense, but she still believed it to a degree. She also still held her other basic assumption that she couldn't be happy without love or attention from men.

I asked her, "On what do you base your belief that you can't be happy without a man?"

She answered, "I was really depressed for a year and a half when I didn't have a man."

"Is there perhaps another reason why you were depressed?"

"I guess I was looking at everything in a distorted way . . . but I still don't know if I could be happy if no one was interested in me."

I said I didn't know for sure if she could be happy without a man's interest either. I asked if there was a way she could find out.

"Well, as an experiment, I could *not* go out on dates for a while and see how I feel."

I told her she had a good idea. Although it has its flaws, the experimental method is still the best one around to find out the facts.

She was able to stick to a "cold turkey" regimen. For the first time in her adult life she wasn't attached to a man—either in her mind or in reality. After a brief period of unhappiness, she was delighted to find that her well-being wasn't dependent on another person.

Distorted self-images. Many patients' negative beliefs involve false ideas about personal attributes—a version of what one person called a "hound complex": humorless, old, ugly, nonverbal, and dumb. The most common one is believing you're ugly.

Nearly every depressed woman I see believes she is ugly. None of them, however, meets the dictionary definition, "aversive to look at." Almost all of them are in the average range of appearance.

Their problems about being ugly are self-created. Research in social psychology has found it okay to be average looking—people don't treat you badly if you're average looking. Research has found if you're extremely attractive, people will give you more breaks when they first meet you, but this special treatment quickly drops off as they get to know you. Similarly, if you're exceedingly unattractive, people will give you fewer breaks when they first meet you, but this changes as they get to know you.

Your appearance is continually changing and it's a mistake to misperceive these changes as ugliness. It's true you may look different at forty then you did at twenty, but this doesn't mean you're ugly.

Therapists use different methods to correct distorted self-images. One therapist told me, "When my patient said he was ugly, I said I was sorry to hear that because I thought he looked like me. And it was true. We asked the receptionist. She said we did look alike. And the patient didn't think I was ugly, so he had to rethink his belief."

It's difficult to change beliefs about ugliness because ugliness is subjective. How can you prove it one way or the other? The most useful technique is focusing on what you want out of life. Plenty of women could be considered ugly, yet they have good jobs, boyfriends, and happiness. Forget for a minute about being ugly. What do you want? Do you want a particular job, a boyfriend, happiness? Once you decide what you want, go after it and learn that good looks are in the eye of the beholder.

Impossible expectations.   Some people rely heavily on absolute rules for their lives, usually phrased as "should" . . . "ought" . . . "must" . . . "have to." Words like these often are cues to beliefs so self-defeating and inflexible that you don't have the freedom to enjoy your own successes or the chance to learn from your own failures. They can stop you from setting priorities and deciding for yourself what you want to do. By continually giving yourself absolute orders (in the form of *shoulds*), you become anxious, frustrated, and disappointed—since you can't possibly carry all of them out. Moreover, many are contradictory ("I should be pretty" . . . "I shouldn't be vain").

Comparison is a dangerous pastime. If you compare yourself to others, you'll feel either false pride or inferiority. Another kind of comparison can be even worse—comparing what you *should* do to what you *are* doing. Instead of comparing yourself to another person, you're comparing your behavior with the rigid, impossible standards of an ideal behavior or a perfect person.

You'll know you're misusing *shoulds* in your life if you discover an abundance of them among your automatic thoughts. Similarly, discovering that you intensely believe the *shoulds* to be correct, absolute, and ideal is a signal to start questioning them.

If you run into problems because your personal rules become too severe, absolute, and rigid, restructure them or abandon them as unworkable.

Betty Lawson thought she *should* never make mistakes. Because, like everyone, she did make mistakes, she was setting herself up for disappointment and accompanying anxiety and depression. Often people find support for their *shoulds* from their experiences. From Betty's point of view, her rule prevented something bad from happening. Magical thinking like this is difficult to disprove. However, you can change self-defeating *shoulds*:

1. *Keep in mind that* shoulds *are arbitrary.* There's no absolute way you have to lead your life. You can have guidelines that make life easier, but these aren't absolute, universal laws. Suppose, for example, you have a rule that you don't hurt other people's feelings. Generally, this is a good idea; but there are times when for your own best interests or theirs you have to say something that may hurt ("I'm sorry to rush you out the door, but I have to get up early tomorrow" . . . "Since you asked, Mom, that hair color doesn't suit you").

2. *Don't act on yor own absolute orders.* Every time you act on your negative beliefs, you strengthen them. Betty thought, "The house should be immaculate," and strengthened this be-

lief by dusting the tops of the doors and drying the sink after she ran some water.

Try this method. First, state the *should,* or write it out. Betty wrote, "I should be concerned because Laura [her daughter] isn't doing her homework."

Second, predict what will happen if the rule isn't followed ("If Laura won't do her homework she'll get into trouble with the teacher and that'll be terrible").

Then test the prediction. Betty decided *not* to check on Laura's homework and to revise her rule according to the results of the experiment. Laura didn't do her homework. *And* she got into trouble with the teacher. *But it wasn't terrible.* Laura learned the consequences of not doing her homework. Because of the experiment, Betty told Laura that in the future she would have to take responsibility for doing her homework. This helped Laura increase her own sense of responsibility.

Betty worked on changing her belief from "I should be responsible for other people" to "It would be better if those I care for did what was best for them, but I can't take all the responsibility for them."

3. *Change counterproductive contracts.* Shoulds, oughts, musts, and other absolute rules for behavior are really personal contracts you made with yourself years ago as a child. Perhaps your mother told you to give up an immediate source of pleasure or comfort ("Share your cookies, darling"). She implied that you would receive something better as a reward ("You're a nice girl for sharing").

There's nothing wrong with sharing or postponing pleasure. But if in the process of learning to share you also began to make rigid and unrealistic contracts with yourself, such as "Being nice will always earn me a reward," you could be in trouble.

I asked Betty how this concept of personal contracts applied to her system.

She said, "I guess my contract is that if I'm perfect, people will love me—I guess because I believe without love I can't be happy."

I asked, "When did you draw up this contract?"

"Probably when I was a child, from what my mother told me. She's a lot like me."

"If you had a business, would you let a child draw up the contracts on how it should operate? And would you contract the controlling interest of the business to other people?"

Betty realized that this is what she seemed to have done.

Personal contracts often are unworkable and maladaptive because the terms are vague and open-ended. In Betty's case, "being perfect" and "others' love" are relative concepts. There's no end to how perfect you have to be and no way to tell how much love you have to have to be happy. Remember that you can always renegotiate your contracts.

Fairness. Negative underlying beliefs often revolve around ideas of fairness—what you or others deserve when certain acts are performed. You may believe the world, God, and society are grossly unfair.

One of Eva McBride's basic beliefs was that *life should be fair*. She believed that it was unfair that she didn't get what she wanted out of life. This belief helped to keep her depressed. She felt sad because other people had more money, better husbands and children, got all the breaks, and didn't have to work as hard.

She didn't see that many situations in life are naturally unfair: There's no symmetry in the way good things in life are handed out. People are born with different abilities. Fortunate and unfortunate experiences happen randomly.

You can't make a special claim to favored treatment or magical protection against adversity without experiencing some disappointment. Upsetting yourself about the unfairness of life won't change it. Eva came to see that she could change her attitude—even if she couldn't change the external situation. Sometimes you *can* change unfair situations. But if you can't—becoming depressed will only make things worse.

You may think that others should act differently, but you're just giving yourself an added burden—worrying about what others should or shouldn't do. It might be better for you to use that energy more constructively, though this isn't to say you shouldn't try to make the world a better place if you can.

Fairness is often a matter of personal opinion or bias. The employee believes, "I do the work around here and produce the product. I should receive more money. It's not fair." While the owner believes, "I produced the capital. I invested it. I took the risk. I should get more money instead of having to give it to the workers."

Fairness is not a concrete entity; it is a hypothetical, made-up construct, an ideal. But though no one can define fairness and unfairness, the concepts often cause great irritation and unhappiness.

Instead of viewing the world in vague and abstract terms, decide what you want and take the steps to get it. If the goal seems worth the effort, you'll have a better chance of getting it if you're not bogged down worrying about being treated unfairly.

Eva tried an experiment: She carefully observed and recorded for two weeks the reactions of other people to her self-sacrificing behavior. She found that the actual consequences of her behavior were different than what she expected. Instead of appreciating her, people discounted her. She decided that she should change her philosophy from "The meek shall inherit the earth" to "The meek shall inherit dirt."

Her therapist, Steve Hollon of the Center for Cognitive Therapy, pointed out that this turnabout also represented an extreme way of looking at the world. Remember, your actions have a range of consequences—some desirable, some not. Many consequences are unanticipated. The best policy is to develop flexible guidelines that allow you to have rewarding relationships—guidelines that don't subordinate your interests to other people's.

Self-fulfilling prophecies.   Most beliefs that lead to depression are self-fulfilling. If you believe that you can't be happy without approval, you'll probably be unhappy unless you get it. By predicting the consequences, you bring them about. You can change these beliefs by realizing that they're not only self-fulfilling, but also self-defeating.

I talked to Sandy about her belief that not being loved leads automatically to sadness.

I asked her, "Not being loved is a nonevent. How can a nonevent lead automatically to something?"

She said, "I just don't believe anyone could be happy without being loved."

"This is your belief. When you believe something, it dictates your emotional reaction."

"I don't understand that."

"If you believe something, you're going to act and feel as if it's true, whether it is or not."

She said, "You mean, if I believe I'll be unhappy without love, it's only my belief causing my unhappiness."

"Yes. And when you feel unhappy, you probably say to yourself, 'See, I was right. If I don't have love, I'm bound to be unhappy.'"

"How can I get out of this trap if this is what I believe?"

"You could experiment with your belief about having to be loved. Force yourself to suspend this belief and see what happens."

If you have a similar problem, pay attention to the *natural* consequences of not being loved, not to the consequences created by your belief. For example, imagine yourself on a tropical island with delicious fruits and other foods available. Imagine that the primitive people who live on the island are friendly and helpful, but don't love you. None of them loves you. How do you feel in your fantasy? Would you be depressed?

Sandy said she'd feel relaxed and comfortable. She repeatedly challenged her belief. She eventually came to see that it didn't necessarily follow that if she wasn't loved she would have to be unhappy.

Advantages versus disadvantages. You may hesitate to discard self-defeating beliefs because you fear you'll lose something important or something bad will happen to you. You may see the advantages of changing the belief, but the disadvantages may seem greater. Try not to structure your experiences as no-win traps with the disadvantages always outweighing any possible advantages.

To get out of a no-win situation, list the advantages and disadvantages of your belief and correct any distortions. One patient changed her belief ("In order to be happy I have to be perfect. I should *never* make a mistake or show my flaws") by listing the *advantages* to giving up her belief:

"(1) Without this belief I could do a lot of things I've been avoiding—like learning to drive a car. (2) If I were more open, I would have more friends. (3) I wouldn't be so anxious about making mistakes or depressed because I did make one. (4) I would be able to accept the reality that I'm not a perfect person."

She listed the following *disadvantages* to changing this belief: "(1) I've been able to do exceptionally well in school and on my job. (2) What I do, I do well. (3) Because I avoid a lot of things, I've avoided a lot of trouble and problems."

We discussed the disadvantages. I asked her, "This belief may have helped you on your present job, but how has it helped your long-range career plans?"

"Actually, it's held me back. I feel I'm overqualified for this job. If I had more courage, I'd work for a bigger company in a more challenging position."

I told her, "Dread of making mistakes often blocks people from taking chances. What about this belief: What you do, you must do well?"

She said, "That's true. I have the highest ratings at work."

"Is there a point of diminishing return?"

"Yes. I told you, I bring work home every night and go in on the weekends. I do a lot more than is demanded or expected of me."

She was eventually able to see that believing she had to be perfect had its drawbacks.

Self-evaluation.   Do you believe that people and events outside yourself determine your worth? Do you need others' approval? If so, you're placing yourself in a one-down position. Approval, like success and achievements, is open-ended and nonconcrete. If you think you need the approval of other people to survive, you'll never get enough of it. There isn't enough love, attention, or money around to satisfy illusionary needs.

No one can tell you how to evaluate yourself. You can only concentrate on your traits. But to equate your traits with your total self is an overgeneralization that is likely to lead to trouble.

When you're performing well in one area, it's appropriate to feel good and to evaluate this performance realistically so that you can continue to perform well. And when you're not performing well, it's a good idea to evaluate this realistically too, so you can improve.

But in both cases, the performance has nothing to do with your self-worth, which can't be measured or evaluated.

Long-term versus short-term payoffs. Try to examine the long-term effectiveness of your beliefs, particularly if they lead to depression and yet appear to be working in your favor. For instance, if you believe you need the approval of everyone, you may be extremely happy when you think you have it. If you believe your value depends on your performance, you may be overjoyed when you're performing well. But look at the long-term effects of operating under these rules—you don't get approval from everyone always and when you don't, or if you don't perform well, you get depressed.

Those who continue to work at changing their negative beliefs become less prone to depressions. However, the motivation to change is weak when the formulas are working: for instance, when rating yourself as wonderful leads to euphoria or when avoiding unpleasant situations relieves anxiety. Recognize the long-range harm produced by these beliefs.

Acting against your beliefs. Try *actively* to change your negative beliefs in the course of your ordinary daily experiences. Trace your automatic thoughts back to your negative beliefs, answer them, and act against the negative belief.

Acting against a belief is the most powerful way to change it. If you're afraid to make mistakes, seek out situations where there's a high probability of making mistakes. If you feel compelled to be with others, force yourself to be alone. If you place high value on acceptance, go places where the probability of being accepted is slight. If you're afraid of making a fool of yourself, do something outlandish. If you believe you must have everyone's approval, set a goal of doing one thing a day that goes against seeking the approval of others. You might have to force yourself. Tell yourself, "Even if it's uncomfortable, I'll do it."

You're probably reluctant to act against your beliefs. You can do so in a guarded manner, or you can jump right in. In either event, you're likely to experience discomfort when you attempt to break long-established "rules."

You've acted on your dysfunctional beliefs for so long that they are part of your total system—your mind, emotions, and body. Expect anxiety when you change, but remember that anxiety won't kill you. Anxiety is like weak muscles. If you stay with the anxiety and practice building up your tolerance, it will harden into courage.

Be on the lookout for an inner voice that says, "This isn't the right time," or "There is this or that reason for not doing it." These excuses will stop your efforts. Ignore this voice and force yourself to jump in. This is an example of when you can use the critical-incident technique—doing the opposite of what your instincts tell you to do. At these moments you have a choice—you can strengthen your dysfunctional beliefs or weaken them. Keep in mind that because this isn't your normal way of acting, you'll feel strange. If you stay with it long enough, the sense of strangeness will go away.

Arguing against your beliefs.   One of the best ways to change a belief is to use your own argument against it. One woman believed that her happiness hinged on reaching great artistic heights. She thought about it and concluded that she would have to be as good as the poet Sylvia Plath. But then she thought some more about it and realized that Sylvia Plath was chronically depressed and in the end killed herself; artistic success was no guarantee of happiness.

Following any rules blindly can get you into trouble because you don't see and consider facts that go against them. Bertrand Russell observed that the certainty with which a person holds a belief is inversely related to the truth of that belief. Fanatics are true believers; scientists are skeptics.

XI

Handling the Stress of Motherhood

Tracy's mother died when she was nine. She was brought up by her father and older brother but she never felt close to either of them. When she was in the tenth grade, she started dating George, a high school dropout who was several years older than she was. After they had gone together for a year, she discovered she was pregnant and George reluctantly agreed to marry her. She didn't particularly want to get married either, but she was glad to get out of the house.

She and George were close for a while. He worked in a gas station and she enjoyed fixing up their small apartment. Tracy was happy when Debbie, the new baby, came. Their second child, Tommy, was born when Tracy was nineteen. His birth brought on her first depression. She was depressed off and on for the next eight years—just how badly depended on events in her life.

For instance, George developed a drinking problem and his drinking bouts and periods of unemployment would trigger her depression. She became even more depressed after their third child, Kathy, was born.

George had become a long-distance truck driver and was gone for weeks at a time. When he was home, they rarely talked; they didn't seem to have much in common. Tracy suspected he might have a girlfriend in another state.

Tracy said, "Then the best thing happened. Mrs. Butler moved next door." Mrs. Butler was a widow with grown children. She and Tracy were good friends immediately. She became like a grandmother to Tracy's kids. They talked almost daily and visited frequently. Mrs. Butler helped Tracy out in many ways. She would babysit so Tracy could get out to a church meeting or a movie. Tracy said the best part was having someone to whom she could *really* talk.

After Mrs. Butler moved in, Tracy started to feel better. She thought matters would sort themselves out and that she might even go back to school when the kids were older. George's trucking job meant that money was less of a problem.

The winter after she moved in, Mrs. Butler became sick and was taken to the hospital where she died. Tracy went into a severe depression. She wanted to kill herself but didn't because of the children. The more depressed she became, the more the problems with the kids multiplied. The youngest, three-year-old Kathy, had asthma and Tracy spent a lot of time taking care of her and running her to the doctor's. She was also worried about her ten-year-old. She was afraid Debby was spending too much time with the older, rougher kids in the neighborhood.

Tracy, who was under a great deal of stress to start with, found herself even more overwhelmed. *Stress,* one of those words that's used a lot but not often defined, is simply how you respond physically and psychologically when your demands outstrip your resources. The demands may be either ones you place on yourself or ones the world places on you. Tracy developed stress because she saw a major resource for handling the demands on her as wife and mother—Mrs. Butler—disappear. This left her with more than she thought she could handle.

Severe stress or a series of stressful events can trigger negative beliefs that lead to depression. Tracy's negative beliefs were formed when her mother died ("I have no control over anything" . . . "I'll always be disappointed if I count too much on someone"). When Mrs. Butler, who was like a substitute mother, died, these beliefs were reactivated. The stress of the death along with the stresses of raising children became too much.

The type of stress that leads to depression is usually related to a

particular vulnerability. For example, if you have underlying negative beliefs about your health ("Any health problem leads to unending suffering" . . . "I can't endure pain"), the stress of a major
illness such as cancer or a long series of minor illnesses could
activate these beliefs.

A certain amount of stress is inevitable: You will always face
problems that don't have ready solutions. While too much stress
can immobilize you, a certain degree is needed to motivate you to
find solutions.

Many depressed people are hospitalized to lower demands on
them and thus lower their stress. However, the demands are often
too low in a hospital. They don't have the stimulation needed to
get better—so they vegetate. It's important that you don't try to get
rid of all your stress; rather, you want to learn to keep it at a
reasonable level.

How much stress can you tolerate before there's a breakdown in
your system? It varies. A few people thrive on high levels of stress.
One such woman said, "I'm lethargic and dull unless I have dead-
lines to create pressure. I feel like a lizard unless I'm solving a crisis.
When things are going too smoothly, I'll change jobs or sell my
house to create some excitement." This particular woman is well
adjusted but does have problems with people who don't like even
minimal stress because she's continually in motion. Other people
find change and stress extremely uncomfortable, and they try to
avoid them as much as possible.

At times it may be a good idea to cut down on your demands.
You *can* lower your stress by withdrawing and cutting out some
pressures, but this may lead to depression. Other ways of handling
stress may be less dangerous.

If you aren't normally bothered by depression and you have a
mild bout of it, going to bed and treating it like a mild case of the
flu might help. But if you have a moderate to severe depression of
any standing, this isn't a good idea. The treatment for an acute
problem is usually the wrong treatment for a chronic one. Pain
researchers find that bedrest and painkillers are good for acute back
pain, but that they're the worst treatment for a chronic back problem. Similarly, if you go to bed when you're mildly depressed and
stay there too long, you can develop a full-blown clinical depres-

sion. That's why you have to control mild depressions before they grow.

If you could change your life to match certain available statistics, you could protect yourself from depression. First, you'd be a man (they have less depression); then you'd try to have enough resources to handle life's demands (money, good health, abilities and talents); you'd avoid severe losses (marriage, job, home); and you'd have a person in whom you could confide, who supports you through thick and thin, and who gives you good advice (husband, friend).

More realistically, however, you could learn from those who have experienced severe stress. Why does a fourteen-year-old girl, the only surviver of an airplane crash in the jungles of Peru, come out alive after two weeks when another person dies of exposure after only one night outdoors? Why does one person survive in an open raft on the ocean when others in his party don't? Investigators have found that survivors don't give up and get depressed. Survivors also don't get anxious and excited; they stay calm. They accept the situation. They keep their emotions under control by not jumping to conclusions or exaggerating the situation. They don't make negative predictions ("It's hopeless, why try") and they don't rely on positive predictions ("I'll just sit here until a helicopter comes to save me"). Rather, they focus on the task in front of them ("How can I stay warm, get water" . . . "How can I figure out where I am"). They're too busy staying alive to exaggerate the situation.

This is a good strategy to use with your problems. The more you can focus on solutions, even partial ones, the better you'll be able to handle the stresses in your life. The solution may be to get more information or to tolerate uncertainty until an answer turns up.

I know this is easier to say than to do; but with practice you can become a better problem solver—and this is one of the best ways to lower your stress.

Remember, it's *perceived* demands and *perceived* lack of ability to handle the demands that cause stress. Distorted predictions and expectations that go beyond the facts make the stress worse. Tracy, for example, would hear stories of kids in the neighborhood smoking pot and then automatically think that Debby would have drug problems, too.

Tracy worked at becoming aware of her *predictions*. When she started to get upset about her problems, she'd think, "I don't know what to do now; that's a fact. But that doesn't mean I won't in the future; that's a prediction." You can't always test or check out predictions, but knowing they're predictions and not facts can save you a lot of trouble.

Philosopher Alfred Korzybski said that the secret of happiness lies in keeping your expectations low and motivations high. Try to keep both your positive and negative expectations about the future to a minimum. If you expect the worst you're likely to bring it about, and if you expect the best you're likely to be disappointed —and depression is fed by disappointment.

You can use stress to your advantage by recognizing it for what it is. Stress is your body's way of telling you, "Something's wrong. Something needs to be changed, either in your environment or (more likely) in your thinking." Use feelings of stress as early warning signals of problems.

MOTHERHOOD AND STRESS

Most stress revolves around getting along with others. Since child rearing is a major area of stress for many women in their young and middle years, it's important to learn stress management procedures to use with children—always remembering that these methods can be applied to other areas of your life. Even if you don't have any children, you can use these methods to handle other stresses in your life.

Fertility and depression. Women's problems in motherhood aren't limited to raising children. Take for instance the depression that follows the birth of a child. At one time this was believed to be due to hormonal changes in the newborn's mother. Many researchers now believe the three-day baby blues that many new mothers go through is not a true depression—just a mood swing. You're actually much more likely to experience depression when your baby is a year old or so. However, women with unrealistically positive expectations about their baby ("He will be perfect" . . . "She'll be easy to care for" . . . "He won't interfere with my life") are the most vulnerable to depression right after the birth of a child.

Scientists have also speculated on the relationship between the loss of the ability to have children and depression. One school believes that the loss of childbearing ability makes you depressed because you no longer feel "fulfilled" as a woman. To support this, they cite studies that find a high degree of depression in women following a hysterectomy. Depression has been found to be three to four times higher following a hysterectomy than following a comparable operation such as a gall bladder removal. However, studies can be misleading. Dr. Dennis Gath, a research psychiatrist at Oxford University, studied depression following hysterectomies in depth and found that a high proportion of women who had hysterectomies *were depressed to begin with.* The hysterectomy actually reduced the depressions of fifty percent of the women. The physical discomfort of, say, heavy menstrual periods may have kept them more inactive and so more depressed. I'm certainly not suggesting that you have a hysterectomy to cure your depression; rather, I want to point out that there is little evidence to support the claim that loss of childbearing ability, naturally or surgically, leads automatically to depression. However, you *can* make yourself depressed if you choose to put a negative meaning on it.

Society and mothering. Over the last ten to fifteen years, millions of women have experienced a strange type of mass demotion in their jobs due to no fault of their own. It wasn't in the newspapers. Many women took years to realize it; others refused to accept it and so weren't affected by it. Who was demoted and why? As a result of changes in society, many women in traditionally female occupations (secretaries, nurses, receptionists, and especially housewives and mothers) have come to believe that their status has been lowered.

The movement toward equality of the sexes, while good in the long run, does have some short-term drawbacks. As we expect more women to achieve professionally, those that don't meet society's new standards are often looked down upon by themselves and others. For example, sociologists have noted that the increasing number of positions open for women in medical schools relates directly to the number of nurses who think of themselves as failures for not becoming doctors.

Many women accepted their demotions as signs of their own personal shortcomings. Their self-demeaning attitudes lowered their self-esteem, which in turn lowered their resources for handling stress. Many also suffered from the patronizing behavior of others —ranging from the relatively mild, "I couldn't get along without the little woman," to the extreme, a boss who asks his secretary to pick out the black jelly beans before he gives them to his wife. But the real threat to their self-esteem stems from accepting these social changes as demotions.

Society puts mothers in a real bind. While on one hand, the importance of the mother's role is stressed (the "hand that rocks the cradle" school), at the same time her role as "only a mother" is discounted. You can escape this bind by not accepting it, by not making value judgments. Mothering is a job that's different than others—not better nor worse, just different. Granted, it's a hard job, with lousy pay and tough hours, but just because it's a hard job doesn't mean it's second rate.

You can get yourself into trouble if you use outside approval of your mothering—your husband's gratitude or your children's accomplishments—as the paycheck for being a mother. This is an elusive currency. It's better to take what enjoyment you can directly out of being a mother and not to count on outside approval.

Self-created demands. Most of the stress over children is self-created. Demands on you come from within. Take for example the woman who couldn't decide whether to have a baby or not. She structured this as a no-win decision: No matter what she decided, it would be the wrong choice.

She was creating stress for herself in two ways. First, she was demanding the impossible: to know beforehand what the result of her decision would be. Second, she created stress by demanding she make the right, perfect decision. Her internal, self-created demands led to stress.

She finally did decide to have a baby, which led her to create more stress for herself. Before, her internal demand had been for a perfect decision. Once she decided, she began to demand she be pregnant right away. This type of stress often prevents pregnancy. Many women become pregnant after adopting a baby because the adopted child removes their internal, stress-creating demands. This woman was eventually able to lower her stress by changing her *demand* for pregnancy into a simple *preference*.

Stress and small children. Although Tracy had many real problems with her kids, she created many others. She increased her internal demands by taking on greater responsibility for their welfare than she could control. For example, she thought it was her duty to protect them from all adversity, be it sickness or the teasing of other kids. She was constantly on guard. She also increased her stress by *demeaning* her performance as a mother. By putting herself down she made herself depressed and less able to handle the duties in front of her.

Many women increase their burdens by believing, "I have to get it all together!" But as one woman with three small children put it, "How do you organize ants?" The answer is, "With great difficulty." When you have three small children, you can bet that at any given time at least one will be sick or having problems.

To increase your tolerance for stress, accept that there will always be unsolved and unresolved problems. An accepting attitude can calm down stress. As I said before, stress is your body's way of saying, "Hey! Something's wrong." By accepting it, you're in effect saying, "Thanks. I've got the message. You don't need to keep reminding me."

When one of Tracy's kids fell down and hurt himself, her first thought was, "Oh, no! Not this. I can't take it any more." But by learning to take the opposite tack ("What do we have here and how can I handle it?"), she was able to diffuse most difficult situations before they escalated.

You also might be second-guessing how badly your child is feeling. This can increase your stress. When one of Tracy's kids was sick or having trouble with a playmate, she often felt worse than the child. This didn't help the child, but it *did* cause Tracy distress. She overcame this by teaching her children to tell her (the best they

could) when they were really sick or hurt and by distancing herself
from their everyday problems and concerns.

Closely related to overemphathizing is another common mistake:
believing difficulties are bad for your children. Many women
strongly believe this. Sherry would walk her seven-year-old to
school in the morning and go to great lengths to see that he had
friends to play with in the afternoon; she always had activities
planned for him in the evening so he wouldn't be bored. She
quickly intervened in his difficulties—fights with playmates, trouble
with schoolwork. She was continually anxious about his welfare.

I talked at length with her about the importance of children's
experiencing adversity—rejection, pain, boredom. I suggested she
could intervene if her son didn't seem to be solving the difficulty,
but that he should have the first go at it.

Only by experiencing problems when they are young can children learn to handle them later. Children need to inoculate themselves against later difficulties and problems. Sherry was depriving
her son of opportunities to develop independence and experience
in handling problems.

Many depressed women and men come from overprotective
families. They're raised with an unrealistic idea of what the world is
like. When they run head on into inevitable problems later, they
don't have the resources and experiences for handling them.

The Supermom syndrome. You may have unrealistic standards about being a mother. The excessive demands you place on
yourself, which usually develop out of misconceptions about being
a parent, almost guarantee that you'll fall short. Remember, your
circumstances affect what you can do as a parent. For example,
because Tracy had three children she didn't have the same amount
of time and energy she would have had with only one child—or if
she had had a husband that pitched in to help. She had to settle
for an approximation of how she would like to mother in an ideal
world. She had to learn to expect situations to be incomplete and
not to berate herself because one child was going uncared for at a
particular moment. A sense of incompleteness comes with the territory of motherhood.

If the bad news is that you can't be an ideal mother, the good news is you don't have to be. You may have bought the idea that if you make some mistakes you'll ruin your child's life. You may mistakenly believe that your every move is going to make a lasting impression on your child.

Your anxiety may be worse if you don't even know what your mistakes are. There's always conflicting advice on how to raise children. For example, many women are worried when their children wet the bed. Somewhere along the way they've picked up the idea that this always indicates an emotional problem. But more often than not, bed wetting is the result of a slightly different developmental rate of the child's control or of sleeping too soundly. In nearly every case the child outgrows it, but you can turn it into an unnecessarily stressful situation if you put too much emphasis on it.

Time management. One of the best ways to manage stress—particularly if you're the mother of small children—is to manage your time. Tracy began to use a few simple but effective time-management principles. First, she realized that she could only do one thing at a time and that there were important activities that she had to do—making meals, washing, paying bills—and if she didn't do these she would be in a bind. So she listed what she had to do and did the most important things first.

You can do the same. List the five or six activities you have to do each day. Rank them by importance and do them in that order.

Tracy also started to schedule pleasurable activities and time off for herself. Only by seeing your own interests as priority items can you keep up your energy.

One of the best ways to increase your resources is to use outside agencies—church, neighborhood, and volunteer groups and other social agencies. Often the people that need this support the most are the last ones to use it.

When I asked Tracy if she thought about getting a part-time job, she said she'd like to but that she didn't know how she could manage the time. However, she was willing to explore the possibility. Once she started looking she was able to find a subsidized daycare center for her youngest child so she could work a couple of days a week.

Medical sociologists have found that mothers of young children who have few resources are often depressed. However, if the woman has some type of outside job, the likelihood of her getting depressed is only half that of mothers who don't have jobs.

A job can give you perspective on your problems. Tracy was glad to have a chance to talk to adults at work and make some friends with whom she could go places. An outside interest doesn't necessarily mean a job—any activity that you enjoy outside the home could serve the same purpose. You might sign up for an evening course or take up an active sport or hobby.

Living with an adolescent.   Much has been written about the depression women suffer when their children leave home—the "empty-nest" syndrome. A recent study, however, confirms a common clinical impression: Fathers are bothered more by this than mothers. Men often are so busy with their work that they don't have a chance to really know and enjoy their children. So when they leave home, the fathers believe they've lost forever the chance to know them.

Occasionally depressed women suffer the empty-nest syndrome. But more often the woman is depressed because the adolescent is *still* at home. Mothers appear to have more trouble when their children are in adolescence than at any other time.

Alison Lurie captures the spirit of many mothers in her novel *The War Between the Tates:*

They were a happy family once, she [Erica Tate] thinks. Jeffrey and Matilda were beautiful, healthy babies; charming toddlers; intelligent, lively, affectionate children. There are photograph albums and folders of drawings and stories and report cards to prove it. Then last year, when Jeffrey turned 14 and Matilda 12, they had begun to change: to grow rude, coarse, selfish, insolent, nasty, brutish, and tall. It was as if she were keeping a boarding house in a bad dream, and the children she had loved were turning into awful lodgers—lodgers who paid no rent, whose leases could not be terminated. They were awful at home and abroad; in company and alone; in the morning, the afternoon, and the evening.

The relationship between mothers and adolescents is often difficult—especially between mothers and teenage girls. This difficulty is often exaggerated when one is depressed. Cheryl Townsend and her fifteen-year-old daughter, Barbara, were in continuous battle with each other. They might fight over anything, but it was usually about Barbara's weight.

When Barbara was young, Cheryl had to struggle with her to finish her meals; but when Barbara started to gain weight, they began to fight over her eating too much. Barbara would get upset when her mom told her not to eat candy and cake, yelling back at her, "It's none of your business, you miserable old bitch."

Like many mother/adolescent relationships, theirs was touched with ambivalence. When most people say they're ambivalent about a person, they really mean that they switch back and forth from like to dislike. They don't hold both points of view at the same time. Schizophrenics, however, can hold two opposing ideas in mind at the same time; they can have true ambivalence. The relationship between mothers and teenagers often comes close to this true ambivalence. Living with a person you both hate and love at the same time can be extremely stressful.

While you can improve most relationships by moving closer together, this doesn't usually hold with your adolescent children. Often you need more distance and less involvement—a degree of separation—before you can come together.

Cheryl's stress was worse because she believed her relationship with Barbara was abnormal and shouldn't be that way. But she lowered her stress by accepting the situation and realizing it would probably pass. Like Cheryl, you may be worried that your teenager won't make it as an adult. This worry is usually unfounded.

The ratio of adult behavior problems to adolescent problems is quite small. Cheryl, for example, was worried about Barbara's laziness. Most adolescents could be considered lazy. But the number of lazy adults compared to the number of lazy teenagers is small.

Many parents criticize their children for being too concerned about what the other kids will think. But really, how your child fits in with the other kids is important. Many adolescents develop trouble when they move too far away from what the other kids do. I usually draw a bell-shaped curve to illustrate this (see p. 218).

Sociologists have found that seventy percent of adolescents fall into the middle group (C). They break some rules—occasionally smoking marijuana, skipping school a couple of times, experimenting with alcohol and sex. And ninety-five percent fall into the wider middle group (B-C-D): some (B) break more rules and may even be arrested once or twice and others break very few rules (D). But the serious deviants, those who break a lot of rules and come to the attention of the courts (A) or those who break no rules and become socially isolated (E), are both small groups.

Rules for children differ according to when and where they grow up. Children from urban, high-crime areas may have brushes with the law several times and still not develop into chronic delinquents. But in a small town in Iowa, one brush with the police could start a child on a downward turn into the delinquent group.

Once your child is outside the limits of peer acceptance, problems can develop. Here, referral for outside help may be indicated. But remember, your son's or daughter's norms are different than yours and as long as they stay within their general peers' norms they'll usually be all right—even if they don't act as you wish they would.

Cheryl said that while she could see that her daughter was in the middle range of the bell curve, she still couldn't understand her daughter's behavior. Barbara's moodiness and loud outbursts baffled her.

While many mothers empathize too much with their small children, they often lack empathy for their adolescents, who themselves have so little empathy and regard for others. But you can deal better with your adolescents by seeing their world from their eyes.

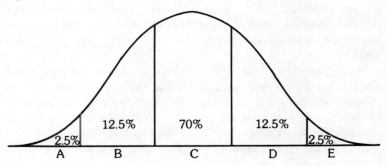

Consider adolescence as a sort of emotional disorder. Typically, teenagers are so self-absorbed, preoccupied with their own changes, that they can't be bothered relating to their parents and other adults. You might try to recall how you felt at that age to get an inkling of what they're going through.

Maintaining consistent limits and rules, however, is a good idea with children of all ages. And you can apply another principle to the raising of your children—*natural consequences.* Your son's or daughter's irresponsible behavior has its own natural negative consequences that usually act as a check on his or her behavior—if you allow them to happen.

In Barbara's case, the natural negative consequence of overeating was gaining weight. Her mother really had little control over what she ate (other than not bringing fattening foods into the house). Once Cheryl took this stance of relying on natural consequences, their relationship started to improve. When Barbara began to complain about being fat, Cheryl simply pointed out that it was the natural consequence of her own behavior and that she was the only one who could do anything about it.

If your son borrows the car and returns it on empty, the natural consequence of his irresponsibility is the loss of the privilege of driving—at least for a while. If he skips school and he's caught, the natural consequence is for him to go and face the vice-principal—without your intervention to smooth the way. If your daughter doesn't clean her room, the natural consequence is that she has to live in a dirty room. And if she doesn't pick up her clothes, she won't have clean ones to wear.

Adolescents are continually growing and changing; there's no reason to assume they're going to stay the same. Even late adolescents (nineteen to twenty-five) are developing. Young people, especially between nineteen and twenty-five, need a period of time to figure out what they want to do, to run possible life plans through their heads, to reorganize themselves.

I call this "time on the sofa." One of my uncles, after graduating from college, worked at odd jobs but spent most of his time daydreaming on the sofa, much to my grandparents' dismay. One day he abruptly announced that he was going to law school, which he did. That ended his year on the sofa.

This family story has stayed with me over the years and I've seen many friends and patients and their children going through similar periods on the sofa. Some people go through it when they're eighteen, others not until their forties. It's much easier when you're younger because it affects fewer people. Dropping out of college for a year to work or to travel has become almost a standard rite among students.

One woman said, "But what if my son never gets up off the sofa?" I told her the probability of this was low, but if he didn't, he would have to live with the consequences. And as long as you don't intervene in the natural consequences of his not working (by giving him money), he's likely to get up and start moving on his own.

She went on, "But he keeps bugging me for money and wants to use my car all the time."

Although your child's requests can be persistent, you can be just as resistant. But be prepared for the requests and demands to escalate until he *really* realizes you mean no. This woman eventually learned not to be so reactive to her son's problems and to let the natural consequences operate.

Much of your stress with your son or daughter may be caused by their sudden change from children to small adults. The way one's life can be turned upside down almost overnight has been called the "strange but exact truth." But not all changes are bad.

Alison Lurie describes Erica Tate's situation two years later:

Of course they are older—Jeffrey is 16 now and Matilda is 14—and therefore out of the house more. They are also marginally cleaner and more polite when in. Erica really has very little to do with them; she maintains certain rules and schedules, but has more or less given up trying to control what they wear or eat or read or watch on TV. In return they are minimally agreeable to her, like people forced by a war or flood or some other natural disaster to share living quarters. They have even made a few gratuitous gestures of goodwill: Jeffrey, without being asked, took down all the storm windows last month; and Matilda brought Erica's stereo back down stairs.

Once you're able to control your own reactions you may find, as Erica did, that your children change for the better.

The Stresses of Your Older Years

"OLD people are inadequate, obsolete, and a drain on society," Eunice Oliver said at our first meeting. "I can see why no one wants to be around me. I can't keep up with what's going on. I don't have anything to say to people."

Somewhere along the line, Eunice bought into a pack of negative beliefs about growing old and now that she was sixty-five herself, these beliefs were deepening her depression.

An executive secretary, she'd been active and productive until she turned sixty-five and retired. At the same time, she also resigned from clubs, stopped seeing old friends, and in general began to say no to life. The less she did, the more depressed she became. Everything seemed to support her belief, "Once you turn sixty-five, it's all over."

One out of every five women over sixty-five is depressed. And if they have physical problems, the chances of being depressed are higher. Although older people make up only ten percent of the population, they account for twenty-five percent of all suicides. The President's Commission on Mental Health found that most older Americans' depressions go untreated; and until recently, the mental health community has ignored their problem. Since older depressed people don't cause much trouble, their plight is ignored.

When you get older, new demands (job changes, retirement, geographical moves) frequently join forces with cutbacks in resources (less money and energy). When your demands outstrip your resources, you feel stress, and prolonged stress can lead in turn to depression. The first line of defense against depression is to learn to handle stress better.

Multiple losses—not only of jobs and power but also of people close to you—are a major source of stress for older people: Parents, brothers and sisters, husbands, wives, and close friends die, and situations change. Learning to cope with multiple losses is just one of the challenges to living a depression-free life.

Mislabeling depression.   When you get older, your depression is more likely to be misdiagnosed—usually as hypochondria and senility. Do you regard *nervousness, lack of energy, sleep difficulties, loss of appetite, hopelessness,* and *unhappiness* as parts of the natural aging process? Do you use them as evidence that you are old and useless? If so, you're making a mistake. These are symptoms of depression and not signs of aging. When a twenty-year-old acts this way people say, "What's wrong?" When a person in her seventies acts this way, it's "What can you expect?"

Eunice's daughter and some of her friends didn't help; they endorsed, and at times initiated, many of her negative ideas about growing old. When Eunice mentioned that she'd like to go to Europe someday, her daughter went into a long tirade, "At your age you should be thinking about slowing down, not about starting something new!"

Eunice said at our first meeting, "Things have gone downhill since I turned sixty-five. Everything was going all right until then."

I pointed out how arbitrary this was; she was drawing an imaginary line at age sixty-five that represented "old age."

She came back with, "Society says when you turn sixty-five you're old."

"Well, *old* is a relative concept." I asked, "Do you think there is a greater difference between two twenty-year-olds or two sixty-five-year-olds?"

"Well, I guess between two sixty-five-year-olds."

She was right. Studies have found that greater differences, both psychologically and physiologically, exist among older people than among younger people. It makes little sense to talk about older people as if they are all the same.

I also pointed out that she had done well last year (when she was sixty-four) and that was actually her sixty-fifth year of life. She came to see how little sense it made to change her self-concept just because she had had a birthday. Many people panic or give up when their age ends in a five or a zero.

She also saw how her belief became a *self-fulfilling prophecy;* by acting as if the belief were true, she made it so. For example, she was extremely anxious at social gatherings where the people were younger than she was. She felt like a second-class citizen. "They think I'm trying to act younger than I am because I wear bright clothes."

Later she was able to answer this type of thought with, "I don't have any evidence that they think that. Even if they do, I'm not going to wear dowdy clothes just to please them." By repeatedly responding to her own anxiety, she learned to control her social anxiety.

Barbara Walters, forty-nine, uses a similar technique when she finds herself becoming nervous in social situations. She tells herself, "I am the way I am; I look the way I look; I am my age." She reports that using this simple method is a great help in calming down.

Ageism. Many of Eunice's anxiety-causing thoughts were related to ageism, the belief that the old are innately inferior. The worst effect of ageism is that you can start to believe the negative opinions of others. You can become prejudiced against your own age group. Since stereotypes about the old are ingrained and often demeaning (just watch TV), it's hard not to buy into them. When you're older, you're in a continuous battle against adopting and acting out these beliefs.

You're more inclined to follow the age-related dictates of society ("At my age I shouldn't go to dances, roller skate, travel with a backpack, ride a bicycle, or use bad language; I should dress more conservatively, stay home at night, and invest in a burial plot").

In short, "Walk, don't run."

The older you get, the more restricted and rigid the rules: It seems as if aging is a crime and restrictions are the penalty. Learning to avoid negative attitudes about old age is a real problem for every aging person. When you're depressed, this can be an even bigger problem. You're more likely to believe, "I'm too old to have sex, to enjoy new experiences, or to have fun in general." So one of your first jobs if you're depressed is to look for and examine your ageist attitudes.

Paralysis of the will. One result of ageism is the belief that you're too old to start new activities. You may believe that it's too difficult, dangerous, or complicated, or that you're too vulnerable and weak to handle it.

To overcome this, plant a seed of doubt in your mind ("Maybe I'm mistaken, maybe I can do more than I think I can do"). Consider your beliefs ("Life is over when you're old" . . . "Old people are no fun") as opinions, not facts. Realize that opinions that may be doing you more harm than good should be examined before you accept them. Ask yourself, "What is there to gain by trying" as opposed to "What is there to lose by not trying?"

Josephine Ford was blocked from starting new activities. She'd retired five years earlier after an active career as an associate newspaper editor. She had no children and her husband had died three years earlier. She had enjoyed going to concerts in the past with her husband, but hadn't gone in several years.

When I asked her why she couldn't go she said, "It's too much of a bother to get tickets—they'll probably be sold out anyway. I can't go alone and there's no one I can go with. Even if I go, I won't enjoy myself."

She did agree that these hypotheses should be tested out—not accepted out of hand. She set up a series of experiments.

First, she analyzed her hypotheses: (1) It'd be too much trouble to get the tickets; (2) they'd be sold out; (3) I can't get anyone to go with me, and (4) I wouldn't enjoy myself.

Then she called the theater and found that they had plenty of tickets and that she could reserve two. She disproved hypotheses 1 and 2 immediately. She called a friend to see if she wanted to go. Her friend was going out of town that weekend, but suggested she call a mutual friend. She did and her other friend was glad to go, thus disproving hypothesis 3. At this point she was willing to test out hypothesis 4. She went to the concert and enjoyed it. She had disproved all four of her ideas.

By testing out her other negative beliefs, she found that she *could* still enjoy herself. Subjecting her thoughts to tests helped her to emerge eventually from her depression.

Another common age-related belief can also cause you trouble, that is, thinking that you lose all of your resources once you reach some magical age. Some of your strengths and resources may be temporarily blocked by your depression, but they can be easily regained, often quite rapidly.

One woman in her sixties came for treatments after her husband died. She said. "He supported me my whole life. I don't know what to do without him. If I were younger I could start over, but I'm too old."

She was overlooking her capabilities. She had run the family business for the last few years, during her husband's illness. She came to realize that she could continue to run it. This brought back her energy. During the next year she actually expanded the business.

Life review. You may be looking back critically over your life. It's normal to go through a period of review as you move from one life stage to another, to take stock of what you've done and what you want to do in your next period of life.

Problems arise, however, when you focus on past failures and build a case against yourself from them. You may go over old mistakes again and again in a vain attempt to change them. In the meantime, today slips away. You can get stuck in your review and have trouble moving on.

This was the problem with one seventy-four-year-old woman I saw. Her depression stemmed from her conclusion that her life was a total failure. She based this theory on two facts: She had been divorced, and one of her children had ended up in a mental institution.

We discussed these issues a number of times before she was able to see that being a mother and wife was only part of her life. She was able to see that for the most part she'd led a full life in the past and could continue to do so.

Whenever I submit a manuscript for publication, I always hope the editor isn't depressed. Depressed people have a way of only seeing shortcomings. It's not a good idea to review anything when you're depressed—restaurants, movies, books. And it's an especially bad time to review your whole life.

Remember: *Don't take inventory of your life when you're depressed.* You're much more likely to see what's missing than what's there.

Your perception of growing old. Growing older does, however, require getting used to a number of real changes. Careers end, children move away, husbands and friends die—and while your resources and physical abilities are diminishing, society continues to change and place new demands on you. Many people have problems making these lifestyle changes.

Dr. Hans Thomae of the Institute of Psychology in Bonn, Germany, has spent a number of years studying people who successfully adjust to aging. His findings are remarkably similar to observations at the Center for Cognitive Therapy. He found that *how you view growing older is more important than any other aspect of aging.* Although there are internal (biological) and external (social) factors in growing older, the most important single factor is the *meaning you assign to aging.*

For example, how you think about retirement in the years prior to it directly affects how much you enjoy it. If you expect it to be a bleak period, you're likely to have a hard time; but if you look forward to retirement, you're likely to enjoy it and have fewer adjustment problems. It's obvious that good health and enough money help, but Dr. Thomae found that how you regard retirement is more important than money or health.

Your overall perception of growing old—and the adjustment that follows—is related to how well you balance what you want with what you have. If you believe you've accomplished what you want in life, you'll make a better adjustment than if there's a big gap between what you want and what you have. Consequently, if you have problems getting used to being older, you can improve your life by creating a better balance between your achieved and desired goals.

You might be able to reach a better balance by staying active. One woman, for example, was depressed because she was forced out of her job when she turned sixty-five. She returned to school and fulfilled a life-long ambition by getting a college education. Once she recognized that she had control over her life's course, her depression left her.

Self-defeating thoughts. I'm not saying "Look at the bright side and everything will be okay." Rather, I'd suggest that you see the world as it really is. One way to do this is to correct your thinking errors.

For example, Mrs. Hector told me, "No one wants to be around old people. Yesterday my landlord didn't speak to me when I walked by him. I don't think he likes having old people in his building. I'm afraid he's going to ask me to leave so he can get young people in who'll pay more rent. I don't know what I'll do then. Nowadays you're either young and have money or you're old. And if you're old, no one wants you around."

She was making a number of thinking errors. She was *overgeneralizing:* While it is true that some people dislike and avoid older people, they aren't in the majority. She was *jumping to conclusions* about her landlord and not giving him the benefit of the doubt, since she had no evidence that he was going to evict her. She was *catastrophizing* by putting the worst possible light on the situation. She was using *either/or thinking:* a person is neither young nor old; rather, a continuum extends from youth to old age and a person's place on the continuum is not determined by numerical age. A baseball player may be old at thirty-five with respect to his athletic function, while a senator may be young at sixty-five.

Mrs. Hector's "homework" was to talk to the landlord and find out where she stood with him. When she mentioned the incident, he apologized and said that he must have been daydreaming because he didn't remember seeing her. He also said that he was happy to have her in his building, and that he liked having older tenants. They were reliable, and because many didn't work, they helped keep an eye on the place.

I don't mean to be a Pollyanna about the elderly's plight, nor do I believe that all of their problems are in their heads. The aged in our society face numerous real problems: loss of income, serious health problems such as loss of sight and hearing, the death of close relatives and friends, and increased vulnerability to the hazards of modern society. Still, many of these concerns have a psychological aspect. See Table 18 for some other examples of self-defeating thinking.

Practical problems. Working to solve your practical concerns can actually be good medicine for your depression. One patient was depressed and anxious because her husband's upcoming retirement would mean less income. I asked her husband to come in and we discussed their budget. It became clear that they had enough money to live on, but that they would have to stop the regular allotments they were giving their two grown children. It was painful for them to tell the children, but it relieved much of her anxiety.

TABLE 18
Examples of Self-Defeating Thoughts About Being Old

1. There's nothing to live for.
2. I'm obsolete.
3. No one wants to be around me.
4. Things aren't as good as they used to be.
5. Kids today don't know how to act.
6. I'm too old to learn new ideas.
7. I shouldn't do anything that is inappropriate for my age.
8. My kids owe it to me to have me over more often.
9. If I join the new senior citizens' club, they'll think I'm lonely.
10. There's no need to be friendly to the girl who lives next door; she's too young to be my friend.
11. The butcher tries to cheat me because I'm so old.
12. The doctor doesn't want to be bothered with me. He says I'm fine when I feel bad.
13. Exercising won't do any good—when you're old you're rusty.
14. I can't wear the scarf my kids gave me—it's too youthful for me.
15. I'd like to have dinner with Mr. Jones, but my kids would think I'm silly.
16. Mr. Jones and I are too old to hold hands and act romantic.
17. I can't invite my teenage grandkids to visit; I'm too old to show them a good time.
18. I can't go swimming in my kids' pool. I'm too old to wear a swimsuit.
19. I'm too old to get a pet.
20. My kids and grandkids should call and visit more. They should respect me.

The more you know about community resources the better you'll be able to solve practical concerns. Social agencies can provide help with housing, health, legal services, and transportation. There are also specialized programs like Foster Grandparents and athletic programs for the elderly.

Loss of memory and the ability to concentrate. Sometimes what looks like a practical problem may actually be a problem you've created in your mind. For example, you may believe that you have lost or are losing your mind, when you really haven't. This is a common problem with depressed older people.

When you get older you'll experience a slight decrease in your ability to remember or to solve abstract problems. This loss, however, is generally so slight as to be only a mild annoyance. But many depressed people become so convinced that they have suffered serious memory loss that they convince both doctors and family members of it, too. They may frequently end up labeled as senile.

In an important study on memory among the elderly, researchers at the University of Chicago found that many memory complaints weren't related to actual ability to remember but to depression. Older individuals with actual memory impairment often didn't recognize they had problems.

The researchers also found that family members made unreliable observers. They generally agreed that their relative had a memory impairment. But in actual tests, the patients' memories were better than half of the relatives' memories! My observations corroborate this experiment: Complaints about loss of memory and ability to concentrate are more often signs of depression than signs of brain deterioration.

Dr. Corbitt is a good example. Before her retirement she'd been a university professor, the author of several books, and a national leader in her field. She valued her mind highly. When she began to believe that she was losing her ability to think, she went into a deep depression. She was considering suicide because, as she told me, "Now that my brain is gone, what's the point of living?"

Like many older people, Dr. Corbitt was caught up in a vicious cycle. She became depressed; as a result, her thinking slowed down a bit. She then began to believe that her mind was going; the more convinced she became of this the more depressed she became. She'd even managed to convince her husband that her mind was gone. She, like many depressed women, mislabeled her own symptoms.

Instead of accepting Dr. Corbitt's diagnosis of her problem, I gave her a series of tests and memory tasks. I asked her to read and to memorize passages out of books. As she began to prove to herself that she could still think and remember, her depression lifted and thoughts of suicide vanished. If there had been any real signs of brain damage, I would have referred her to a specialist.

Grief reaction. One of the realities of growing older is that many of those close to you die. Often, people don't let the natural process of coming to terms with death unfold, so their grief is prolonged or turns into depression. If someone close to you dies, be aware of the factors involved in resolving grief:

1. *Denial.* Immediately after the loss you'll probably go through a period of denial. You won't believe the person is gone. You'll find yourself making plans that include the other. In general, you'll be acting *as if* the person isn't dead.

   At first, denial can be adaptive; it gives you a chance to make sense of the confusion. Richard Lazarus, a major stress researcher, points out, "In severe crisis, denial buys preparation time; it lets the person face the grim facts at a gradual, manageable pace." However, if your denial goes on too long, it can prolong your grief.

2. *Emotions.* Sadness is the most useful emotion to have when you've recently suffered a loss. Sadness leads you to look at the reality of the loss. By thinking about the loss, you're moving toward accepting it. Accepting it is how you get over it.

   On the other hand, guilt isn't helpful. Patients with prolonged grief often feel guilty, believing that they could have prevented the death or treated the person much better. Guilt often wards off your sadness. One woman said, "Guilt doesn't feel as bad as sadness." Guilt also implies that the situation could be different or changed, while sadness is more final. One of the first steps to accepting your loss is overcoming your guilt.

3. *Avoidance.* In the first stage of grief you probably won't want to do things or go places or be around objects that remind you of the person who is gone. It's important, however, that you start to approach the things that bring up these memories. The memories will bring on sadness and the sadness will help resolve your grief.

People with a prolonged grief reaction avoid painful memories and acceptance of the loss. One effective treatment of prolonged grief is to flood the patient with memories of the person who is dead. While this can be extremely painful (and should be carried out by a competent professional), it does help the person accept the loss.

4. *Role of others.* If you're going through a loss, you may not know how to respond to others—what to say, what to do. Their reactions to the loss complicate this uncertainty. Some people can be very helpful and supportive, while others can make you feel more guilty and wrong. Most people don't know what to say to *you* either.

Often, people's expectations are contradictory. One person might expect you to be extremely mournful and tearful, while another expects you to act stoically like your old self.

How should you act? Most cultures ritualize mourning; for example, you'd wear black for a year. But in our culture there are no rules: You can act the way you choose. However you decide to act, remember that you don't have to talk to people who aren't helpful.

On the other hand, be sure to talk to *someone* about how you feel. Your friends and family want to provide support after your loss.

However, if your grief period is too long and postponed, you'll find that there isn't as much support available. One of the arguments against giving drugs to someone going through bereavement is that drugs mask grief at a time when others are there to provide support. Later, when you stop taking the drugs, your support system may be gone, as friends and family return home.

Your overall goal is normalization of your life so that you can get on with living as happily and productively as possible.

Mildred Lane couldn't get over her depression until she came to terms with her grief over her husband's death. They'd been married forty-two years. In normal grief reaction you reconcile the loss of an important part of your past with the need to move on without the other person. Most people get through this painful process. Others, who hold certain beliefs that turn grief into depression, don't.

In Mildred's case, her beliefs were related to helplessness. She found comfort simply in talking about her irrational ideas, such as her anger at her husband for dying. What finally helped Mildred was concluding that her husband wasn't completely gone because he'd left an important part of himself with her. With the realization that he would want her to get on with her life and not to get bogged down in depression, she became more self-reliant.

Physical problems.   While you should go to your family doctor for any undiagnosed physical complaints, you can work on the psychological aspects of illness yourself. Researchers have found that your state of mind can help in managing a range of physical ailments such as diabetes, stroke, and other neurological disorders.

Flora Wayne suffered from arthritis, in addition to depression. She discovered that the pain became worse whenever she would worry about her problem. She learned to control her pain by forcing herself to think about something else.

I suggest the following methods for coping with a physical problem:

1. *Recognize and change unproductive thoughts and exaggerations about the problem* ("I can't put up with it" . . . "Why me?"). This isn't easy, and it takes time, but you can learn to do it.
2. *Don't talk about the problem.* Talking about your aches and pains not only is unpleasant for others but intensifies your own awareness of them. Flora found it helpful not to talk to her husband about the pain.
3. *Stop activities that may remind you of the problem,* such as extra visits to the doctor's office. If you have chronic pain, don't read medical journals as a hobby.

4. *Learn coping skills that can take your attention away from the discomfort.* Something as simple as starting to read when the pain occurs may distract you from it.
5. *Do what the doctor tells you and take your medicine as prescribed.* Many women with physical illnesses are so overwhelmed with depression that they forget even the most basic relief procedures.
6. *Keep an open mind.* One patient blamed her depression on a pain in her stomach. She'd had two extensive medical examinations and nothing physically wrong with her was found, yet she refused treatment when told that it would be primarily psychological.

Children. Many depressed older people have unrealistic beliefs about how their children should treat them. Maybe they don't visit or call often enough. Perhaps you remember a time when children took care of their elderly parents. If so, you may expect more from your kids than what they consider reasonable.

Hazel Upton fluctuated between anger and depression. One moment she would think her kids were selfish for not calling or visiting more; the next she would berate herself for being a failure as a parent. She came to see that her children had developed their moral and ethical values from many life experiences over the years; her parenting was just one of the elements in their education.

Social interaction and help from others. Hazel also suffered from some rather autocratic beliefs, which were not in her best interest, about how others should treat her. She didn't speak up when slighted because she believed others should know enough to treat older people with respect; when her children called, she became angry with them for not calling more often, which caused them to call even less; she didn't initiate social contact because she believed that at her age she was entitled to have people come to her. With work, she turned most of her self-defeating attitudes and actions around.

Rosemarie had other sorts of problems. She had moved back to her hometown to be near her relatives. They were quite attentive initially, but then gradually spent less time with her. She didn't know why. She became depressed and came in for treatment. She'd never asked her relatives why they'd lost interest in her, so her therapist suggested that her daughter and granddaughter come in for a session. The daughter said that her mother didn't listen to others, that she only wanted to talk about herself, and that she didn't acknowledge gifts and attention when they were given to her. The granddaughter agreed. Rosemarie was greatly taken aback. Later she was glad she had the information.

She started improving her social skills. Social contacts that are rewarded or rewarding tend to be repeated, so she started rewarding those who spent extra time with her. She acknowledged their thoughtfulness and tried to make her conversations more satisfying to them. She also started asking questions to let the person know she was listening. Within six months, Rosemarie's daughter noted a remarkable improvement in Rosemarie's way of relating to her and to other family members.

Ask someone close to you, such as your husband, your child, or a friend, to give you feedback on how you interact with others. Ask him to be honest and objective. It may be hard to do, but the suggestions he gives will justify the effort. Others *can* help you with your depression.

One elderly woman believed that she was unable to find any pleasure in life. She asked her daughter to help her keep a record of the times when she actually did enjoy herself. With her daughter's help, she began to recognize all the little activities that brought her pleasure.

Some general guidelines for coping with the depression of aging:

* *Make an effort to meet new people.* Social isolation increases your vulnerability to depression. You need people to talk to, people to help you keep your thinking straight. Don't rely on your children for all of your social life. Twenty percent of all people over sixty-five never have had children, yet they have good social lives.

When you meet new people, don't expect them to be exactly as you would like them to be. Part of being a friend is accepting the shortcomings along with the qualities you admire or enjoy.

Learn to appreciate the whole person, just as you would like to be appreciated.

- *Part of good mental health is taking chances.* Follow up a first meeting with a phone call. Force yourself to go to places that cause anxiety, places where there are crowds, for instance. Make an effort to learn something new, even though you might not be successful at what you try. The experience of learning something new offsets the risk. The mind is like other parts of your body— you use it or lose it. Furthermore, if you don't take chances, your life becomes increasingly restricted. With restriction come irritation, pettiness, and—worst of all—boredom for all concerned.

- *Make your own decisions.* Too often older people let others make their decisions, ranging from where to eat to where to live. Within reason, try to do what *you* want to do. Keep in mind that making good decisions depends on being open to new information, to the opinions and ideas of others. Tell yourself that decisions are, after all, reversible: If you move to a place you don't like, you can always move again. Remember, as a general rule, not to make major decisions when you're depressed. Wait until you feel better and your mind is free to think clearly.

- *Develop tolerance of others.* Our society often casts the aged as weak and incompetent, yet they may see themselves as active and competent. This social typecasting is so strong that you may resolve the conflict by yielding to the pressure of the stereotype and adopting more negative self-concepts. As a result, you may become angry at those you believe are responsible for this unfriendly and destructive bias.

It's not surprising that many old people are constantly angry —if you consider the way others use them. Hazel Upton resented people she didn't even know calling her by her first name. She also resented being told what to do instead of being consulted first about her choices.

Another woman was angry because, "Friends and relatives are always comparing me to other old people—usually to some ninety-five-year-old woman who climbs mountains."

It's important to stand up for your rights and to ask others not to patronize you, but chronic anger (expressed or not) causes more harm to you than to those with whom you're angry. And anger has a worse aspect: It drives off would-be friends just when you need them the most. People in general are quite ignorant about the process of growing old, and the best stance to take is one of tolerance—if possible, humorous tolerance—of their ignorance.

- *Don't buy society's stereotypes of the old.* What's the best way to deal with people who are ignorant about aging? Don't make a big issue out of your age. Don't use your "years" as an excuse for not doing something. The fact that you don't want to do something is reason enough. But don't go to the other extreme and hide your age as though it were something to be ashamed of.

  Some older women never let anyone see their social security checks for fear that their age will be revealed. They're simply surrendering to the stereotype. Your age is a neutral fact; there's nothing intrinsically good or bad about it.

- *Investigate volunteer work.* Many older people have skills highly valued by hospitals, nonprofit arts organizations, museums, schools, churches, and temples. Even political organizations usually want someone to help with the phones. To line up meaningful volunteer work takes persistence, but the payoff in terms of what you can contribute and gain is worth it.

- *Don't overlook the effects your body has on your mind and emotions.* Most older people take some medicine. The older you are, the greater the possibility of a drug reaction. If you're concerned about your medication and its effects, talk to your doctor. Don't just decide on your own to stop taking it. To keep track of how the medication affects you, write down the time at which you took it and how you felt afterward, and report this to your doctor. If necessary, get a second opinion from another doctor.

- *Try to exercise.* Exercise is one of the most beneficial ways to maintain your health. Walking is an excellent way to build your energy level, stimulate your metabolism, and maintain muscular strength. Yoga exercises can be learned in local classes—or even from a TV program—and can be adapted to your own capacity. Dancing is not only good exercise, but it's fun—and pleasure is an essential ingredient of healthful living. Whenever possible, enrich your exercise experience with some pleasurable accompaniment, such as playing music while exercising indoors or taking a friend along on your walk, even if it's only a friend of the canine variety.

- *Watch your nutrition.* Sometimes depression is exaggerated by malnutrition, known as the *"tea-and-biscuit" syndrome.* It isn't always easy to cook for yourself, or perhaps it doesn't seem worth the effort, but it's crucial that you have nutritious meals. In recognition of this problem, many recipes (and entire cookbooks, in fact) have been written to help the single person—young or old—enjoy the preparation of tasty and nutritious meals for one. Think of yourself as your own guest. Make everything as tasty and as aesthetically enjoyable as you would for a guest you especially want to please.

- *Don't be afraid to go for counseling.* You may believe you aren't entitled to such help. You don't want to be a burden or a bother to others. If the situation were reversed, would you insist someone you love seek treatment if he were suffering and in need of help? Some older people refuse to go for counseling because they mistakenly believe that it would indicate that they're "crazy" or "ready to be locked up." Once they get into counseling, they realize that precisely the opposite is the case. If they were candidates for an institution, they probably would lack the good sense and initiative to seek treatment.

  Although some mental health workers have a bias against treating older people, many counselors enjoy their contacts with older people. Studies indicate that most older patients respond well to therapy. I've found that not only do the older patients respond quickly to treatment, but in general they make more progress more rapidly than many of the younger patients. They don't seem to want to spend a lot of time in therapy; they're more interested in getting better and moving on to live their lives in a more richly satisfying way.

- *Build self-reliance.* At each life stage you must meet specific challenges in order to become a self-directed and self-reliant person. When you're young, it might mean breaking away from your parents to lead your own life, or in your middle years, forming a balance between what you want and what others want from you at home or at work. The elderly often have trouble maintaining a positive self-image because their increasing dependency interferes with their desire to be self-reliant.

When an older woman becomes depressed, she may find people around her assuming she's more dependent than she really is. Eventually, she may give up and let others take over for her; she doesn't want to run the risk of being considered eccentric, cantankerous, or even stubbornly self-reliant. To avoid this, it's important for you as an older woman to carry on with the activities that you know you enjoy—especially those that contribute to society and put you in touch with others.

XIII

Developing Self-Reliance

A woman "needs the man she loves to help her stand." So goes a popular song. A commonly seen bumper sticker takes the opposite point of view: "A woman without a man is like a fish without a bicycle." These two seemingly dissimilar mottoes share a point of view. Thinking that you can't live without a man is as extreme as believing that you shouldn't even bother with men. The first thought leads to dependency; the latter to isolation; and both frequently lead to depression.

After patients are over their depression, I often suggest that they work on becoming more self-reliant. Many patients aren't concerned about future depressions. They often say, "Why should I worry about that? I know I won't get depressed again." I remind them that self-reliance not only buys insurance against future depression, but it's a way to increase your enjoyment of life.

I also remind them that getting depressed is just about the worst predicament that you can get into. If something unfortunate happens to you (you lose an eye) it may affect a specific area of your life (your vision), but far worse, it may lead to depression—and depression affects *every* aspect of your life, making you unable to enjoy the good things left to you, such as your family and friends (or in this case, your other senses).

After you get over depression, however, you often forget how bad it was. You shouldn't forget, because you have to be on guard against getting depressed again. You'll always be vulnerable to depression.

Dependency and isolation. People at the extremes of life often have the most trouble. If you're too rich or too poor, too smart or undereducated, you're likely to have more problems than the average person. Similarly, if you're too dependent on other people or too isolated from others, you're more prone to depression. The antidote to both dependency and isolation is self-reliance.

When you're acting in a dependent way, you believe you can carry out activities *only with the help of others*. One woman, for example, wanted to see more movies, but because she had no one with whom to go, she didn't. She had a number of reasons for not going alone ("I can't decide on what movie to see" . . . "I won't know what to do if someone bothers me" . . . "If I see someone I know, I'll be ashamed about being there alone").

How does dependency relate to depression? Intensified dependency is a major symptom of depression. If you're mildly depressed you may *feel an urge* to have more and more done for you, an urge that goes beyond any realistic expectations for help. In moderate depression, the *wish* for help is elevated to a *need* for help. You want others to make phone calls for you and intercede on your behalf in everyday affairs. You seek help before trying to do anything yourself. In severe depression, you *want someone to do everything for you*. You don't want advice on solving problems, you want someone else to solve the problem. In one case, a patient wanted the psychiatrist to adopt her children and raise them for her.

But dependency is only one side of the problem. The isolation of many women who withdraw from others plays an equally big role in depression. When you're acting in an isolated way, you believe you can adequately perform on your own, *but not with others*. One of my patients went to the movies alone five or six times a week—sometimes twice in the same day. Although she complained of loneliness, she wouldn't ask others to go with her ("Other people won't like the same movie I do—they might ruin it for me" . . . "I'd be uncomfortable watching the movie with somebody" . . . "I won't be able to discuss the movie intelligently afterward").

If you actively avoid others and want to be by yourself, you may notice that the desire for withdrawal increases when you become more depressed. You become more and more of a loner and spend your time thinking of diversion. You may lose yourself in escapism —reading, going to movies, watching television, taking tranquilizers, or drinking. You may have fantasies of going to a deserted tropical island or moving to a strange city. One woman said, "I'd like to run off to someplace like New Orleans where no one knows me and become a typist or something." In severe cases, you may hide from others. One woman didn't answer the phone or the door. She spent most of her time in bed and when others approached she hid under the covers. Some respond to their isolation by increasing their dependency on alcohol or drugs, or on excessive eating or smoking.

Rapid social change has knocked the props out from under many traditional institutions. Church, family, and other cultural traditions once provided specific guidelines on how people should lead their lives. Although often narrow and constrictive, the guidelines provided consistency and reduced dilemmas.

With their disappearance, people began to use others' reactions as guides for how to act, think and feel. The result can be over-reliance on the opinions of others, which leads to dependency and depression. Or, fearing dependency, you may avoid others, which leads to isolation and depression. Both dependency and isolation mean that you're giving too much power to others.

HOW TO INCREASE SELF-RELIANCE

The solution to both isolation and dependency is to develop self-reliance. As a self-reliant person, you'll have confidence in your ability to handle new and difficult situations—including dealing with other people. I should point out here that I'm not talking about a general lack of confidence. You have confidence, but of what? When you're acting dependently, you're confident that you *can't do it on your own*. When you're isolated, you're confident you *don't need or want anyone else*.

Self-reliance training. Most people develop self-reliance as children. Wise parents encourage and even push their children to try activities on their own, giving them many chances to fail or succeed without the help of others. Through such training a person forms a self-image, a set of beliefs about her competency.

However, often a person has not developed adequate self-reliance as a child or has had her sense of self-reliance weakened by depression. Fortunately, there's another way to develop a healthy self-image: *You can give yourself self-reliance training.* This isn't as difficult as it might sound. You can rapidly increase your sense of self-reliance by putting yourself on a gradual but persistent program.

When I explained this to one patient, Lillian Morris, she said, "Even *you* say it takes a child years to learn to be self-reliant. How can I possibly teach myself in a short time?"

I told her that children usually take six or seven years to learn to read at a reasonable level, yet an average illiterate adult can learn how to read quickly. Educational psychologists found during World War Two that new recruits from isolated areas such as Appalachia could learn to read in a few months—because they were motivated. They saw the benefit in being able to read and were developmentally prepared to learn. The same holds true for learning to be more self-reliant.

1. *First, you must remove any blocks you have to being self-reliant.* One of the most common is confusing self-reliance with dependency or isolation. Lillian, for example, thought that acting less dependently would turn her into a social isolate. And many isolated people fear that moving toward self-reliance leads to dependency. You should know the differences between the three ways of acting. In Table 19, I've compared dependency, isolation, and self-reliance, and in Table 20, I've given some examples of each.   Another major block to self-reliance is underlying beliefs that predispose you toward dependency or isolation.

   You may have formed beliefs about yourself and the world that are conducive to dependency and isolation. Some common beliefs that lead to dependency are: "I don't measure up to others" . . . "Bad things happen when I stand up for myself" . . . "The world is a dangerous place" . . . "I have to be able to do something perfectly before I will do it at all."

TABLE 19
Comparison of Dependency, Isolation, and Self-Reliance

	Dependency	Isolation	Self-Reliance
Interpersonal behavior	Leans on others. Other-directed. Overly focused on others.	Avoids others. Social isolation. Overly focused on self.	Moves toward others. True relationship based on sense of independence.
Seen by others	Helpless. "Needy." Clinging.	Aloof. Narcissistic. Closed.	Mature. Capable. Open.
Self-disclosure	Overdisclosure.	Underdisclosure.	Discloses appropriate to situation.
Choices	Constricted range of choices.	Constricted range of choices.	Wide range of choices.
Feelings	Moves from one extreme to another. Feels helpless.	Typically flat. Feels alienated.	Appropriate to situation.
Fears	Fears being alone, becoming social isolate.	Fears being with others, becoming dependent.	Few interpersonal fears.
Self-evaluation	Indirect self-acceptance based on others' opinions.	Indirect self-acceptance based on own achievements.	Direct self-acceptance. Minimal self-evaluation.
Assumptions	I need others. I can't work alone.	I don't need anybody. Others let me down.	I don't need others but I enjoy them.

TABLE 20
Examples of Dependency, Isolation, and Self-Reliance

	Dependency	Isolation	Self-Reliance
PATIENT IN THERAPY			
Number of problems	Overwhelms therapist. Therapist has to distill problems to manageable number.	Underwhelms therapist. Therapist has to draw problems out.	Brings in enough problems to work on in session and no more.
Problem solving	Wants therapist to solve problems; believes it's therapist's job.	Won't let therapist help; believes should be able to solve problem on own.	Forms alliance with therapist to solve problems.
Mechanics of therapy	Tries to extend length of session.	Misses sessions. Doesn't return phone calls.	Follows appropriate limits in therapy.
Termination	Doesn't want to end therapy. Returns for treatment even when can handle problems on own.	Premature termination. Doesn't return for treatment until problem is severe.	Terminates when ready and returns when appropriate.
MARRIAGE			
Trust	Overtrusts husband's ability and undertrusts own.	Undertrusts husband's ability and overtrusts own.	Trusts husband's ability and own.
Decision making	Asks husband to make nearly all decisions.	Makes decisions unilaterally without husband.	Can make own decisions based on all available information. Shares decision making.

Control	Gives up control easily to husband.	Doesn't give up control to husband.	Can lead or follow.
Crisis	Overreacts. Wants to share all aspects with husband.	Underreacts. Won't let husband in on thinking.	Works with husband to solve problem.
EMPLOYMENT			
Job-finding strategy	Expects agencies and others to find job. Takes another along on interview.	Doesn't tell of looking for work, thus misses opportunities.	Doesn't hide unemployment, and seeks job on own.
Level of employment	Often underemployed due to lack of confidence in own ability.	Often underemployed due to lack of confidence in interpersonal skills.	Employed to potential.
On the job	Has work checked excessively.	Doesn't ask for help for work not sure of.	Asks for help in work can't do on own.
Perceived by supervisor	Lacks initiative; easy to manage but lacks self-management.	Not team player; goes off "half-cocked."	Responsible, can be counted on.

Typical beliefs that lead to isolation are: "Other people will let me down" . . . "Every time I get involved with others they hurt me" . . . "If I do something for others I'm in debt to them" . . . "If people find out too much about me, they'll use it against me." . . . "When people get to know me, they find out I don't measure up." These negative beliefs must be discovered and changed. (See Chapter X).

2. *The next step is to take stock of your self-reliance.* You'll find that you already have a base on which to build and you'll be able to see what skills need to be reactivated and sharpened. For instance, you may find that you're extremely self-reliant on your job but overly dependent in intimate relationships.

You can ask yourself the following questions to see where you lack self-reliance. Do I take care of my basic needs: cooking, clothing, transportation, housing? Do I have my own source (or potential source) of money? Are my emotions dependent on others' actions or events outside myself? Can I go out to social events, parties, meetings by myself? Can I enjoy myself alone? Can I make decisions on my own? Do I trust my own judgment? Do I have confidence in my taste? Do I have close friends? Can I accept help from others? Do I isolate myself from others at work?

From these questions make a list of self-reliant activities you want to work on. Although you may not want to face these situations yet, just making list is in itself a first act of self-reliance.

3. Based on your list of situations, *deliberately choose at least one situation a day in which to be self-reliant.* Gradually you can increase the number of times per day, or you can choose one situation during the day and another one during the evening.

Choose a situation that is challenging but not so difficult that you won't attempt it. For example, you might decide to rewire a lamp instead of having someone do it for you. Or you might make a difficult phone call that you've been putting off.

To avoid discouragement at the beginning of your self-reliance training, think of your life in day-tight compartments. Instead of worrying about how you're going to become more and more self-reliant, just concentrate on carrying out your intentions for twenty-four hours. When the next twenty-four hours come along, concentrate on them alone.

4. *Keep a detailed record of what you do, when you do it, and most important, how you feel while doing it and after you finish.* You might also want to jot down any misgivings you may have had before attempting it. Note whether your predictions of a "bad" result came true.

After you've had a few self-reliance experiences, write down what they mean to you. After you get used to keeping your detailed records you might want to add more details, such as a rating of your degree of self-reliance on a scale of 0 to 100, or a rating of the degree of anxiety associated with your action. Remember, the act of keeping good records in itself indicates self-reliance.

5. *Gradually increase the number of self-reliance activities.* In order to make the most of this step, study your records to see if you've left out any important activities. The most formidable enemy of self-reliance is avoidance. If there are important tasks you've been putting off, write them down for scheduling.

6. *Analyze and take on more complicated activities,* such as some of the self-reliance skills you want to reactivate. For instance, suppose you've been avoiding living on your own. Write down the various steps involved, such as sorting out your money, looking in the newspaper for an apartment, deciding on the area, all the way up to getting the phone turned on after you move in. Decide how many of the tasks on your list you can tackle in one day, schedule accordingly, and then do them. Other more complicated activities—such as taking a trip by yourself, starting school, or finding a new, more challenging job —can also be broken down into separate tasks.

When you're ready for more complicated action, pause and notice how you feel about yourself. Often when you move from helplessness to resourcefulness, you find yourself making a cognitive leap. You become motivated to aim at more difficult assignments.

Keep in mind that self-reliance skills take a while to develop; they usually can't be switched to full power overnight. Realize that it may take six to twelve months for your new self-reliance behaviors to become automatic. Don't run the risk of discouragement by attempting too much at first.

Motivation. When you start acting more self-reliant you may feel strange. Lillian Morris felt odd when she began to act more emotionally self-reliant and decided not to take her children's or husband's problems as her own. She said, "I feel like it isn't the real me . . . like I'm doing something that I'm not supposed to do."

But by not backing away from her strange feelings, her new ways of acting started to feel more natural. Eventually she found she didn't have to force herself to be self-reliant.

If you have a problem with social withdrawal or isolation, you might feel like a phony when you move toward people. Many people go back to their old habits rather than wait out this discomfort. But you can overcome this block if you *expect* and *accept* these feelings, instead of using them as reasons or excuses for avoiding the difficulty of the moment.

To reinforce your motivation, you might want to pretend that you're someone whose strength and self-reliance you admire. One patient who had difficulty returning unsatisfactory merchandise pretended to be her sister, who was a self-confident and self-reliant individual. The patient was surprised at how easily she fell into the role.

Another way to keep your motivation up is to remind yourself why you want to be more self-reliant. Most people's self-change programs (jogging, dieting, or carrying out New Year's resolutions) usually fail—mainly because they forget why they started them in the first place. You can avoid this by periodically reviewing your reasons for wanting to be more independent.

If you want to increase the chances that you'll carry out your intentions, try the *"out-on-a-limb"* method. Make a decision that involves the completion of many smaller tasks. One person, for examply, decided to go on a camping trip alone. She was forced to become self-reliant in many small ways to survive the trip. Another person invited some friends over for dinner. He had to plan the meal, shop, cook, and clean in order to live up to his expectations of himself.

Or you can try the *commitment* technique. Before you carry out your self-reliance plan, tell others about it. One woman, for instance, wanted to increase her self-reliance by spending the weekend by herself in New York City. She told everyone that she was going to do it, made hotel reservations for two days, and promised friends to bring back catalogues and postcards from the various museums she planned to visit. This helped her avoid the temptation of staying in her hotel room for the whole weekend.

Another way to boost your motivation is to *make a production out of your self-reliance activity.* A woman who had become depressed after her husband's death had stopped going out to dinner because she had enjoyed it so much in his company that she couldn't bear to dine alone in public. When she was over her depression, she decided to practice her self-reliance by going out to a restaurant by herself. She found that she could carry it off more confidently by asking the waiter for a better table, asking to see the wine list, and in general doing all the things which she had relied upon her husband to do.

Sex roles. Dependency often shows up in connection with what people perceive as sex roles. Many men, used to having women take care of the cooking, cleaning, and children, feel helpless if they have to do this themselves for any length of time. Some women feel inept, helpless, and dependent about car maintenance, income tax preparation, financial arrangements, household repairs, and other so-called "male jobs."

To overcome this type of dependency, you can gradually learn how to handle challenges that are roadblocks to the development of your self-reliance.

Some women are afraid that others will be turned off if they become too self-reliant and that they'll end up lonely instead of self-reliant. Test out this idea by asking some of your relatives or acquaintances how they feel about your becoming more self-reliant. Don't be surprised if some of your friends haven't even noticed a change. But also be prepared for some encouragement. Generally, competency is more attractive than helplessness.

Some warnings. Occasionally close friends or relatives contribute to your dependency by taking over responsibilities that should be yours. As you gain more self-reliance, you may find yourself in conflict with such people.

Practice assertiveness by simply expressing what you consider to be your rights. Explain that you need to develop your own abilities and that you don't want to miss any opportunities to practice. It's important that on your road to self-reliance you discuss this issue with significant people in your life. In fact, you could schedule such a discussion as one of your important self-reliance training activities.

You may begin to feel anxiety over self-reliance activities. Interpret this as a good sign, a signal that you're demanding more of yourself, taking more risks—in short, improving.

As you progress in becoming more self-reliant, expect some setbacks and discouragement. All human progress is subject to unevenness. You can overcome temporary difficulties by making sure that you stick to your schedule in spite of discouragement. Promise yourself a reward of some sort for your stick-to-itiveness, or deny yourself a reward if you don't carry out your plan. One woman didn't watch any television until she had performed her scheduled self-reliance activity. Another woman read her favorite magazine for an extra half-hour if she increased her number of self-reliance activities.

THE BENEFITS OF SELF-RELIANCE

When you adopt a self-reliant lifestyle, you'll find your life becoming richer. Here are some of the ways your life will be improved:

1. *You'll become less vulnerable to emotional disorders.* When you're emotionally self-reliant, you're in charge of your feelings. You still have the normal range of feelings, but you don't react to others' actions or to events with extreme emotions.

   I recently saw a fifty-five-year-old woman in therapy. She had led a rich and varied life, but she'd always remained emotionally dependent on her husband. This had become progressively worse over the years. His rages and irate behavior would send her into deep depression.

   Our explicit therapeutic contract was for her to become emotionally self-reliant. She said if she wasn't able to do this she was going to get a divorce. We worked on specific ways she could learn to control her emotions. She made quick and excellent progress and learned how to maintain control over her emotions despite how her husband acted.

2. *Your self-esteem will go up.* The more you move from helplessness toward resourcefulness, the better you'll feel about yourself. What you think and feel about yourself depends largely on what you do. You watch how you act and then evaluate yourself accordingly.

One patient was initially reluctant to go anywhere by herself. After she'd successfully spent an enjoyable day in the city by herself, I asked her she felt about this.

She said, "I felt real good about it."

"Why do you think you felt that way?" I asked.

"Well, I did something I didn't think I could do."

"And what does that mean to you?"

"I guess it means I'm more capable than I thought." As she did more for herself, her feelings of inferiority began to disappear.

3. *You'll become more efficient.* The belief that it's easier to get someone to do your work for you is a common fallacy. Your life runs more smoothly and efficiently when you can take care of your own business. People will spend three days trying to get someone to type a report they could do themselves in an hour.

A writer I know tried to increase his writing time by building up a support staff to take care of his daily demands. He had someone do his shopping, make his reservations, schedule his appointments. He finally got rid of this support system because he found he had to spend so much time telling other people what he wanted and correcting their mistakes that he never had any time for writing.

One woman made learning to drive one of her self-reliance goals. Once she started to drive, she made several discoveries. She found that many people over the years had secretly resented having to drive her around. She also discovered that because she didn't have to spend so much time arranging and waiting for rides, she had much more free time.

4. *You'll be able to handle everyday stress more effectively.* Researchers have found the more you believe you can determine your own fate, the better you'll be able to deal with stress and meet challenges.

One woman I saw found her job stressful because she had to work with some difficult people. On a Friday she had a bad quarrel with several co-workers. Over the weekend she became quite depressed about facing them Monday morning. She decided that she would be emotionally self-reliant and not upset herself over her co-workers.

When she went in on Monday, rather than acting angry and cold to the others and feeling self-conscious, she used the critical incident technique. She came in with a smile and asked pleasantly how her co-workers' weekends had been. Though caught by surprise, their response was a positive one, which set the tone for the rest of the day.

When you decide to take control over your life, you increase your resources for handling stress.

5. *You won't be intimidated by others.* You'll be intimidated by others if you believe you need something from them—the more dependent you are, the more you'll be intimidated.

When you're self-reliant, you're not intimidated by others because you know you don't need them to take care of you or to give you a stamp of approval.

For example, Linda Young felt intimidated about many matters after her divorce. When she had overcome her depression, she decided to develop self-reliance about car maintenance, primarily because she'd always been intimidated by mechanics and gas station attendants.

She started by learning how to pump her own gas at a self-service station. Next, she learned how to change a tire. Finally, she enrolled in a course for women on car maintenance, and eventually became more than adequate in taking care of her car. She discovered that auto mechanics was largely common sense. She also realized that she'd been working with machines her whole life (women, in general, handle more machines at home and in the office than men). She had just had a block about doing what she hadn't tried before. Once Linda realized she wasn't dependent on the mechanics' whims, she stopped being intimidated by them.

6. *Your relationships with others will improve.* When you believe you need others to support you, you drive them off. A vicious cycle begins. The more they move away from you, the more you try to grab on.

The opposite happens when you're self-reliant. People will be less guarded and more relaxed when you don't act like you want something from them. Because they'll feel more comfortable, they'll move toward you.

When you're self-reliant, you'll also be more comfortable with yourself. You won't feel that you have to act in ways calculated to please others.

Your true self—how you really are—is nearly always more attractive than your social facade. When you're self-reliant, you feel free to be yourself and this makes you a better person to be around.

7. *You'll increase your freedom.* When you're depressed, your freedom is severely limited. Your feelings and behaviors are constricted. You don't feel like you can do much of anything.

Self-reliance is at the other end of the continuum. Here your freedom is maximized—you can invent your own life. For example, you may stay in a relationship or on a job because you want to, not because you believe it's your only option.

You're free to make your own opinions, judgments, and decisions. You can follow your own gleam rather than be swayed by others; and you can see reality for yourself rather than let others define it for you. You can yield to the truth but not be devastated by it.

When you're self-reliant, you can recognize and act on more choice points—moments when you can make a choice to direct your life or let events or other people direct it for you. These moments are windows in time. If you look out these windows, you can see the outcomes of your different choices. One choice can lead toward dependency or isolation and depression; another toward self-reliance and a depression-free life.

RECOMMENDED READING AND AUDIO TAPES

Beck, A. T. *Cognitive Therapy and Emotional Disorders.* New York: New American Library, 1979.

Beck, A. T., and G. Emery. *Anxiety Disorders and Phobias: A Cognitive Perspective.* New York: Basic Books, 1985.

Beck, A. T., A. J. Rush, G. F. Shaw, and G. Emery. *Cognitive Therapy of Depression.* New York: Guilford, 1979.

Beecher, W. and M. Beecher. *Beyond Success and Failure.* New York: Pocket Books, 1981.

Burns, D. *Feeling Good.* New York: New American Library, 1981.

Burns, D. *Intimate Connections.* New York: New American Library, 1986.

Ellis, A. and R. Harper. *A New Guide to Rational Living.* New York: Prentice Hall, 1975.

Emery, G. *Becoming More Self-reliant* (audio tape). New York: Psychology Today Tape Club, 1985.

―――. *Controlling Your Depression Through Cognitive Therapy* (audio tape series and workbook). New York: BMA Audio Cassettes, 1982.

―――. *Emery News* (newsletter). Los Angeles: L.A. Center for Cognitive Therapy.

―――. *Overcoming Anxiety* (audio tape series and workbook). New York: BMA Audio Cassettes, 1987.

―――. *Own Your Own Life.* New York: Signet, 1984.

―――. and J. Campbell. *Rapid Relief from Emotional Distress.* New York: Fawcett, 1987.

————. *Stress-free Home Study Course* (audio tapes and workbook). Los Angeles: L.A. Center for Cognitive Therapy, 1986.

Reynolds, D. *Playing Ball on Running Water*. New York: Morrow, 1984.

Books and audio tapes by Gary Emery are available from:

L.A. Center for Cognitive Therapy
630 South Wilton Place
Los Angeles, California 90005
213-387-4737

Index

About the Author

Gary Emery, Ph.D., received his doctorate from the University of Pennsylvania, where he worked with Aaron T. Beck, M.D., in helping to develop cognitive therapy. Over the last ten years he has combined his graduate training in sociology and psychology to help people better understand how they can use their minds to lead happier and healthier lives.

He is Director of the Los Angeles Center for Cognitive Therapy, Assistant Clinical Professor in the Department of Psychiatry at UCLA, and a Clinical Associate in the Department of Psychology at USC. He lives in Los Angeles with his wife and son.